TUBBY

The Story of Coach Raymond
and Championship Football
at Delaware

TUBBY

The Story of Coach Raymond
and Championship Football
at Delaware

by
Harold R. Raymond
and
Al Cartwright

**Serendipity
Press**

TUBBY
The Story of Coach Raymond and
Championship Football at Delaware

Dedication

To my parents, who made it possible.

Tubby Raymond

To my championship home team:

Mary, Al Jr., Mary Jane, Debbie and Laurie.

Al Cartwright

Acknowledgments

Noted below are three people from the University of Delaware who gave unlimited assistance — making it possible to publish this book.

Elbert Chance, Director, Alumni Association
Ben Sherman, Sports Information Director
Debi Teel, Senior Secretary, Football Office

Also a special thanks to Linda Spinelli, amanuensis, for keeping staff tempers on an even keel.

The Publisher

Publisher's Notebook

Bring a famous football coach and a top professional writer together and you have a BIG WINNER.

This autobiography, TUBBY, is a classic example of proficient collaboration between the subject, Harold Raymond, and the writer, Al Cartwright. The combination made publishing this book especially attractive to Serendipity Press.

Featured in TUBBY are the ups and downs of Raymond's career — to his present position as head coach of the Fighting Blue Hens of the University of Delaware. . .1979 National Champions, NCAA Division II. *Sports Illustrated* characterized the Blue Hens as the winningest Division II football team of the last decade. *Time* magazine documented their winning against major college teams — Colgate, Rutgers, Villanova, Boston U., and William & Mary. One coach said, "They're absolutely overwhelming. They should play teams like Ohio State, Notre Dame and Alabama."

The blend of Tubby Raymond's coaching technique, his integrity and the University of Delaware policy which insists that athletes be scholars, has produced football teams acclaimed by coaches, writers, broadcasters and fans. The score over Tubby's thirteen years as head coach: 119-38-2.

Other coaches have won championships in various college football divisions but Tubby Raymond, with a special quality of leadership, stands equal to the best and much superior to most.

Is there a secret to acquiring athletes who are also real students?...no athletic scholarships, no mercenaries, no money under the table. The dominant criterion at Delaware: "Football is an educational opportunity." They don't buy MEAT ON THE HOOF at this University.

No wonder they keep repeating, in locker rooms and on campuses: "He must be quite a guy to develop top teams year after year!"

A noted professional football player and later a successful coach said, "I could never coach a college team with all the frustrations of working with 19-year-old athletes." Tubby can deal with this. He understands students' problems and knows how to communicate with young people. He is decisive and effective — always the General in charge of his "troops." Bear Bryant calls him Napoleon.

It would take a plethora of adjectives to describe Tubby Raymond.

Anyone meeting him is left with a strong impression. A dramatically handsome individual with a commanding presence . . . proud, eager and enthusiastic. His energy and tenacity remind one of a bull terrier — noted for courage, endurance and never "giving-up." With all his charm, he's as cocky as a bantam rooster. Sometimes intense and unrestrained, there is an expansiveness about him that makes him appear larger than he is. An expressive face, at times a twinkle in his eyes, or a strong piercing gaze which makes you feel he is reading your character. Occasionally a telling touch of sensitivity comes through. He gets widespread satisfaction out of life — his family, his job and the success he has established.

You can take him or leave him. He may amuse you or annoy you, but he won't make you yawn. In a crowd he seems to charge the atmosphere with excitement. This is no mediocre man. He is articulate, resolute and invites confidence. Whatever he does, he does with dedication and flare.

Al Cartwright possesses literary power. . .as a journalist he has received substantial acclaim and is known nationally. For twenty-five years he was Sports Editor for the Wilmington News-Journal papers. . . presently a feature columnist. His walls bear witness to his talent:

- The Headliner Club Award for being "the most consistently outstanding sports columnist in the United States."
- Ten times his columns were selected for BEST SPORTS STORIES
- Winner of the first annual writing contest of the Thoroughbred Racing Associations
- Twice winner of John Hervey citations for columns on harness racing
- In 1980 elected to the Delaware Sports Hall of Fame

With his customary skill Cartwright has driven every nail home — a "bang-up" job of research and writing. TUBBY is excellently crafted — resulting in a book of vital interest to any sports fan — and especially to Blue Hen football devotees.

J. Blan van Urk

Contents

Foreword

Tubby Raymond called me up to ask me a couple of questions about a book I had written in conjunction with John Underwood of *Sports Illustrated*. He told me he had been asked to write one, too, and wanted to know if I had enjoyed the experience — during the writing and after publication. Then he asked me if I'd buy a book that he had written. I'm afraid I'm going to have to. He didn't say anything about sending me a free one in exchange for the advice.

But the answer is yes, I'd buy a book by or about Tubby Raymond, because nine years ago I bought the little guy himself, as a man and as a football coach. That was when we were fellow coaches in the summer All-American Game in Lubbock, Texas. He is a special person, this University of Delaware coach, and so is his pretty little wife. We've felt like family ever since.

Tubby and I hit it off like we'd been coaching together for years. He has an outstanding personality to go with his football knowledge, and it was no problem at all for me to figure out how he can get maximum effort from his young men. And he must be getting maximum effort, judging from the Delaware record.

I've often said that if a man could live without coaching football, then he should. He should give up the game and try to do something he cannot live without — even choppin' cotton, if that's his thing. No man can be a successful coach unless he has the dedication of Tubby. Incidentally, maybe this book of his will tell me how he got that name. To me, Jackie Gleason is tubby. Tubby isn't tubby. Don't they have grits in Delaware? Or do they just serve them in the press box? Tubby's short and trim, but he has the command of a general. And also the swagger.

When we first met, I wasn't so sure he had a sense of humor. I always try to find out quick, and I found out he likes to needle and likes a laugh just like I do. That's why I could tell him before the Lubbock game not to look for me after the game if his defense did poorly, 'cause I wouldn't even go in the locker room. And that he might not see me even if we won, because I'd be too busy getting my picture taken and remembering not to mention any of the assistant coaches.

Tubby could coach anywhere in the country, and I know he's had many opportunities to leave. The size of a school has nothing to do with your coaching ability; it's the size of your players. I'm not surprised he has chosen to stay with the Blue Hens this long. Some people like a way of life and they stick with it. Some run here and there.

I was the run-here-and-there type. I guess I had an exaggerated opinion of my coaching ability. In retrospect, the best job I ever had might have been the first one I ever had — assistant coach at University of Alabama. But I wasn't the normal run-of-the-mill assistant, I guess. I thought to be successful, you had to go out and climb whenever there was a mountain available. I don't feel that way now. Certainly Tubby's a great success with that mountain up there in Delaware.

I sort of envy him. If you asked me if I ever wanted to coach at a school on a lower level, I'd say yes — right now. There's one right here in the state of Alabama that plays the calibre of football that Delaware does, and I've said to myself a lot of times that I wouldn't mind working there. It's a good little program, away from the recruiting circus and the other heavy-duty stuff that goes with coaching at a major university. I'd have more time to enjoy life and rough around with the grandchildren.

I've never heard anything but compliments about the Delaware football program, even before I met Tubby. I know coaches who have gone there and borrowed some of his offense. We've fooled with it ourselves at Alabama at various times, but never have adopted it basically. Everytime I play Notre Dame, though, I think about it.

Some coaches are great recruiters. Some are blackboard experts. Still others do their best in the trenches, right on the field on Saturdays. I don't know just where Tubby's strength lies. I have the feeling he gets a high rating in all those categories. I definitely know he's a winner. It doesn't make any difference where you're winning — it's something I respect.

I will close by wishing my friend I call "Napoleon," good luck with his book. I was flattered by the reaction to mine. I know it was well-read in the Southeastern States, which is our territory; I don't suppose anybody cared enough to pick one up in other places. I don't think I would be especially strong in Delaware, for instance.

But I know you'll peddle at least one of yours in the Southeastern States, Tubby. I got the hint. But if you ever sell the movie rights, you owe me one. Tell them you want the Bear to play the title role.

Paul W. (Bear) Bryant, *Head Coach*
University of Alabama's Crimson Tide
June 1980

1

Saturday Mornin' Comin' Down

Saturday Mornin' In Albuquerque . . . wonder what Kris Kristofferson could do with that one as a song title?

That was, crazily, the only extra-curricular thought that ran through my mind as I sat on an equipment trunk (and yes, all you foes of Short People, my feet did touch the ground) outside our stadium locker room this beautiful, sunny December 1979 day way out there in New Mexico. It ran through my mind and right out of it. This was three months to the day since the University of Delaware had opened its football season and my mind was even more of a football than it usually is. So there wasn't any room for any Kristofferson possibilities to be lingering. I had said just about all that could be said to a team that was going out to play for the National Championship of NCAA Division II in an incredible fourteenth game of one season. They had to be sick of me and I was sick of plotting and inspiring and cajoling and barking over all those weeks, so with maybe an hour to go before a television-commanded 11:30 a.m. kickoff, I went out the door and put my little body on the trunk and sought the therapy of privacy.

For the championship game, the University of New Mexico's stadium had been christened the Zia Bowl. My American Indian isn't too good, but I seem to remember an

Albuquerque host telling me that Zia means Four Seasons —
the four seasons of nature and the four seasons of a human's
life. I have experienced football seasons that seemed like four
in one, but I don't think that is what the Indians had in mind.

The opponent, Youngstown State. The pageantry was
forming; the spectators were coming into the park. Not that
many of them, because here was a team from the state of Delaware and another from Ohio about to abuse the logic of neu-
trality by running into each other in New Mexico, a site that
had been chosen before any one knew what the match-up
would be.

We had been there before. Not in Albuquerque, but in
the championship game. We had been there before and come
away empty. For the fifth time in nine years, we were in the
playoffs, and for the third time in six years we were in the
finals. We got murdered in one championship game in Sacramento, Calif., and shaded by a point in the other in
Longview, Tex. So we were 0-for-2 when it REALLY counted.

Our fans were saying "Let's get it this time," and that battle
cry did more to irritate me than to hype me. Within several
pre-game hours, I felt this terrible pressure, mixed with not a
little touch of terror, and finally, resignation: That whatever
happens is going to happen; I have coached the best that I can.

I wasn't naive enough to believe our track record of getting
to the title game was enough to satisfy our Delaware fans — or
was I? Sitting there on the trunk, watching the Delaware fans
come into the park with their blue tams with the gold tassels,
waving pennants, I had the feeling they were more excited than
I was. What did they want — blood? The answer had to be yes.
The answer couldn't be only "Gee, we got to the big game three
times, even if we did get beat — again." The problem was Coach
Raymond's.

We're national champions now, and I still feel it is an
under-rated accomplishment just to get in a position to strike

for it, but I don't argue it any more. I've convinced myself that nobody wants to hear that Sunday school lecture. I have learned it is the nature of the fan to crave, almost demand, total success — and never mind all that garbage about offering mere participation in the playoffs as a standard of success.

The night before, I had told the troops that just being where they were was a far greater accomplishment than, for example, Ohio State's going to the Rose Bowl. Delaware is not Ohio State — thank heavens — but this is not a ridiculous analogy. Ohio State had qualified for the trip to Pasadena by winning its conference, playing an eleven-game schedule. That did it for the Buckeyes. We had to go through our regular eleven-game season, emerge with a record good enough to be selected, and then start playing do-or-die in the playoffs — three times, if we were lucky. If we didn't do, we died, immediately.

We knocked off Virginia Union and then Mississippi College in the first two rounds and if we could do the same to Youngstown, that would be our thirteenth victory of the season — and no other team in the country would be able to make that statement.

Despite those Saturday morning flashes of terror ("We're not even going to get off the ball, we're not going to do anything right"), I had a pretty good idea we were going to make that statement. The University of Delaware, 1979, was a relatively well-balanced football team with an offense that, in my opinion, could not be stopped. I had been blessed with an offensive line that probably was the biggest and strongest in Blue Hen history. I can't conceive of Delaware's ever having had any better football players on the line than Garry Kuhlman at right tackle and Herb Beck at right guard, off what they had shown me this long season: Kuhlman, 6-feet-3, 263 pounds, and Beck, 6-2 and 247 and on his way to a Little All-American selection.

Those two had come to us from the majors, which they had decided wasn't for them — Kuhlman a transfer from Penn State, returning to his home town, and Beck a transfer from the University of Georgia who wanted to be a little closer to the front porch in Drexel Hill, Pa.

I had myself a three-year starter at center in Mike Donnalley, and exceptionally team-oriented people on the left side in Tom Toner and Joe Booth. We had Jaime Young and Jay Hooks at what the new football terminology calls skill positions, the ends, but nobody is going to tell me that the Kuhlmans and the Becks and the other inside linemen aren't skillful. Hooks gave us that old sports-page bromide, lightning speed, at the spread-receiver spot and we hadn't had that for some time. If you have a tight end who is strong enough to block and do the things that you need for the ground game, and also have the footwork and the hands to give you a receiving threat, you are in good shape. Jaime Young did those things.

I was getting ready to unleash a backfield that included the swiftness of Lou Mariani and the power and the elusiveness of Gino Olivieri. We had started to play Olivieri at right halfback because he would be behind Beck and Kuhlman, and with Gino's blocking ability, that gave us an element that could drive the ball all by itself. Bo Dennis at 6-3 and 220 was the biggest and strongest fullback we've ever had at Newark. At quarterback, well, I'd just have to call Scott Brunner incomparable.

I also was going to unleash a defense that never really understood me. Here I was, a Coach of the Year a couple of times, going into another championship game on national television — and I had a communications gap with my defensive platoon. I felt as if I were singing "My Way" and umpteen big young guys were singing it right back at me.

We had won twelve ball games and in every one of them I had criticized the defense. The polite way to say it is that I had been very analytical about their performance. It's not that they were rookies; many of them had played in the championship game the year before and played extremely well. To nutshell it, they gave up more yardage against certain teams than they should have. The inconsistency had become a concern. Opening day, they totally dominated Rhode Island and bingo — they suddenly stopped and allowed Rhode Island to move.

I got a red neck right there. I realized that the defense already was showing signs of developing a tendency to play when they wanted to play. The football philosophy at Delaware is that a team or a player play their very best ALL the time. It is an educational aspect to this game, and there is no sense in approaching the game otherwise. I do not demand that we shut out and/or minus-yardage everybody we play. I do demand consistency.

We gave up more yardage against C. W. Post than some of the poorer teams C. W. Post played. We had completely stopped Temple — in many ways, we were dominating Temple in our annual Big Game, this time in our own park — and then we gave up seventeen points in the last quarter and blew it.

You never knew with our defense. We spotted Villanova twenty-one points early in the game and then the defense turned itself completely around, as though we had done a master job of substituting for everybody, and the very same guys shut the Wildcats off in the second half. We won the game, but I let the defense have it. I blistered them. They were having too many lethargic innings.

"Delaware's much-maligned defense" started showing up in newspaper stories.

I concede that we — the coaching staff — and mostly me, could be at fault. The offense always gets the spotlight. We go around the country speaking at clinics about our Wing-T offense and its documented effectiveness and nobody ever says anything — or is asked to say anything — about the other half of the team. Thus, the defense has to feel a little left out.

From an individual coaching standpoint, my responsibility is the quarterback. This means that I spend much more time with the offense than I do the defense and I may create some resentment. In fact, I KNOW I do. It surfaced last season when several of the defensive players asked if they could meet with me.

"All we get is criticism," they complained. They had something of a case, but their beef upset me. They still weren't digging my philosophy. If this gang really had the personality of a successful defense, then they would have reacted differently. Rather than talk about it, they would have gone out and demonstrated their hardness. And that's what I told their committee.

But this defense apparently wasn't going to react My Way. So I decided before our trip to Albuquerque that I wouldn't get on the defensive players. It was their football team. They were the ones who were going to do the playing. They had the responsibility. It's your game, gang.

Harold Rupert Raymond, your friendly — sometimes — philosopher. As I said to myself, we had an offense that couldn't be stopped. I would pass this feeling along to the offensive players, but leave the ever-popular "if" loophole, Like, "If you play up to your capacity, you can move the ball on ANYONE."

At the same time, I might tell the defense I didn't think they could stop Don Knotts, or even Mrs. Don Knotts, or insults to that effect. A defense definitely has to be ugly and irritable to play well.

In a move to correct the inconsistency, we made a change for Youngstown. We slid Ed Braceland, who had played defensive end, back into the defensive tackle position he had filled the previous season. This gave us mobility we needed. He was in the front four with Mike Bachman, a two-year starter, and Greg Larson and Jamie Bittner, the ends. Jamie had a knee problem, but we felt he was ready to play.

Steve Panik (with that name, you gotta become a coach, Steve) hadn't always been able to play at his best because of injuries, but he also got the OK to start at linebacker with Al Minite and Mike Wisniewski. Vince Hyland at cornerback was extremely excited about appearing on national TV. Whatever turns 'em on, I'm all for it. Mark Howard was the. other cornerback, Robbie Woods and Bob Lundquist the safeties.

Woods had moved into free safety ahead of John Oberg because of his mobility. Lundquist had played strong safety for our injured captain, Jim Brandimarte, all year.

Hyland was going to have to cover Jim Ferranti, Youngstown's disgustingly capable receiver. We had decided to let Vince flip-flop, or go to the side of this threat. We had erred in the planning of a regular-season game against Youngstown, when they confused us by using Ferranti as a flanker, running him in motion to the opposite side of the field; thus, we had the wrong man covering him. That would have been Mark Howard, a very fine football player in his own way but not nearly as experienced as Hyland.

Now we decided to put Hyland to the wide side. If Ferranti was there, we would have Vince in the right place. If Ferranti went into motion, we also would have Hyland on him. And if Ferranti worked to the sideline, Howard would be more than capable of handling him within a restricted area.

I wondered how they all would react to the crowd — the lack of a crowd, that is. We were used to playing to full houses of 20,000 at Delaware Stadium. Now we were getting all steamed up to dash out into the Zia Bowl — and face 4,500 displaced Delawareans and Ohioans and thousands of empty seats. I had discussed this with the team. I reminded them they might think they were playing on a corner lot, from the size of the audience, but that a nationwide audience would be watching on television.

I left my warm perch at the Zia Bowl and rejoined the athletes. The coaches called out the names of the starters, defensive and offensive. At the hotel, after the morning meal and the group meetings, we had announced the makeup of the specialty units — the kickoff team, the receiving team. There was no need to repeat this. Our squad meeting had been held in the lounge, with me standing in front of the bar and the ball players spread out all over the place. Anybody walking past might have thought we were winding up an all-night party.

We have a set of procedures we follow before every ball game. I feel very strongly about being organized this way, especially for road games. It calls for a demonstration of total concentration. If you do things consistently, if you follow a schedule faithfully, you are apt to get a much more at-home climate. The players expect these progressive steps and it eases the tension.

At the stadium, we reviewed the offense and the defense, with little asides to certain players — not all of them complimentary.

Ever since the 1974 team requested it, we say the Lord's Prayer before each game and follow it by a minute and a half of silence for the renewal of personal commitments.

That's how we observed the countdown for Rhode Island on opening day and how we got ourselves together for Youngstown in the big one three months later.

We charged out into the sunny stadium. Saturday mornin' — not Sunday mornin', Kris — was about to come down in the form of the kickoff.

2

Crowned with a Cowboy Hat

For all of you out there who had their TV sets recalled by the finance company before the game and who also did not receive their Sunday papers of Dec. 9, 1979, the final score was Delaware 38, Youngstown 21. We had gone all the way. "Finally!," said so many people, and "Finally!," said the headlines. I tried not to let that bug me. I was not totally successful.

I'll talk about the actual ball game a bit later.

We had first played Youngstown, the next-to-last stop on the schedule, at Youngstown. It was a dilly of a game, one in which we were down 24 points at halftime and came back to win by 51-45. A shootout, the press called it.

Every football team has its unique path to where it's going. We had played our best offensive football of the year in that last half at Youngstown, and the next Saturday we defeated Colgate but played rather poorly. We were Flat City. But that's what happens so many times to a team that expends so much emotional energy on one game and wins it and then, perhaps subconsciously, takes the next test for granted, as if they are going to play but a game of cards. Whatever, there was a letdown after the tremendous excitement of the victory in Ohio.

We were selected for the playoffs. In the first elimination, we began to come back to our capability at the expense of Virginia Union and then produced our best whole game against Mississippi College in the semi-finals.

It didn't make any difference to me who we played in the finals, even though, as it turned out, we were going to see Youngstown for the second time in a month. Just in case there was any cockiness in the ranks, I told my players that if they were looking for a soft touch, they weren't going to find it in the championship game. Nobody gets that far without being a good team. But I think the mountain we had to move to conquer Youngstown in that first meeting was too fresh in their minds to have our guys suffering from fat-headedness.

We had made a tactical mistake in 1978, the year we reached the finals and lost to Eastern Illinois. We played an eleven-game schedule and practiced the same as if we were playing eight or nine games. That is, we scrimmaged every Tuesday. We started to ease off a little on Thursday, but generally speaking, we had two full workouts every week — and when we got into the tournament we followed the same routine. We were bumped and bruised and emotionally tired by the time we saw Eastern Illinois.

So the next season, we planned ahead. I felt we had a fair shot to return to the playoffs, so we did not scrimmage after the fifth game — just in case. We did some contact work in advance of the sixth and seventh games, but after that there wasn't any hitting at all. Once into the playoffs, we cut our workouts by a big thirty minutes.

There are only a limited amount of things you can do with a football team. I have to smile when I think what Dick Vermeil of the Philadelphia Eagles did last year, during the same period we were getting ready for the finals. The Eagles were about to take on the Dallas Cowboys in the National Football League playoffs. These clubs had already met twice that season, and thus I couldn't understand why Vermiel was watching game films twenty hours a day.

It doesn't matter whether it's professional or college or high school — the things you do well all year are the things that are going to do well for you in a post-season game. The small special gimmicks and tricks you might whip up may cause some concern for the opposition, but not much. What you do is stick with the basic moves that have advanced you this far.

The point I am trying to make is that from our seventh game on, we decided our level of execution was pretty fair, and we stayed with what we had. Another thing: The longer you play, the greater the injury risk both in combat and in practice. In 1963, Dave Nelson's Delaware team won a national poll championship by sweeping an eight-game schedule — and now we're talking about a possible preposterous FOURTEENTH game.

You play that long, people show wear and tear and even the equipment reflects the extended season. The ball players have physical and emotional problems. You just cannot have them at peak pitch every Saturday over a three-month period. Summary: fourteen games are too many to play when you're going to college. I say that even though we won the championship. I feel, rather, that we ESCAPED with the championship. We were not at our best.

Without getting too deeply into X's and O's, I'll touch on our Game Plan for Youngstown. I capitalize it because that's how some fans refer to game plans — with awe, and intrigue and a touch of religion. I have this crazy thought that some day a coach, when asked about his game plan by the press, will reply "I didn't have any." But the coach won't be me.

There has been a creeping trend towards a defense that uses an eight-man line. The general front is seven men, with a four-deep secondary. The last several years, some teams have brought an extra man up on the line of scrimmage. In our offensive case, this hurts our running game but at the same time it gives us a chance to probe, with passing, what is a short-handed secondary.

Youngstown had tried this eight-man business against us our first meeting. Actually, they tried literally everything. They had a multiple defensive scheme — just about every defense I've ever seen or even heard about. They were heavily defense-minded, but the eight-man line was the thing that nagged at me the most.

We intended to challenge this by showing them a bunch of formations from the double wing, or in the double-wing category. This means there would be four deep Delaware receivers at any time, making a three-deep defense impossible. I think we wiped out perhaps a third of their defensive plot with this action. They didn't handle it very well, particularly in the turnaround second half.

We also intended to do a lot of shifting, which makes multiple-defensing difficult. But despite all the shifting, we hit them with our regular bread-and-butter offense. I do give them credit for limiting us to 187 yards on the ground, but our Scott Brunner's passing was more than an equalizer.

We made some defensive adjustments of our own. The option is a special football play for Youngstown, and when you face it you must have people responsible for meeting its three threats: 1. the carry by the fullback, 2. the quarterback keeping the ball and 3. the pitch to the tailback. We had been a little lacking in these assignments at Youngstown.

The big change we made involved No. 3: We would hammer the tailback on the line of scrimmage as opposed to bringing up a back to take care of him. Robby Robson, the Youngstown tailback and a great runner, had hurt us badly. We decided to try and take that opportunity away from him, and it worked. He did run for 127 yards at Albuquerque, but it took him 27 carries. He had more than doubled that yard-age the first time we saw him.

But we had to sweat before anything clicked.

Those flashes of pre-game terror I had experienced seemed justified, for too long a time. If we hadn't made so many mistakes early, we would have run Youngstown right out of the southwestern United States. We were tight a whole quarter. The tension was obvious. Both Lou Mariani and Bo Dennis fumbled the ball away, Bo when he was going into the end zone. Jaime Young dropped a touchdown pass right in his hands on our very first drive. We knew the sun was going to be a problem — the field was laid out east-west — and Jaime got it in his eyes and was its first victim.

You only get so many opportunities in a game, and we were abusing them. We fell behind 21-7 with less than five minutes to go in the first half — but we went into the locker room with a 21-21 tie. This is what is known as playing football the hard way.

After a scoreless first period — and our own shoddy play made it that way — we spotted Youngstown a touchdown. But we bounced right back on a 74-yard bomb from Brunner to Jay Hooks that our spread receiver caught at midfield.

Now Youngstown retaliated with its own 80-yard touchdown drive, but our plan to contain Robson on the pitch from his quarterback was getting results. He contributed only seven yards to this drive, in four carries. Then we pulled a couple of boners — a shanked punt by Mike Schonewolf and a holding penalty — and Youngstown scored again and had us down three touchdowns to one. But that was the last they were to see of our end zone.

We hit them with two touchdowns inside of four minutes and forty-four seconds to get the halftime tie. Youngstown fumbled Schonewolf's punt and Herb Beck pounced on it around the 50. Now the breaks were beginning to even up. Brunner passed to Young to put us on the 30 and on fourth down from their 33, we called for an exciting play that our guys love to see: the fake field goal.

Brandt Kennedy lined up to kick it and Schonewolf, one knee on the ground, was the holder. Contrary to public opinion, the knee on the ground does not down the ball. The holder has special dispensation. He can do whatever he chooses with the ball, run with it or whatever, even with both knees on the ground — although I have to think he would do better running on his feet.

Hugh Dougherty was the cornerback protecting the "kicker" on the left side. At the snap of the ball, Dougherty ran to his right, three yards behind the line of scrimmage. Schonewolf, who is a quarterback and can do these things well, fielded the snap and made a backhand flip to Dougherty. The right side of our line, the strong side, blocked "down," or to the inside, and Dougherty ran off-tackle. Youngstown's outside defenders, intent on blocking a field-goal try, rushed right in without opposition and found the barn empty.

This was a vital play for us. Dougherty took it inside the 5 and almost scored. We did score when Brunner passed to tight end Phil Nelson.

Vince Hyland, the guy who couldn't wait to get on national TV, got on it as a star when he intercepted a pass and ran it back 61 yards for a touchdown with 18 seconds to go. When Kennedy placekicked his third straight point, we were even on the scoreboard.

And now I knew we were going to win. I just KNEW it because of what had happened in the first game. We had started to hurt them in the second half — and by that I mean our physical power was taking its effect on them. Our experience as a playoff repeater, our strength all came together in the second half of Shootout II, the same as it had the first game.

I was extremely confident we would play well the second half. The defense, again, played when they wanted to, and they wanted to that second half. They made a commitment at halftime to simply go out and win the game. In my opinion, they won it.

We broke the tie in the third quarter when Brunner and Hooks collaborated on a 75-yard touchdown play, and in the last quarter Kennedy, on fourth down with 17 yards to go, kicked a 47-yard field goal and Oliviere ran 34 yards to score after Gregg Larson recovered a Youngstown fumble.

As Scott Brunner told the reporters, the defense was the key. We had put the pressure on our defense because of the bobbling we did in the first quarter. Brunner called it their best game of the year. Over the last 34 minutes, we held Youngstown to 134 yards and, more important, no points.

Cornerback Hyland did his job on Jim Ferranti, Youngstown's elusive Little All-American wide receiver, who made only three catches — and one of those came with seconds to go, while we were already celebrating. Hyland had asked specifically to be assigned to him, in both games, despite Ferranti's reputation. Vince, who also played well in the 1978 finals, seems to save his best for the big ones.

Brunner was slightly magnificent in demonstrating his marvelous skills for the last time as a college player. We couldn't move the ball on the ground, so we decided "Let Scotty throw." And Scotty responded "There is no risk at all. I'm fine."

It was a team that accepted the responsibility of Delaware tradition in general and their own in particular. I'm making all this sound pretty calm, but I flipped out when the game ended. I remember going bananas with the help of Jim Brandimarte, our captain incognito, as I called him. Jim never played his senior year. What began as back spasms turned into a pinched muscle and he required surgery to fuse six vertebrae. Jim came back to stand beside me on the deck at all games, and he remained the captain. He wore his game jersey over his street clothes. He was a great leader, and when I traditionally turned over the team to the captain for one minute together in the locker room before each game, I knew they were in good hands.

Somewhere in Youngstown, there is a TV commentator who may still be eating his words. I heard him when we watched the Betamax of the first Youngstown game, at a party that Saul Savitch and Bob Hooper threw for the coaching staff. When we were trailing 33-7 at halftime, he had commented that the Wing-T is not a come-from-behind offense, and that all his listeners could expect Delaware to change its attack immeasurably. He had to be kidding. With the same offense, we scored every time we had the ball. And in the title game, the Wing-T came from behind against the same opponent all over again. Our offense, whether ahead or trailing, was just plain dynamic.

I have a great deal of respect for Bill Narduzzi, the Youngstown coach, and I believe the feeling is mutual. We have had these great wars, and no two coaches ever got along better. During that first game, there was a great deal of compliments being exchanged by the players . . . "Nice shot" . . "Nice play" . . . and they were helping each other to their feet. At the final gun, both teams met in a spontaneous display of uninhibited admiration, what Ted Kempski, our offensive coordinator, calls the Stanley Cup routine. It was a mass exchange of handshakes and compliments.

Narduzzi had come over and put his arm around me. "You little bugger," he said, "you won this one, but I'm gonna get your ass in the playoffs."

When the shooting was over in the Zia Bowl, here came

Narduzzi again and he was not in possession of any part of my anatomy.

"I want to tell you one thing," he declared as we shook hands. "There is no question about it: You have the best football team. If you played us a hundred times, you would beat us a hundred times."

This mutual respect, this great tribute from a defeated coach in a game of this proportion, is what intercollegiate football is all about. Or is supposed to be all about.

Friends who saw the game on TV told me I looked pretty collected on the sidelines, even when we were butchering things, even when we were down three touchdowns to one.

I hope I'm that way every game. I should be, because we are extremely well organized. I'm proud of that. We know just what we are going to do and thus a great deal of jumping around and gesturing and over-coaching on Saturday isn't in the picture. Fritz Crisler, my old Michigan coach/guru, always said more football games are lost on Thursdays than on Saturdays, meaning you should not overwork the team on Thursday and you should have a fresh team at game-time.

Let me give you an example of how we're wrapped. Say we're on offense and it is third down. Mike Schonewolf, our punter, automatically jumps up from the bench and runs over to Ed Maley, our defensive coordinator. Mike points to each defensive player on the punting unit, and counts them. If there is an injury in the ranks, he will remind Maley that there is a position that needs a change; usually, this change already has been made. If we fail to make the down, and our decision is to punt, all I have to do is wave my right index finger and the punting team takes the field. There isn't a whole lot ot coaching in that.

When we get into field-goal range, the kicker, Brandt Kennedy, will have his team ready to go on the proper down, just like Schonewolf. All this can be done without histrionics. Some teams require this calm approach to leadership and if I think that's what they need, I'll provide it. They need both to see poise and to demonstrate it. We have been blessed to have back-to-back quarterbacks with extreme poise in Jeff Komlo and Scott Brunner.

Let us say that I was not too organized personally once the championship celebration started. I had had nothing to eat or drink since 8 o'clock that morning. My throat was evidence that I had done a lot of shouting in that dry air.

As I came out of the stadium I ran into Skip Loessner, who is an assistant to our university president, Art Trabant. Skip just happened to have a healthy supply of Coors beer in the trunk of his rented automobile. People seemed to be helping themselves. I was so thirsty I could have handled anything, and I fell victim to the tantalization of the Coors. I simply had to have one, and did.

When we reached the airport, the players, now free from the training restrictions after some seventeen weeks — and certainly all of age — invaded the bar. It got to the point where all the overpowered bar would serve was beer. They yelled to me to come in and have my picture taken with them and the trophy, and Al Minite and some other big spenders wanted to buy me a beer. Euphoria ran rampant.

The airport also included a shop that sold cowboy hats. Dave George, George Thompson and a lot of other folks who made the trip to root for us all had been in there to buy hats, and were wearing them. I seemed to be the only bareheaded Delawarean.

I had to be part of the show. I went into the store and after trying on several, with the encouragement of Jaime Young, I picked out a camel-color suede number. It was ME. It all but had my name on it. Just what I wanted. I didn't even blink when the clerk said "That will be fifty dollars, please."

Three hours later on the airplane, after dinner, I sat there looking at my investment and said to my wife, Sue, "What on earth am I going to do with a suede cowboy hat that cost me fifty bucks? I doubt that Gene Autry ever spent that much on one."

"You are going to wear it, that's what," Sue said.

Now you can't get it away from me. I wore it all winter, everyday. I love it. And it's sort of symbolic. After all, we did win the big shootout in the West. And I wouldn't look nearly as dashing just wearing holsters, or spurs.

To some people, the following is going to be placed among the same un-American activities as kicking Lassie and booing Kate Smith, but I must say it: I am not in favor of college football playoffs. For the first time, the University of Delaware has won a national championship on the field. I would rather the title be decided off the field. By the polls.

When you are involved in a playoff system like the Division II Championships, it means the sudden-death destruction of all the participants save one. It is a pyschologically brutal system. The championship is not worth the physical and mental anguish a team must experience to survive.

For example, we had gone a terribly long way — and I don't mean geographically — to get into the 1978 finals in Longview, Texas, and we lost by 10-9. I fully realize that there were a hundred and thirty-four other Division II teams that had to be wishing they were in the game. But I have never seen a team that was so emotionally destroyed — and there is no other verb for it — as Delaware that day.

Playoffs make no sense to me. I think it is a case of professional-football mores oozing into amateur football, and we are missing the boat. They never are going to talk the major colleges into playoffs, and I don't blame the majors. Their bowl setup is far superior to this elimination torture.

I do not offer the polls as a perfect solution. For every "official" No. 1 team, there are four or five others seriously claiming to be No.1, and a bunch more insisting they are just as good. But I see nothing wrong with sending a lot of people home happy with their contentions.

I liked the old Division II setup, when eight teams were selected to play four regional "championship" games around the country — period. In our case, it was the East, and this was when we were making all those Boardwalk Bowl appearances in Atlantic City. It meant just a single post-season game for each participant to determine a geographic champion, and it meant four teams had the pleasure of being successful. And to allegedly settle any arguments over which was the national champion, the polls could take care of that.

OK, so I've kicked Lassie and booed Kate Smith. So sue me.

3

Why Couldn't They Call Me Rocky?

Winning the National Championship had its empty side for me because it happened in a year in which I lost my parents. My mother died in February and my father passed away the last week in August, when we were preparing for our opening game.

In reviewing my bittersweet year of 1979, I thought of Ray Meyer, the DePaul University basketball coach, who has been around a long time. In 1980, DePaul was ranked No. 1. In the NCAA basketball playoffs in March, DePaul got knocked out of the Western Regionals by unranked UCLA in a stunning upset. Ray Meyer put the defeat in perspective. He said to the reporters after DePaul had gone down to defeat for only the second time: "So what? . . . None of our players lost their lives."

Delaware goes all the way in its football division and brings the title back from New Mexico after a nationwide television audience had seen our performance. So what? Mom and Dad didn't see it, nor could I tell them about it, and I won't ever see them again. There is absolutely nothing that can balance such a loss.

I had been away from home since I was 18 years old. I became engrossed in my own activities and my own career and perhaps I didn't give my parents quite enough time. Perhaps? I KNOW I didn't.

They were always very, very encouraging, and if I have had any success as a parent, and I think I have — with Sue's help, or her leadership — then the credit goes to Mr. and Mrs. Ira Russell Raymond.

I know I have been criticized — at least by innuendo — by friends and neighbors that I didn't sit on my sons, Chris and Dave, and make them do enough work around the house. Neighbors would see me doing the chores — mowing the lawn, clipping the hedge — and sometimes they'd wonder out loud to me, "So where are the boys?"

They were playing baseball, or football, or playing something, that's where, and that was all right with me. They went on their way and I dragged out the lawn mower and the shears. I thought it was really important that I handle it this way because this was a carryover from the way my parents had treated their son. Sure, I had jobs to do around the house when I was a kid, but if I had a ball game to play — even a pickup game — they gave that priority.

All that had taken place in the metropolis of Flint, Mich., a mean industrial city with matching winters. It is the seat of Genesee County and just south of Saginaw Bay, which is a tributary of Lake Huron — or don't lakes have tributaries? Anyhow, I grew up on the Michigan peninsula. Detroit was just to the south of us and so was — and is — Canada, the Windsor, Ontario, part of Canada. I used to win a lot of quarter bets when I first came East. I would tell skeptical people I had been brought up in a city in the United States that was well north of Ontario. I don't bet that one anymore. The word got out.

Flint was an automobile town, a General Motors-dominated town. In the early '30s, things were not going well for the Raymonds — and millions of others around the country. Athletics were a lifesaver for the Depression kids in Flint. Nobody went on vacation, but somebody could always scrounge up some baseball gear or a football, and that was the beginning of my interest in athletics. It was sort of a self-defense interest. I think it was the materialism of the baseball equipment that drew me to the position of catcher.

My father had a rural background, the Bay City area. He had to go to work his senior year in high school, dropped out and landed a job in Detroit. In an automobile plant — where else?

Dad eventually went back home and married Pearl Brundage and they settled in Flint-land. He went to work in a store, a haberdashery, that his brother ran. It didn't work out. The store died on them, as did a lot of other things in the 1920s. Dad then tried his hand at selling life insurance, which was another license to starve during that period.

I couldn't have been more than eight years old at the time, but I still remember a family conference we had one night in the kitchen. Things were grim. My father did not have a job, nor any prospects of one. We really didn't know what we were going to do.

But out of the blue, Dad happened across a job as a telephone operator for the Buick Motor Division. It was night work. This didn't exactly put us on Easy Street, but I can recall how happy my parents were that Dad had come up with something in an extremely lean job market. He stuck at it, and that was the beginning of a thirty-five-year career with Buick. He became an officer in Plant Protection, in charge of a shift, and retired comfortably in that position.

The Raymonds were four strong. I was the baby. My sister Jane is now Mrs. Charles Brown. She went to the University of Michigan and earned a degree in sociology, then raised a family in Saginaw. She and her husband still live there. Jane will agree with me — we are the products of a very happy home.

Dad had been a bit of an athlete. He played some high school football. My early estimate of him as a physical specimen was that he was enormous, but he really was only a little bigger than his heir Harold when heir Harold reached maturity. I was always "Harold" to Mom and Dad.

I think the Harold came as a concession. Dad had wanted me christened Ira Rupert, which was his grandfather's name. Mom objected. Dad managed to sneak in Rupert in the middle and Mom somehow came up with Harold. I'll get into the "Tubby" business a little later.

Dad's brother, my Uncle Irvin, had played professional football. The two of them were interested in seeing that I got every chance to participate in sports, and took me to the first football game I ever saw. There I was, sitting between them, six years old, watching Flint Central High School play Flint Northern High School in one of those Thanksgiving Day classics. I was captivated by the atmosphere of the game. I felt completely in love with football as my father and uncle patiently explained what was going on, without trying to overwhelm me, and I've been having a romance with the game ever since.

We lived in a neighborhood that is best described as rather poor. My parents didn't have to buy my shoes one at a time, but I went long spells between getting them two at a time. They bought our house in Flint for $2,400. A coal furnace supplied the heat. I did the carry-out-the-ashes-and-bank-the-fire routine in the cellar every night. You burn a lot of coal in Flint.

I never had any problems physically as a kid. I mean, I wasn't sickly. The only thing that got hurt was my feelings sometimes.

The family included a little Boston bulldog by the name

of Jingles, and we always had a cat somewhere around the estate. I never was much of an animal person, though. At the risk of sounding awfully narrow, I must confess that much of my boyhood was spent playing ball. I wonder if Jingles ever forgave me?

I went toddling off to school at Longfellow, which went from grammar grades through junior high, and I managed to make them all without stumbling — and also without alerting any Rhodes Scholar scouts who might have been in the area.

I would say I was a better-than-average student. I worked hard at it, I know, because we had decided at home that I might have a future in the field of medicine. So I realized I needed good grades to get into any pre-med school that would have me.

Funny thing: As economically tough as things were, it was always understood that Jane and I would go to college, somehow. No question about it. In retrospect, it was almost a laughable situation — but it turned out to be just what my parents had ordered. They always wanted their kids to be better off than they were, and they told us the route was in education. That was something that had not happened to them. They were not about to see it not happen to their daughter and son.

From Longfellow, I moved in to Flint Northern High. A boy named Pete Fusi moved right along with me. We were inseperable. During our senior year, Michigan State tried to recruit the pair of us. He was a two hundred and thirty-pounder but an exceptional third baseman, too, and he did indeed go on to play football at State. He now is principal of a high school in Genesee County.

I had another neighborhood buddy in Dominic Tomsi, and we were to move on to the University of Michigan arm in arm, shoulder to shoulder, stout-hearted men, and all that stuff. Dominic had a lot more going for him than I did. He captained the Wolverines and was their Most Valuable Player his senior year. He's now with Buick in Flint, supervisor of a process engineering division.

I wonder whatever happened to Mrs. Short, or Mrs. Davis, two of my favorite high-school teachers? I suppose there must be a Mrs. Short and/or a Mrs. Davis in everybody's secondary-school background. They were sweet and very competent ladies. After our championship victory in 1979, I received a very cherished letter from a Miss Lyons, who had been dean of girls at Flint Northern. She said she was combining a hello with congratulations and it was a delicious name out of the past, one I hadn't heard in about forty years. What a wonderful fringe benefit it is to be remembered by the Miss Lyonses of the world.

OK — let me replay the broken record of how I happened to be saddled with the nickname of Tubby. I hope by now I have painted a picture of a very sports-minded neighborhood. The kids I was trying to hang around with and impress were at least two years older, about my sister Jane's age. I was trying to compete with them, and if I may be kind to myself, I was a bit on the heavy side. What I lacked in years I made up for in pounds. Years later, Mom told a reporter I had been "clump."

The other kids started calling me Tubby, at first in derision. The name stuck because, I hope, they had accepted me. I wasn't enthralled with my new handle; in fact, I despised it. I got into a few tussles over it. But I've been Tubby ever since, even though the baby fat melted away. What was cute at six to some people — has become a burden at fifty-four. Oh, well. They could have called me something a lot worse. But why couldn't they have hung a label on me like "Scrap Iron," or "Rocky"? Rocky Raymond — now that really sings.

I guess I had enough street fights to be Rocky. When they

started taunting me with "Tubby," I would take on the taunter at bare knuckles if he was no more than a foot taller. Modesty prevents me from disclosing my won-and-lost record as a sidewalk pugilist.

I also fought in the basement of a kid named Harry Carlquist, but this wasn't grudge stuff. This was educational. Harry could box; I was just a pitcher and a catcher. We would put on the gloves almost every day. Harry became a very good fighter in Golden Gloves competition and went all the way to the national finals. I also wanted to get into the Golden Gloves, but my parents sat on that pretty quickly. They said baseball and football were taking up enough of my time, and they weren't about to raise any prizefighter.

You never heard of Eddie Krupa, but to young Harold Raymond he was just about the greatest human being that ever was. He was an All-State football player at Flint Northern, my boyhood idol. He went off to Notre Dame, and I just about went into shock when I learned he never made the football team. I couldn't imagine that happening.

Mickey Cochrane, Charley Gehringer, Hank Greenberg — you've heard of them. Merely baseball Hall of Famers, and they were the great Detroit Tiger stars of the day and my very own personal favorites of all the big leaguers. Every year a trainload of Flint kids would be treated to a ball game at Tiger Stadium. We'd sit in the real cheap seats, in the outfield. Goose Goslin was with those Tigers. I remember him vividly, mostly because of what he would do before a game He'd throw baseballs into the stands, in the direction of us kids, but we'd never get them because he would deliberately bounce the ball off an I-beam and it would come back to him.

This trick dazzled me — the accuracy of his throws. Later, I found out those I-beams were more than a yard wide. The Goose had a pretty good target.

In case you are losing interest in this rather one-dimensional childhood, the dimension being sports, let me quickly announce that I really did know that girls existed. I dated very little, though, with Jean Adams or Lois Caister or Madelyn Groshak. I have no idea of what has happened to them, and I have the impression the feeling is mutual. (Trust me, Sue).

The first real job I had, one that enabled me to stay in spending money and buy the family some presents, was in a drug store. Herman Heinemann's Pharmacy, corner of Dayton and Detroit. I was a soda jerk (and there will be no wise remarks from the balcony, please) and generally messed up the place.

Herman Heinemann was a kind, wonderful man, too kind to say then — as he did just last year — that he never thought his drug store would survive me because I was always dropping things and breaking them.

I worked there till I started to go out for football in high school; I quit because I didn't have time for the job. Mr. Heinemann tried to discourage me for a couple of reasons. He said I wouldn't be good enough to make the team and even if I did, it would detract from my intentions of becoming a medical doctor.

But he had no chance of dissuading me, as much as I respected him. Despite the wide difference in our ages, he was one of my very best friends. I enjoyed his company. Such a fine man. I had been working for him for some time before I found out he had a daughter named Sue. Little did we know that Sue and I would grow up to make Herman Heinemann my father-in-law.

4

Let's Hear It for U-High

When I was playing for Flint Northern, my high school coach, Guy Houston, told a sports writer I was "small but hard and determined." I guess that about tells the story.

I had never given anyone the impression I was Frank Merriwell reincarnated as an athlete. I did finish third in the state wrestling tournament one year, and even my father was surprised. I did it by default — the guys I was supposed to wrestle kept getting sick.

But you had to be a pretty good football player to play for Guy Houston and Flint Northern. We were in the Saginaw Valley League, the toughest in the state. As a tenth-grader, I made the junior varsity team and was promoted to the varsity the last two games. My junior year we went undefeated and the next season we lost two. That was the year I was picked third-team All-State.

I want to talk some more about Guy Houston, who had more to do with influencing my future than anyone else. Somewhere along the line, he planted something in my tiny brain that made me want to be like him, to be in the same business.

He died early in 1972, but he was aware that I had made Coach of the Year the previous season, and hearing from him was a very pleasant thing for me. He had retired from Flint

Northern after twenty-four seasons, during which he turned out ten undefeated teams.

In his day, he was an outstanding football player at Western Michigan University, where the old-timers still talk about his fleetness of foot. By the time I got involved in it, he had probably the best high school football program in a state that was loaded with perenially strong teams. I played mostly guard and linebacker and spent part of a season as quarterback.

The University of Michigan coaches used to say, and probably still do, that any one who can play in the Saginaw Valley League can play at Michigan. I kind of put an interruption to that theory when I showed up at Ann Arbor, but you get the picture. In addition to the league games, we went as far as Aurora, Ill., which has to be three hundred miles away, to play. That's how they spread the high school schedules in the Midwest.

Houston was fiery, a hard guy, a master disciplinarian. He had to be. Our high school was a melting pot, located in an industrial area, and the way Houston handled his athletes set the tone for the entire school. Race relations were entirely different from what they are today, but the coach was extremely frank and open with both his black and white kids. There were a lot of ethnic groups. Most of the parents were first-generation American citizens.

The city of Flint was extremely fortunate to have Guy Houston. You could say the same about a gentleman named Charles S. Mott, who was a principal stockholder in General Motors Corp. He established a Mott Foundation that contributed heavily to the city's recreation and sports program. There were something like 4,500 kids playing baseball, all the way from what now is called Little League up to semipros who had the pleasure of playing in Atwood Stadium, where I later played as a minor leaguer. They also had football clinics for youngsters on Saturday mornings. By the time I got to high school I was pretty well indoctrinated in football and baseball.

I mention Mr. Mott here because Guy Houston worked for his Foundation part of the year. Our coach also was dean of boys, and later the principal. When I was graduated in 1944, I took a lot of Guy Houston with me.

Northwestern and Michigan State had expressed an interest in me as a football player, but this was wartime and I went off into the aviation cadet program, first to Birmingham Southern College. By the time I got out, I had flown ten training hours in a Piper Cub. The security program of the United States wouldn't stand for any more. Somebody else did the piloting.

I was lucky enough to stay involved in athletics. At Spence Field in Moultrie, Ga., they had a bunch of pro baseball players and they needed a back-up catcher, who turned out to be me. I spent a month at Maxwell Field in Montgomery, Ala., and practiced with the football team. It was at Maxwell that I got the suspicion it might be tougher than I thought to play at the college level. Still, I wanted the opportunity. The two Big Ten schools that had contacted me in Flint weren't exactly barber colleges.

A guy named John Kobs wasn't much encouragement, though. When I was sprung from the service after two years, I took a trip to Michigan State to see Kobs, who was the freshman football coach. He took one look at my five feet eight inches and said "What happened?", like I had been wounded or something. But he was seeing all of me, and he didn't like what he saw.

That's when I decided what-the-heck, if I'm going to college I might as well go to the best. So I went to Michigan on my own, with the help of the GI Bill. This was in September of 1946, when freshmen were eligible to play for the varsity. I was among about one hundred and ninety candidates, many of them back from the service after interrupted college careers, who reported to the Wolverines' canonized coach, Fritz Crisler.

The coaching staff had a good pipeline around the state and knew me from Flint Northern. I got a preferential locker and started practicing with the varsity — but not for long. After three days, they decided I wasn't big enough and sent me to the freshman squad. That's when I was finally convinced I was a member of the Little People. It hurt.

Now I was at the bottom of everything, lost in a mass of one hundred and thirty football players. Coach Crisler announced he was going to have a fifty-five-man varsity squad and would augment this with twenty-two players who would play a junior varsity schedule and also "demonstrate," which is a gentle word for suffer. When you demonstrate, you take the part of a player on an upcoming varsity opponent and they throw you in to scrimmage the varsity. Cannon fodder.

But I was picked as one of those twenty-two players, after two weeks of auditions, which was good for my morale. Irv Wisniewski, later a long-time assistant on the Delaware staff, was a member of our brave troops. So was Bob Hollway, later head coach of the St. Louis Cardinals and now an assistant with the Minnesota Vikings.

I was quite pleased with my progress. I started all the Jayvee games as a running guard and linebacker. Little did I know that this was to be the peak of my college football career.

The next spring, I caught for the baseball varsity and went away to play summer ball in International Falls, Minn. I came back on one leg. I broke the other one stealing home — or trying to steal home. That was in early August.

My sophomore football season was over before it began. I was in a walking cast when I returned to Ann Arbor, and I'd go to the football workouts and just watch and eat my heart out.

What to do? I just couldn't cancel out my football ambitions. So I asked Fritz Crisler if I could hang around in some fashion and try to learn what college football coaching was all about. Crisler was great. He arranged for me to go over with the 150-pound team as a coach, figuring I knew the Michigan system and could be of some help. He mentioned that there was a young graduate assistant over there coaching the ends, new to the Michigan operation. That's how I met George Allen. THE George Allen, later an outstanding and controversial coach in the National Football League.

That was my first taste of coaching, and it was delicious. It was the year Michigan qualified to go to the Rose Bowl. Coach Crisler told me that if I could scrounge up a ride to Pasadena, I could come back with the team on the train because Pete Elliott and Irv Wisniewski were returning earlier to join the basketball workouts, and that would leave a couple of seats for me and another injured player.

We got out there by car, with Dick Wakefield as chauffeur. He was the first of the baseball bonus babies, signed out of Michigan by the Detroit Tigers for what then was an astronomical sum. He had his very own bonus-baby automobile. We had a great time with Dick, who was sort of a free spirit. In Pasadena, I had the advantage of a Michigan football player and none of the disadvantages. I made all the social scenes, including dinner at the home of Tom Harmon, Michigan's all-time halfback, and his actress wife, Elyse Knox. And I sat on the bench as we creamed Southern California, 49-0.

By the time I reported for football my junior year, they had decided I might have the makings of a quarterback. Bennie Oosterbaan, formerly the backfield coach, had succeeded Crisler, who retired, as head coach. They knew and I knew that I wanted to be a coach, and they figured my playing quarterback would help me. I think they also figured I'd never be an All-American at any position.

So I turned out to be the third-string quarterback, and the demonstration man in scrimmages against the first level. I'd try to run the opposition's plays that the scouts would bring back each week. I think I still hold a University of Michigan record. One day I was pretending to be Perry Moss of Purdue. Moss would have thrown up at my act. I must have gone back to pass thirty-six times and haven't got one off yet. To this day, they don't know if I can throw. It made me feel a lot better when they killed Moss, too, on Saturday.

I did manage to get into a couple of varsity games, against Indiana and the Naval Academy. They were routs, in Michigan's favor, which is why I got to play. I also made the traveling squad that went to Michigan State and Ohio State. I never lettered. I was just a dud quarterback who had no business being in that company, but I loved it. I even loved being mussed up as a demonstrator. The referee in one scrimmage happened to be my baseball coach. He kept telling me to get out of there while I was still in one piece. He didn't want his catcher maimed.

I had to give it all up my senior year. By that time I was a physical mess, with a shoulder separation that would pop out at a glance. I had lost a faceful of teeth, and had problems with blood clots. Otherwise, I was beautiful. I had come charging out of high school to become a Michigan Wolverine, and instead had a rinky-dink three years. Despite that, I had the time of my life. But the best was yet to come.

I will forever be grateful to Bennie Oosterbaan. In the spring of my junior year, he took me aside. Unlike the one-liner, he did not leave me there.

"I want you to stop worrying about making the team next season," he told me in his office. "I'll do the best I can for you. You can be on the training table. We'll play you when we can. We'll take care of you and you can travel, too.

"But I want you to consider this: There's a coaching job open here in town, if you want it. It's at U-High. I know you want to be a coach, and I think you're going to be a good one. My advice would be to start now."

Ann Arbor University High School, on the University of Michigan campus. I jumped at the chance, and I would have grabbed it for nothing. It paid $1,600, very welcome gravy. I was getting an early start in coaching, the only thing I wanted to do. I long ago had forgotten about being Harold R. Raymond, M.D. Just call me Coach.

Bennie Oosterbaan is tremendous. He may well have been one of the greatest athletes of all time. An All-American end at Michigan three years in a row! Plus, a starting basketball and baseball player every year. He was one of the few athletes to be offered professional contracts in all three sports following his graduation.

But he chose to coach at Michigan and he never coached anywhere else. After assisting Crisler, he was head coach for ten years. He had my total admiration and he reached the point of diety when he brought in a one hundred and sixty-four pound quarterback-linebacker-whatever to talk to him and put him on the path to coaching.

Hank Fondy, a friend of mine, was leaving the U-High job to coach at a bigger high school. I had an interview with the authorities and decided to give up my senior year of eligibility, which I am sure came as a blow to the varsity. What it did was open up another seat on the bench.

I had agreed to play summer baseball in Montpelier, Vt., which turned out to be an exhilarating experience. Everytime I hear Willie Nelson sing that old ballad "Moonlight in Vermont," I do a great flashback. And what with looking forward to coaching at U-High, I was living in the best of worlds.

My greatest kick from coaching the schoolboys came from realizing I could put in an offense and have it work. What a feeling. I like paintings. I like to draw, to create with brush and pen and pencil. The first thrill I anticipated in coaching was to create, also, just like painting a picture.

I will try not to sound saccharine when I say that my first crop of boys was an outstanding one, on and off the field. We won six and lost two, but forget the statistics.They were a fine bunch of young men. My first captain was Scotty Crisler, Fritz's son, a big end. Fritz Crisler was out of coaching after bossing the Wolverines for a decade, but he was very much visible at Michigan and I picked his brain whenever I could.

Thirty years later, my first U-High squad threw a big party in my honor. As I had expected, they grew up to be an elite group of citizens: doctors, lawyers, merchants. Morton Cox is one of the top retinal surgeons in the country. Scotty Crisler is an attorney. Charley Erwin had become a priest, and they made him deliver the invocation on his knees the night of the party. As football players, they had given U-High its first conference championship since the Ice Age. A most enthusiastic bunch.

I had agreed to go back to U-High the following season, after my debut as a baseball pro in the cotton fields. This was to be as a graduate student, for I had received my degree — I had majored in mathematics and physical education — and had enrolled for six hours in the fall.

We duplicated the 6-2 record and won another conference championship. It was dawning on me that enthusiasm was the key to coaching success. It was something I had tons of, and it was working for me.

I didn't have much chance to try out my best stuff from the Guy Houston School of Discipline. I do remember one little incident in this realm. We practiced about a mile and a half from the school and everybody had to be aboard the team bus by 4:15, or else. One day, it gets to be 4:15 and I can see Mort Cox in the distance, running like the devil to beat the deadline. But old unbending Coach Ramond ordered the bus door to be closed. We took off and Cox — today's master retinal surgeon — had to run all the way to the field.

The same Mort Cox was holding a dummy during one practice. His attention was diverted by an airplane, and while he was watching it one of the guys slammed into the dummy. "I think there's something wrong with my arm, Coach," he said when he extricated it. There was. It was a weird-looking, angled arm; it had been fractured. We got him out of there via an ambulance.

Mort Cox is turning out to be big in my memoirs. The next year, he told me he was quitting the team. He had simply decided he didn't want to play any more. It gave me a chance to use a technique I still dredge up today. "Quit?" I said, as if Cox were proposing to commit a felony. "There's no way you are going to quit, because I'm not going to let you. The team needs you. You CAN'T quit."

It was right out of a novel — a hokey one. Cox stayed. Thirty years later at the party, he talked about that scene. "That was one of the best experiences of my life," he said, "because when I went on to medical school I felt like walking away from it all many times. Then I'd remember your saying you wouldn't let me leave; I had to go through with my commitment."

The Mort Coxes, they bring pleasure into the life of a football coach. They make it bearable, and then some.

And then there was Georgie Finkel. That name won't mean a thing to you unless you read television credits. He produced the Super Bowl telecast a year ago. Finkel had gone on to the University of Michigan, majoring in communications, and now is a front-line TV producer.

The paths of Coach Raymond and Georgie Finkel were to cross almost twenty years later at the unlikely site of Temple Stadium. Delaware was about to go at it again with the Temple Owls, whom I had grown to dearly hate. Ernie Casale, the Temple athletics director — and because of that never one of my favorite people — had told me Friday that I was to have my offensive team on the field five minutes before the game so that it could be introduced individually on television. This was one of Temple's early TV attempts.

"Wait a minute, Ernie," I bristled. "I'm not too sure I want to do this. If I can't introduce all twenty-two starters, the defensive players too, then I'd rather not trot out anybody."

Casale wouldn't budge. He said it was his ball park and his TV production and I HAD to do it. I consulted with my leader, Dave Nelson. He threw the buck right back to me with "It's your football team. You can do what you want with it."

OK. I did. I told Ernie Casale to forget the introduction of the Delaware offensive team. I would have my club on the field three minutes before the game, as the rules said, and not before. And that's the way it was handled.

Our bus pulled up to Temple Stadium on game day and when I jumped out, a young man approached me. I didn't recognize him.

"Coach, how are you?" he said. "I'm Georgie Finkel, one of your old U-High immortals, and I'm doing the TV production of your game today."

Right away, I felt bad because I had been so stubborn with the introduction bit. I had no regrets over locking horns with Casale, but I told Georgie that if I had known he was involved, there would have been no problem. I would have done anything he had asked.

"That's all right, Coach," he said with a laugh. "I won $20 on this deal, on a bet. I told my people you just wouldn't go for introducing half of your lineup."

5

Remembering the Maine

The fine hand of Bennie Oosterbaan had a lot to do with steering me into the ranks of college football coaches. Where I was steered to was the University of Maine, but I came awfully close to starting out at Florida State. How's that for extremes? Instead of the Atlantic Coast's southernmost state, I chose the one at the top of the map. I would have saved a lot of money on foul-weather gear and anti-freeze had I gone to Tallahassee, but things were to work out beautifully over the long haul.

Bennie called me in the winter after my second season at U-High, and I know he wanted to talk about my future in coaching. He told me there were some people interested in having me work with them and one, Dr. Don Veller, the head coach at Florida State, was going to be in town the next day. Veller had an opening for a backfield coach.

"This will be a good opportunity for you," Coach Oosterbaan said, and he arranged for Veller and me to lunch together. It was an historic lunch for me — my first real job interview in my chosen vocation. I tried to cool it, but I was excited. Veller described his setup. He said he'd get back to me that day; he had to visit a fraternity. He was back within an hour.

"I would like to have you on the Florida State staff," he

told me. "The job is yours if you want it. It pays $4,000 a year."

Four thousand dollars was a staggering sum to a former soda jerk. It sounded like all the money in the world, at least the Midwest. I still don't know why I didn't blurt out "I'll take it!". Instead, I asked him to give me a day or two to talk it over with my family. My hesitation — and I really cannot justify it — was to have a tremendous impact on my career.

The next day, I got another summons from Coach Oosterbaan.

"A fellow named Harold Westerman is here," he said, "and he'd like to talk to you about being an assistant football coach and the head baseball coach at Maine."

Bennie suggested I consider the Maine opportunity very seriously because "it's Michigan family up there." Dave Nelson was a Michigan who was leaving Maine to coach at Delaware, and Westerman was a Michigan — although he had not played football for the Wolverines — who was picked to succeed him after serving as Maine's backfield coach.

You have to understand this Michigan "family" business. The greatest legacy that Dave Nelson and I inherited as student athletes was a complete philosophy of football, Michigan style — principles that were solid, sound, tried and true. If you wanted to go crazy with your own imagination, you could go right ahead. But we always had that background of organization, of teaching techniques, of teaching progression, of breaking down skills.

So when masters like Bennie Oosterbaan, and also Fritz Crisler, said they thought I should go to Maine because of the Michigan connection, I did what they told me. Nelson had put in a good word for me with Westerman, too. He had stopped by to see me when I was playing summer baseball in New England and he was coaching at Maine, and we had some nice talks. I particularly remember one session we had in Keene, N.H., after a baseball game.

Westerman offered me the job after we talked at Ann Arbor. Now I was in a classier neighborhood. He offered me $4,250 and I started wondering what I was going to do with all that money. Would I have any problems with the IRS?

I was to be the line coach. On that same visit to Michigan, Westerman hired my roommate, Bob Hollway, to coach the backfield. I stalled on my acceptance, but not for long. I talked with some people, including Nelson. He said I should go to Maine, adding that at the first opportunity he had to bring me to Delaware, I would be hearing from him.

And thus I came part of the Michigan family, New England style. While Hollway and I were moving in, Nelson was moving out and taking Mike Lude and John Cuddeback with him for his Delaware staff. Dave still calls it a trade.

To get back to the Florida State opportunity, I was more than a little bit tempted by what I had seen of Tallahassee during the war. I had spent a pleasant weekend there. A bunch of us service guys had gone to a dance in the Florida capital and we seemed to have been outnumbered by the girls by 1,000 to 45. My only experience with that area had been a pleasant one — although it had absolutely nothing to do with football. But I liked the territory.

Anyhow, I finally told Don Veller, who had been calling consistently since our luncheon, that I had picked the Maine job because of the Michigan involvement. I must confess that there were to be times during the snows in Maine when I thought I had been sentenced, not hired, and I gave a thought or two to the climate in Tallahassee.

Veller? He's still at Florida State, coaching the golf team. Not bad duty.

Although my contract with Maine was not to begin until fall, they wanted me to report for spring practice, get involved with the installation of the offense and meet the proper people around campus; in general, to get a running start on acclimation. They gave me a little money, not much, for that work.

Tubby and Sue, bride and groom, showed up at Maine three days after our marriage and in another day or two I was looking at football films from 7:30 p.m. to midnight. Sue was learning fast how it was to be the wife of a football coach. More or less in self-defense, I guess, she suggested that she would like to see the films, too, if it would be possible. Harold Westerman thought this was a sensational idea. As one of my favorite Wilmington sports writers would put it, Westy embraced her with open arms.

After my disastrous second season of baseball that year, I gave up all hopes of ever being the new Bill Dickey, short version, and was glad to get back to Maine full-time and into an occupation my mother would respect.

We had our problems. We had a head coach, Westy, who had not played football in either high school or college. He was a basketball player at Michigan. But he did have the background of four years as a Dave Nelson aide. We had Bob Hollway, who never coached at all, in charge of the backfield. We had Tubby Raymond, with all of two years of high-school coaching in his resumé, coaching the line. We also had John Maturo, who came from Michigan as a graduate assistant, helping coach the ends. John is now the high-school principal in Pontiac, Mich. That was our grizzled staff.

Westy was a night man. He figured he did his best work when the sun went down, and he also felt that God would smile upon those coaches who worked longer than others, no matter what the work was. We would hit the office at 9:30 in the morning and often didn't get home until 2 — also in the morning. Many a night we would come up with an idea we thought was a bright one. We'd break out the films to see if it had been done before. If the idea survived, we would take it on to the gymnasium floor and we coaches would have a little scrimmage, trying to decide if the timing was going to be acceptable.

And, of course, we ran up some nice phone bills talking with Nelson at Delaware. He must have felt he was coaching two different universities. It got to the point where I got sick of Dave making the decisions for us after we had been up all night discovering that our brilliant tactics weren't going to work.

But would you believe that we went undefeated that first year, winning six games, tying one? Seven games, imagine that, half of what we played last season at Delaware. At that point now, we're just getting warmed up.

We won the championship of the Yankee Conference and I was in ecstacy. How long had this been going on? I knew we had all the answers now, our Michigan family, and we might not lose another game, ever.

You could say we played conservative football. Our quarterback was Gene Sturgis, and we did everything but tape his arm to his side so he wouldn't throw the ball. I think he passed 24 times in a seven-game schedule; everytime we completed one, they should have stopped the game and bronzed the ball. As far as our offense was concerned, we were playing with a square football.

But our gladiators played well and an extra plum was our domination of the state series with Colby, Bowdoin and Bates. My first line included Jimmy Butterfield, who last year coached Ithaca College to the Division III championship. His brother, Jack, was our fullback. Jack Butterfield became vice-president in charge of personnel for the New York Yankees. I picked up the paper one day about a year ago to read that Jack had been killed in a car accident.

One of our ends was Woody Carville, now the assistant

athletics director at Maine. Nobody ever heard of a spread receiver then, but we invented one in Carville. We had a raft of injuries and were going to play New Hampshire and we needed all the help we could get, personnel-wise. We got the idea that we should put good old Woody out there, spread him about 10-12 yards, because somebody from New Hampshire would have to get out and cover him, thus leaving us more room for our basic stuff.

We discussed this for three hours. "But what are we going to do," I asked, "if they ignore him?" It took us another hour to explore this revolting possibility.

"You don't think we're going to throw the ball to him, do you?" Westerman countered. As I have mentioned, we all looked upon the thrown football as a sacrilege.

"We'll need some sort of pass play if they don't cover him," I argued. You will gather that this was one of the great moments of all time in football planning. As luck would have it. New Hampshire did indeed send a guy out to play against Woody in his strange position. We won the game without having to include what to us would have been a Harlem Globetrotters play.

One of my assignments was to scout. Sue and I had a black puppy, a cocker spaniel we called Touchdown, and the three of us would take off on a scouting mission each week. If you ever have the chance to travel by automobile from Orono, Me., to Burlington, Vt., site of the University of Vermont, don't take it. It is a horrible ride — or was then — over mountains, stones, sticks, hills.

Sue was pregnant at the time and the Vermont expedition was her first. We must have stopped eight times, either for Sue to throw up or for Touchdown to throw up, or both. Because naturally I am going to be the next football coach at Notre Dame, or at least Southern California, my coaching and its responsibilities, like the scouting, must take precedence

The 1920 wedding photograph of my parents, Ira and Pearl. They tell me I look like Mom.

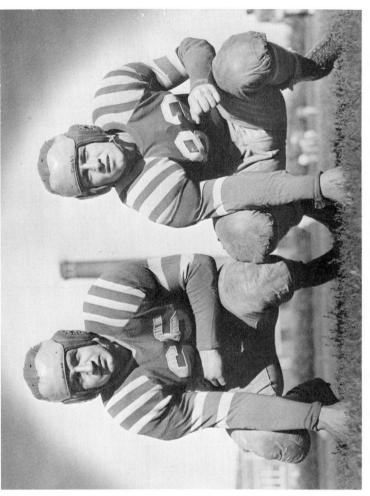

From left to right: Pete Fusi, one of Flint's leading smokestacks and Tubby Raymond. This was when two of the three were co-captains at Flint Northern High.

I'm either showing John Major my manicure or how to throw something I can catch. We were batterymates at Flint Northern in 1973.

I don't know why I look so stern. These two gentlemen provided me with the background that led to whatever success I have had as a coach. Guy Houston (left) was my high school coach and Fritz Crisler my coach at Michigan. Looks like a scene from an Andy Hardy movie, doesn't it?

The circles identify two prominent spear-carriers on the 1948 Michigan varsity. I'm on the right, Irv Wisniewski on the left. The names of the spectators escape me for the moment.

I don't know what I'm doing in this picture, taken at Michigan in 1948. I was a sophomore. Perhaps the team captain, Dominic Tomasi, and Coach Bennie Oosterbaan were welcoming me aboard. Either that, or telling me I can't come in without a necktie.

I'm the middle man in the second row as baseball captain at Michigan. Ray Fisher is the man out of uniform. He was one of the great college baseball coaches.

In 1949, I did some batting-practice catching for my home-town minor-leaguers, the legendary Flint Arrows. Helping with this hokey pose is Manager Jack Tighe, (top left), who later managed the Detroit Tigers.

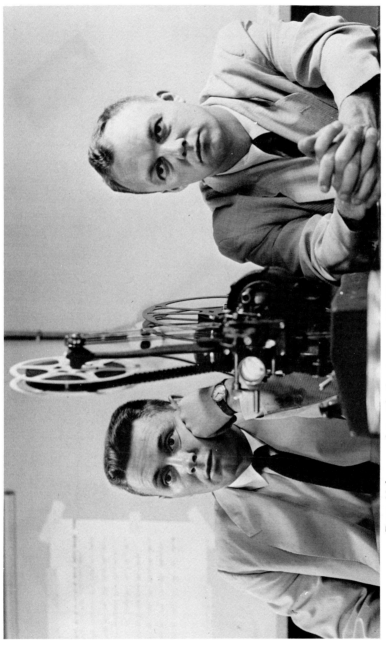

Dave Nelson and I with the inseparable film projector. Not many laughs this day. We were watching either "Camille" or re-runs of a losing game.

This was the day I was promoted to head coach in 1966. Dave Nelson (left) looks as if he is having second thoughts. Like Dave and me, John A. Perkins, then the university president, is a Michigan man.

E.A. Trabant

. . . the university president. When we win, I'm allowed to call him Art.

David M. Nelson

. . . my boss, the one and only Admiral. Football's No. 1 intellectual.

R. R. M. Carpenter, Jr.

. . . the Delaware athletic program's best friend. I almost blew that association the first time I met him.

John J. DeLuca

. . . he went to bat for me and helped make the change that enabled Dave Nelson to concentrate on the athletic directorship while I took over the football team.

Ed Maley
Linebacker Coach

Ted Kempski
Offensive Coordinator

Ron Rogerson
Offensive Line Coach

Joe Purzycki
Defensive Backfield Coach

Bob Depew
Defensive End Coach

Paul Billy
Interior Defensive Line Coach

"Herky" Billings
Offensive End Coach

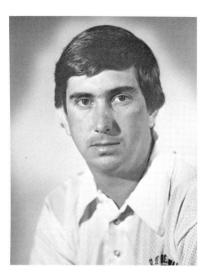

Dr. C. Roy Rylander
Head Athletic Trainer

Keith Handling
Assistant Trainer

Raymond B. "Scotty" Duncan
Assistant Athletic Director

Co-Author, Al Cartwright

Alabama's Paul (Bear) Bryant
. . . he nicknamed me "Napoleon."

over everything — including childbirth. Sue and Touchdown just had to hang in there — neither mountains nor traffic nor the nausea of my passengers would stop this intelligence expert.

We would get home late and I would stay up the rest of the night to have the scouting report ready for Westy. I really didn't wake up until the following Wednesday — then get ready to do it all over again. I've never been so sleepy and tired as I was that first year.

You could not believe the weather that winter in Orono. It was their coldest in 20 years and it seemed to never stop snowing. I had to keep a lamp on in the engine of our car, and a blanket over the hood, so we could get out each morning. One day I opened the front door and I was staring right into a rectangle of snow. Drifts had completely covered the doorway.

Fortunately, Sue had gone back to Flint the first of December, because that's where she wanted the baby to be born. I had tried to talk her out of it, but the way the winter developed, I wished she had left the first of November. Debbie was born the day after Christmas. I was there for the grand event and by the time Sue rejoined me in Maine, she had missed about six weeks of Antarctica.

We had two more winning years with the Black Bears of Maine — who wore the colors of pale blue and white — with records of 4-3-0 and 4-2-1. We tied for the conference championship, and the next season finished second. We were quite comfortable with our competition. The first part of the schedule was the Yankee Conference, and the second part was the state series, so we really had two shots at success.

I was a pretty rigid young coach when it came to rules and regulations, but I got more chance to display it as the head baseball coach. We made up the rainouts, and the snowouts, on the schedule. One morning we decided to play a rainout with Bowdoin, on their field, and I started rounding up my troops. I was looking for my ace pitcher, a boy named Pearly Dean, to tell him he would be the starter. I hurried over to his fraternity house to give him the news, and found him in the basement shooting pool. I also found him with a cigarette in his mouth, a definite Raymond no-no. Dean took one look at me and immediately flipped that cigarette into his mouth with his tongue. It disappeared — the cigarette, that is. He literally ate it!

I was impressed with Dean's act, but he had blown the game — and the season. On the way out of the frat house, I bumped into our captain, Red Merrill, and told him Dean had just quit the team. "That's funny," Merrill said. "I was just talking to him and he didn't even mention that."

I also had another miss-the-bus scene similar to that at U-High. The culprit was David Bates, our third baseman. It got to be 9 a.m. departure time, and we were all aboard but Bates. I could see him running hard in our direction, right down the mall. He had only about 50 yards to go, but I ordered the driver to take off. David was waiting for us at the ball park. He had driven his own car.

I was a hardhead. Today, I'd wait for David Bates. How simple, how stubborn I was. I showed it all over again in my first dealing with a major-league baseball scout. A scout from the Detroit Tigers came in to talk to me and asked me who I thought could play. I immediately mentioned Al Hackett, one of the most natural kid hitters I've ever seen, a left-hander with power. The scout spent the next 15 minutes telling me why Al Hackett was NOT a prospect.

"Well," I said, with all the outrage I could muster on such short notice, "you forget about it. You go back and tell the folks at Detroit never to send anybody to talk to me again because if you've got all the answers, there's no sense taking up my time."

How's that for being a tough guy? Every time I think of that incident, I cringe. I can't even use the excuse that I had been standing in the snow too long. I was a little on the impossible side when it came to diplomacy. Not a very good advertisement for the University of Michigan at times. But I was learning.

What ever happened to Al Hackett, my phee-nom? Don't ask. Although he truly could hit, he had some health problems. He had the only false teeth on the club, but that didn't impress the scout. Nobody ever signed Al, and he went on commuting to school 80 miles round-trip every day.

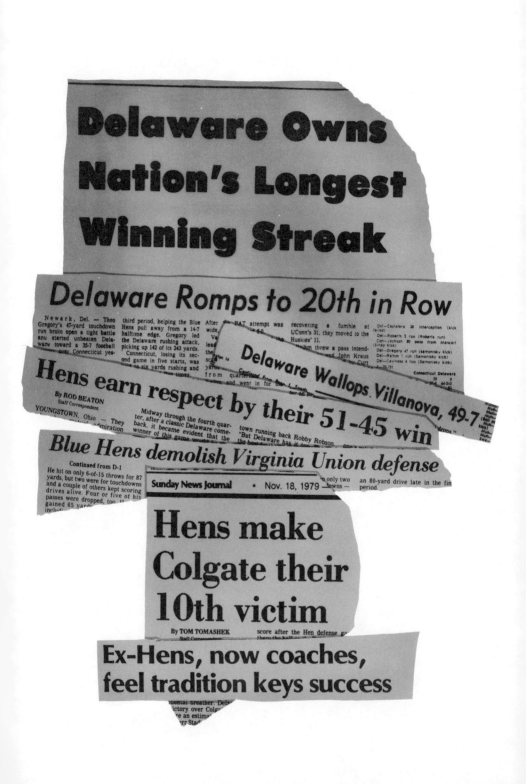

Delaware Owns Nation's Longest Winning Streak

Delaware Romps to 20th in Row

Newark, Del. — Theo Gregory's 47-yard touchdown run broke open a tight battle and started unbeaten Delaware toward a 35-7 football ...over Connecticut yes...

third period, helping the Blue Hens pull away from a 14-7 halftime edge. Gregory led the Delaware rushing attack, picking up 142 of its 243 yards.

Connecticut, losing its second game in five starts, was ...to six yards rushing and ...times.

After ...PAT attempt was ...wide...

Ve...

...Huskies' 11.

...Reihm threw a pass intend...and John Kraus ...by Curt...

recovering a fumble at UConn's 31, they moved to the...

Del—Castafero 34 interception (kick failed)
Del—Roberts 2 run (Roberts run)
Con—Jackson 80 pass from Mancari (Sinay kick)
Del—Gregory 47 run (Samonisky kick)
Del—Reihm 1 run (Samonisky kick)
Del—Caviness 4 run (Samonisky kick)
A—20,751

Connecticut Delaware

Delaware Wallops Villanova, 49-7

Hens earn respect by their 51-45 win

By ROD BEATON
Staff Correspondent

YOUNGSTOWN, Ohio — They ...admiration

Midway through the fourth quarter, after a classic Delaware comeback, it became evident that the winner of this game would ...

...town running back Robby Robson. ...
"But Delaware has it ...the best...

Blue Hens demolish Virginia Union defense

Continued from D-1

He hit on only 6-of-15 throws for 87 yards, but two were for touchdowns and a couple of others kept scoring drives alive. Four or five of his passes were dropped, too. ...gained 65 yards... includi...

...only two...downs —

an 80-yard drive late in the fin... period.

Sunday News Journal   •   Nov. 18, 1979

Hens make Colgate their 10th victim

By TOM TOMASHEK
Staff Correspondent

score after the Hen defense ga... them the ball...

Ex-Hens, now coaches, feel tradition keys success

...mental breather. Dela... ...ictory over Colg... ...re an estima... ...rr Stad...

6

Johnny Bench I Wasn't

Let me tell you about my professional baseball career in one word: Bad. If I were you, I'd turn to the next chapter.

At the University of Michigan, I was delighted to discover that I could still be the same size and play first level in baseball, if not football. I was the varsity catcher for three years, during which we won two Big Ten Conference championships and tied for another. My senior year, they elected me captain. The center fielder on those clubs was Bump Elliott, who later coached the Wolverine football team.

I also played a lot of summer baseball in fast amateur company. Two of those summers were at International Falls, Minn., with a team of college players that was organized to advertise the Mando Paper Mill. We took on all comers in the northern Minnesota area.

The third summer, I went to the Northern League in New England to play for Montpelier, Vt., and my Michigan coach, Ray Fisher. I had been calculatingly ignored by the big-league scouts, who didn't seem to be looking for smallish catchers with no power.

Still, I managed to make the all-star team in New England in a league which had catchers like Lou Berberet, who got to the majors. I also had caught batting practice back home and participated in the infield workouts with the legendary Flint Arrows of the Class A Central League, which was a Detroit Tigers farm team managed by Jack Tighe. Tighe later managed the Detroit Tigers themselves.

The New York Yankees had a team at Muskegon in the same Central League. And it was Muskegon that signed me on the recommendation of Detroit's Tighe — does that tell you something?

Bonus? Are you kidding? My bonus was a warm handshake.

I had this job coaching football at University High School in Ann Arbor, but they agreed I could leave for spring training with the Muskegon club. So I found myself in beautiful Clarksdale, Miss., in a real, live pro baseball camp. It was a strong camp, despite my presence, because it contained names like Elston Howard, Jim Greengrass, Jerry Lynch and Loren Babe, names that any baseball trivia fan will recognize. But they may not know that Howard, later a great catcher for the Yankees, was then a center fielder. And Greengrass, who became an outfielder with the Cincinnati Reds and the Phillies, was a pitcher for Muskegon. Let the record show that I warmed up Jim Greengrass.

I was not exactly encouraged when I learned that my manager was Bob Finley, a former big-leaguer who also intended to be the back-up catcher. They had told me when I signed that Muskegon needed a catcher. Now I was getting the message that they needed a catcher just for spring training. A fellow named Bob O'Neal was set as No. 1, and all I had to do to be No. 2 was to beat out the manager.

Despite the handwriting on the clubhouse wall, I had a pretty decent spring. So I was a little stunned when Finley — no relation to Charley, by the way — called me in and said I hadn't made it. There was some talk I might be shipped to Binghamton of the Eastern League to be the reserve catcher, but Binghamton had big Gus Triandos and my equally large summer league opponent, Lou Berberet, so I was dead there. No room at the inn for the hot shot from Michigan and the Northern League All-Stars.

It came down to a choice. I could stay behind in Clarksdale when Muskegon pulled out, and join the Clarksdale club of the Class C Cotton States League, or be optioned to a club in the Big State League, the Big State being Texas. Because I knew my way around Clarksdale and wouldn't have to start off cold, I elected to stay there. They paid me $300. A month.

Clarksdale was a minor-league affiliate of the Boston Braves. I became the regular catcher for a club that finished a driving seventh, and I came out of the season a solid black-and-blue mess. I only weighed 157 pounds when I started; after a summer in that heat, I looked like I had tuberculosis.

You can look it up, but I hope you won't, in the small print: Raymond, Harold, batted .259 in 80 games, with two home runs.

Permit me to corner you and tell you about one of those home runs. Ready? It was a grand-slam in El Dorado, Ark., on a Sunday afternoon with the temperature about 110 degrees. I can only surmise that the pitcher was weaker than I was.

I grew up some, mentally, in my stint with Clarksdale. I can credit my first raging argument with an umpire.

I was catching and some villain lined a ball down the right-field foul line. He legged it into a three-base hit because, in my opinion, everbody else thought it was a foul ball and our troops played it as such. I charged the umpire, who said it was a fair ball. When I asked him why he hadn't indicated as much, his answer was that he only had to signal when a ball was foul.

Our manager, Chet Morgan, who seemed to be 150 years old to me but in reality was about 35, came out to get me.

"You're wrong, Stumpy," he said to his own ball player.

And hearing that, the umpire threw me out of the game. Getting chased from a game in the Cotton States League was an automatic $50 fine, which was a lot of money.

I still believe the umpire ran me because my own manager said I had no case. Anyhow, now I was REALLY burning. It was more than a young fellow with a red neck could handle. I went back to the dugout and threw my mask in the general direction of Manager Morgan. It just missed him. Then I took off my shinguards and chest protector and tossed them at him, too, barking "If you want some more of this, you can meet me in the clubhouse," or some such adolescent remark.

That night, I was in the local diner consoling myself with a bad steak. I felt a tap on my shoulder and it's Chet Morgan. My first reaction was that he was going to deck me right there and get even for my showing him up in the dugout. My second reaction was to start trying to remember all the fancy boxing stuff I had learned as a kid sparring with Harry Carlquist in his basement.

But Chet Morgan wasn't returning my challenge. He asked if he could sit down with me.

"Son," he said, "nothing that happens on the field or in the clubhouse should ever be taken away from the park. That's all I have to say about today's game. Now I'd like to pay for your dinner — and also your fine."

And he did

There was another incident that summer that now is literally among my souvenirs.

We were playing in Greenville, Miss. I was catching and Jerry Lynch — the Jerry Lynch who had been with me in the Muskegon training camp and who was on his way to becoming a remarkable pinch-hitter for the Pittsburgh Pirates — was the runner on second base for the bad guys in the bottom of the ninth. He is the tying run and he takes off to steal.

Believe me. Trust me. Bet a wing of your house on it. I threw out Jerry Lynch by a kilometer, helped by the presence of a left-handed hitter at the plate. The plate umpire made the call and said the runner was safe. I was outraged, to put it mildly. I carried on so much that the umpire should have chased me right then. He would have, had he, in my out-voted opinion, not blown the call at third.

The next hitter was Ed Sudol, then a big first baseman, later a long-time and great umpire in the National League. On the very first pitch, Sudol knocked it out of sight and we lost the ball game. Sudol was rounding the bases and I was letting the umpire have it all over again, threatening to run over him and destroy him, or at least subdivide him. I kept getting in his way as he tried to get off the field.

That week, I got a letter from the president of the league. I still have it. It goes like this: "Please be advised to pay the sum of $50 for your conduct in the Sunday afternoon game in Greenville, Miss. Obviously, we cannot accept this type of behavior from the participants in our league and I do hope this will be a constant reminder of the type of conduct that we would like to see.

"P.S.: Please be advised to pay the additional sum of $25 for threatening Umpire Stone's life."

You will get an idea of the caliber of my baseball ability when you notice that I have to dredge up a couple of bouts with umpires as some of my few highlights as a pro. But I wasn't the worst ball player in the league, althought it might have been a photo finish. I had a lousy start with the bat, then got hot and hit about .475 for the month of June — and that was it. I really had gone into that season with the idea that I was going to be a Ball Player, capitalized. Then it started hitting me that even if I got anywhere, it would even-tually detract from my football coaching because of the overlapping seasons, and football was where I definitely wanted to be.

So I was determined to hang up the old mask and glove after one punishing season, especially when I got the job at the University of Maine the next year, coaching the line and eventually, the baseball team. But then I got a call from my home-town nine, the Flint Arrows. They had acquired my contract from Muskegon and wanted me to play for them for $325 a month. Baseball was rearing its attractive head again. Good old vacillating me. I had to go for it.

It was the giddiest of times for me. Sue and I had decided to get married that spring, I was getting my teeth into college football coaching right out of college myself and I was jumping up a notch in pro baseball right in my own town. The $325 month was to be on top of the unbelievable $4,250 Maine was paying me. The world was my oyster, which is something I always wanted to say even though I still don't know what it means.

Sue and I were married April 7. Four days later we were at the University of Maine, where I was to assist with spring practice. Some spring. It was colder than whale manure. I mean, it was COLD. I had known some icy stuff back in Michigan, but this was brutal. Right out of Dr. Zhivago.

Mike Lude, making his last appearance before taking off with Dave Nelson for Delaware, was the Maine baseball coach at the time. It is an amazing thing, the Maine baseball program. It has been a quality one for centuries, even before Rudy Vallee started crooning Maine's Stein Song. The kids go out and take batting practice in the snow and wouldn't be caught dead wearing a batting glove. You never hear them scream from the shock of hitting a ball in those temperatures. When I took over as baseball coach the next spring, I found out we had to play in incredible situations.

I couldn't get away from football practice even to throw a

baseball a little bit. Besides, it was always below freezing, and that was no inducement. In Orono, Maine, they don't have many palm trees. Accompanied by my gorgeous, courageous and probably regretful bride, I joined the Flint club on opening night in Dayton, Ohio. The manager was a guy named Steve Bysco, who did not impress me as Hall of Fame material in the leadership department. He had this enormous belly and must have weighed two seventy-five. His steal sign was to breathe on his fingernails and polish them on his stomach.

I introduced myself to Manager Bysco and told him I was a few miles behind the the other guys in conditioning because I had been coaching football — in Maine, yet — and really hadn't had a chance to work out on my own. Manager Bysco was not upset. "I'll tell you what we're gonna do, kid," he said. "We're gonna play you in shape."

Opening night or not, they put me in to catch halfway through the game, and I had to bat against Ryne Duren, he of the bad eyes and the fast ball that had flames on it. He sawed the ball right out of my little hands the only time I faced him. I got the bat on the ball, which was an upset, and the ball went one way and the broken stick another and I was an easy out. It was terribly cold, although after Maine it felt like Florida. The next day, my arm hurt from the little bit of throwing I had done. My debut in Class A baseball was a genuine mess.

Here I am married all of two months and Sue, my bride, is in Flint and I take off on a 14-game road trip with the Arrows, playing towns like Muskegon, Saginaw and Charlestown. In Muskegon, I received a pre-arranged telegram from Sue. The code informed me that she was pregnant. By this time I had been in eight ball games and had one hit, that a cheapie.

I was glad to get off the road and "home" with Sue, such

as it was. It was one of those things generously called a studio apartment — it seemed we slept in the kitchen, cooked in the kitchen, ate in the kitchen. Poor, pregnant Sue, who was finding out how it was to be the wife of a baseball player. Lunch at 3 o'clock in the afternoon, play the ball game, dinner at midnight. Not too sparkling a schedule for a mother-to-be.

To this day, just the mention of that upstairs apartment makes Sue upchuck all over again. It was the worst summer of her life. Mine was just a little better. I lasted until July, plundering the ball at my usual .210 clip. The team was in last place, and stayed there. By now I had the idea that if I was to make a living at baseball, it would be a rather sparse one. While it wasn't hard for me to love people or to have people love me, the baseball system does not adore my type of performer.

The Flint Arrows decided they were going to make a change in catchers and were going to put me in a bow and sling me to Saginaw. But I had had it; I didn't want my standing as a football coach to be defamed before I even became one.

So that was the end of my glorious career in baseball — with the exception of one game, some years later, in the Wilmington Semi-Pro League. I went 1-for-3 at the plate and threw out Ralph Conrad trying to steal second.

In case you missed it, let me tell you again about that grand-slam I hit in El Dorado . . .

7

The Admiral and I

The first contact I ever had with Dave Nelson, he knew nothing about it — because it was with a photograph of him. Henny Youngman might call it a contact print.

When you went to the equipment room at the University of Michigan, you had to deal with Hank Hatch, who was the gear man. Right next to the issue window, he maintained a big bulletin board full of photos of great football players in Ann Arbor history. Tom Harmon, Forrest Evashevski, Al Wistert and Dave Nelson, wearing No. 23.

That's how I discovered what Nelson looked like. The next spring, he was the freshman baseball coach, but I didn't get to play for him. The varsity needed catching help, so Ray Fisher had me with the big guys all season. The frosh worked out on another field; Dave and I would run by each other and say hello. Because I had researched his background as a Michigan halfback, I was in awe of him. He makes light of his ability as a football player, but you should hear the way they talk about the old halfback at Michigan. It is with total respect. No wonder. He won the Big Ten Conference award for proficiency in scholarship and athletics. As a senior, he was the Wolverines' leading rusher with an average of 6.3 yards per carry. As they say in the trade, he could play.

Now we move ahead a few years. I was sitting on the

accept a summer contract so that his staff could go on vacation. He said I could do some studies or whatever I wanted, to get ready for the fall. I accepted, and what I tackled were some defensive studies.

That was how I met Bob Carpenter — and it's a wonder I didn't get fired before the first football was pumped up.

I must say with great humility that I am an intense person and when I study something, I do a pretty good job. So one afternoon, I was doing my defensive lesson. I was the only one around. Dave was away and so was Bob Siemen, his assistant director of athletics.

I liked it that way, because I could concentrate. No interruptions, no distractions. And that's what I was doing, with all the cylinders in my hard head, when a man walked into the office. I looked up and almost said "What the hell are you doing here?" But I didn't. My mother would have loved my restraint. I kept right on working. This interloper — my first impression was that he was a big, tan guy with sort of a William Holden look to him — peered over my shoulder at my papers.

"Mmmmm . . . football?" he asked. I managed a disgusted "Yes," trying to give the impression he was bothering me. This was the first job I had to do for Dave Nelson, and I wanted it to be good. I was anxious to have it completed by the time he got back from vacation.

Then this pesky person introduced himself, sticking out a large hand. "I'm Bob Carpenter."

I didn't know whether to genuflect, crawl under the desk, or leave town. I had heard so much about Bob Carpenter, as president of the Phillies, for the tremendous and influential interest he had in the University of Delaware and for what he had done for its program as a trustee. And here he had been in the office 10 minutes before I even acknowledged his presence. Oh, Harold Raymond, the next Knute Rockne, will you EVER learn?

I managed to pull myself together and told him who I was. That was the start of a friendship. Right then he said he had received a letter in Clearwater from Dave Nelson suggesting that perhaps the Phillies could use me in some capacity. It was to amount to scouting and running a tryout camp in Connie Mack Stadium when the Phils were on the road.

Funny thing. Once we got into the football season, he never spoke to me. He didn't start visiting again until it was over. I figured I had screwed something up, or had offended him in some way, and confronted him with my concern.

"Not at all," he said. "You were busy, and I know you don't like to talk baseball during the football season. So I let you alone."

John DeLuca, now retired from his law practice and living in the Sarasota, Florida area, was Bob's close friend and another super person. He was on the athletic council. Their story goes back many years, to when Bob became interested in the university through his father, the late R. R. M. Carpenter. Bob and John were the men responsible for bringing Bill Murray, who had been coaching in the anonymity of a children's home in Winston-Salem, N.C., to Delaware in the '40s as football coach. Murray was a former Duke star and Bob was a Duke man.

I understand there were a number of people who wanted to hire a name, like a former professional player, who could elevate Delaware to the big time. But that wasn't what President John Perkins, Carpenter or DeLuca wanted to do. They wanted what we have now — a football program that would do the job, be a source of pride for the community and the faculty, meet the needs of the people and be a rallying point for the whole state without being the tail that wagged everything else.

I found Dave Nelson all I had anticipated — a genuine person to work for and with. He was not one to keep his assistants under the thumb. We had constant and long discussions in the staff room; some were really arguments. Which direction are we going, what are we going to run, and so on.

I know there are those who do not appreciate the intellect and the quality of Nelson, and I like to kid the cool side of him. I've often made the joke that he said "Hello" and smiled at me the day I showed up at Delaware — and that's the last nice thing he's said to me.

Dave always listened to his staff. He was very responsive. He would argue like the devil some nights and go out angry, shaking his head. The next morning, he'd come in saying "What was that you wanted to do?" I'd give him my idea again and a lot of times, he reversed his field and said "OK — let's do it."

When I became head coach, with my own staff, I realized what Dave had been doing. He needed time to think, and he really didn't want to give me the idea that anything I said would be automatically adopted. Dave would go home, toss it around overnight and come back with a decision.

He also could lay it on the line for immediate action. Andy Wagner was a very good running back for Delaware for three seasons, his last two in my regime as assistant, and he is a member of our 1,000-Yard Club. He figured in a little incident that showed the tough and the humorous side of Nelson.

We were watching game films one Sunday and Nelson pointed out that Wagner had played very poorly in the game the day before.

"I want you to eat Wagner's tail off first chance you get," he said.

"I don't think he played that bad," was my ungrammatical but nervy comment.

"He played poorly," Dave repeated, firmly, "and I want you to get after him. If you don't care to do it, then I'll be the backfield coach and I'll do it myself."

I grumpily said I'd take care of it. City Hall had scored again. With that, we turned the projector back on and I let out some steam by kicking what I thought was the leg of the table. But I missed and booted what I immediately discovered was Dave's leg, not the table's.

Dave turned the lights on. "And don't kick me, either," he said, dead pan.

It didn't take me long to ascertain I was in a faster league than Maine's, as far as personnel was concerned. I had inherited an experienced backfield corps. We had Jimmy Flynn, Jim Ford, Andy Wagner and Jim Zaiser to run the ball, plus a good-looking soph, Bob Moneymaker. And the quarterback, senior Donnie Miller, was to have a Little All-American year. They were not only fine players — they had sharp minds, which helps explain why they were fine players. They were so good I felt more like a chaperone than a coach. One of my zingers from that season is that I was amazed how quickly they picked up my teaching.

Having been a line coach for three years, I had to do some cramming in my new responsibility. I felt a little inadequate, which may come as a surprise to the reporters who have identified me as "cocky" over the last dozen years. The coaches made it standard procedure to go out on the field with a football every day before the squad reported. We went through the handoff and other backfield techniques and pretty soon it would develop, or deteriorate, into a game of touch. Bob Carpenter took part in a number of these. I made sure he always eluded my touch.

With the seasoning we had among the backs, the learning experience was mine, not theirs. They could absorb and execute quickly. Nelson handled the quarterback meetings himself. I was in charge of the running backs and put in the plays. That was the one-platoon era, so I also was the defensive backfield coach. Defenses then were far less sophisticated than today's two-platoon specialization.

Don Miller didn't look like much of a football player standing still, but he was what the medical association ordered for Dave's offense, for four years. He was a ball-handling magician with a great passing touch. In my time at Delaware, only Tom DiMuzio, Jeff Komlo and Scott Brunner, all big guys — and offensive-platooners — have come along as quarterbacks Miller would have trouble beating out.

When you are as good as Donnie, things go your way. Like the Bucknell game, my first year. Miller was playing defensive safety. I told him he could expect a particular Bucknell pattern in a certain situation. Sure enough, it came along just as we had read it. Miller disregarded all the receivers, ran right into the pattern area and knocked the ball down. Now he had to be careful, for Bucknell had read HIS reaction. He would have to play honest.

The next time, the same situation, Donnie ran deep to his left, to the area in which they would throw the ball. Bucknell instead sent a receiver down the middle of the field on a post pattern (the goalpost is the landmark for the play). There was nobody within 25 yards of him, including Miller, but he dropped the ball. If this had been me defending, the receiver would have caught the ball and gone for a touchdown. With Donnie, it didn't happen.

In another game, Miller was slow handing off the ball to Zaiser, who could get to the hole very quickly. So slow, in fact, that Donnie had to keep it. Donnie kept it to the tune of a 45-yard TD run.

We had opened the season at West Chester, winning

40-6. Miller passed 10-for-15, with two touchdowns, and we rushed for 276 yards. It was a most convincing showing. I went home sitting on top of my little world, but Bud Brusch, a neighbor who still comes to the games, knocked me right off it. It was my first post-game encounter with Delaware fandom.

"You gotta do something with that pass defense," Brusch complained. Here we had clobbered West Chester, and he was knocking the pass defense. West Chester had completed 11 out of 28 for 196 yards and their only touchdown. For that we had to do something?

We swept our first five games. Beautiful. Then we should have been arrested for losing successive 14-13 games to Muhlenberg and Gettysburg. They were successive letdowns. We played poorly. And we never have let Jimmy Flynn forget that he missed kicking the extra points. Forget the 6.8-yard rushing average you had that season, Flynn, and your career 1,387 yards. Where were you when we needed you?

Donnie Miller sparked us into the well-named Refrigerator Bowl in Evansville, Ind., where we beat Kent State 19-7. It was Bleak City.

We rolled merrily along my first six seasons, all winners. Then I learned what it was like to have a losing year. We won two out of nine — my first losing season anywhere, going back to Flint Northern High. I didn't even know it could happen. There were tortures like losing 14-12 to Amherst and 3-0 to Lafayette on successive Saturdays. The Amherst thing never should have happened. Donnie Miller was the backfield coach at Amherst, and we were all tensed up to destroy him. We didn't. And at Lafayette, we had a perfectly good touchdown called back when a block by our fullback, Tony Suravitch, was interpreted as holding.

We tied Marshall 6-6 but another strange call kept us from winning. The Marshall ball-carrier fumbled the ball across the goal-line as he went down under a pile of beef. It was a little roll that went right into the hands of Karl Lorenz, our safety. But the officials claimed Lorenz had stolen the ball when the runner was down. It should have been a touchback, giving us the ball on our 20. Instead, Marshall kept possession and went in to score their only touchdown.

We beat Hofstra and our cousins from Temple on back-to-back Saturdays, and that was it in the victory department. We got shut out by Rutgers and Bucknell and the season was over, not a moment too soon.

It wasn't a fun year. I discovered that there is something traumatic about losing. You also lose confidence in what you are doing, in yourself, in the program. With one exception, losing is non-productive. The exception is that it results in more innovation than would ordinarily be brought out. Innovation rhymes with desperation.

One of the all-time heart-crushing games we played in my tenure as assistant came the next year, 1961, and the egg is all over my face. Ohio University, the defending small-college champions, nosed us out 17-16 with exactly one second left on the clock in our stadium. We had a two-point lead and the ball in our half of the field, first and 10, with about a minute to go. Because Ohio had no timeouts, it was going to be hard to blow this. We — or I — succeeded.

"We are not going to have to punt the ball — we are going to be all right," I told Dave on the phones. "We'll run the clock out."

"Gotcha," said Dave. Our quarterback, Ted Kempski, who now is my faithful aide, understood this. He told the ball-carriers not to step out of bounds. We had to keep the clock going. We didn't get anywhere in three sweeps. Traditionally, and unfortunately, it now was fourth down. "We'll let it go again," I said. "We won't take a chance on a blocked kick."

We drew a five-yard penalty on purpose for taking too much time in punt formation, although we never intended to kick. Now it was fourth-and-15. Our last rushing play gained four yards.

Ohio took over on our 39 with twenty-four seconds to go. They hit a sideline pass to the 30. Then they scrambled into field-goal formation with that big "1" gleaming on the scoreboard. Somebody named Jim McKee kicked the ball nine miles on an angle from the 38, right over the crossbar. Because the goalposts were set 10 yards back, it was an official 48-yarder. The silence in the park was unbelievable. It was a classic come-from-ahead defeat. And I was the one who talked Nelson into playing it that way. But he never mentioned this to anyone. He took the rap. The newspaper accounts of the game jumped all over him for not having called for a punt.

Like Dr. John A. Perkins, the university president, said, "Any fool could have punted the ball. It took some imagination to lose it that way."

In the late 1950s, stories began circulating that Nelson was being wooed by the major colleges, and that he would leave Delaware. He had me squirming. Quite frankly, I thought that if he left that early in my Delaware career, they would give the job to Mike Lude, the line coach, who had been around longer. Still, I was anxious for Dave to get another opportunity because there would be some openings, some growth for me. If not at Delaware, then where ever he went.

Baylor University in Texas was the first to tempt him. If I had been him, I would have gone. But he had access to information I didn't. He saw things he didn't like. For example, Baylor had a big stadium — but they still had a small library. They offered him this and that, but they didn't have the other things he needed academically and he knew he'd never be able to sell himself to the faculty as an equal, nor his program.

He seriously considered going to Indiana as director of athletics and wanted to take me along as baseball coach. The deal was that I would be worked into the football staff, too, but Dave withdrew. He also worked hard to get me the baseball job at Michigan after Ray Fisher retired.

Iowa's winning the Rose Bowl in both 1957 and 1959 with our offense — Forrest Evashevski, Dave's backfield playmate at Michigan, had borrowed our Wing-T — made our Admiral Nelson a hot item. A bunch of strange things happened — or almost happened — in 1957. Dave and I spoke at a clinic at the University of Kentucky and spent some evenings at the home of Blanton Collier, their coach. When I returned to Newark, Collier called to offer me the job as his backfield coach. He apologized for not routing the request through Nelson, but said he couldn't locate him.

I told Collier that was nothing to worry about — but as it turned out, it was. Even though I turned down the job, Dave gave me the cold shoulder for three weeks because he hadn't been involved in the discussion. I think he felt I had become dissatisfied with him and/or Delaware. That wasn't true. I hadn't motivated the offer, but felt flattered to have received it. Dave informed Collier how he felt about the "tampering," too. He felt Delaware offered a better opportunity for me than what I would be "fooling around" with in Kentucky.

Then Dave was romanced by the University of Illinois. He went out there for an interview, and told Mike Lude, Irv Wisniewski and me, his three gun-bearers, he would meet us in New York and give us the scoop. This sounded big.

It sounded bigger when he saw us. "We're all going to Illinois," he said. "It will be announced in four or five days. In the meantime, you guys go to Florida for a little vacation."

We suspended our recruiting and went to Miami. Twice

a day we bought newspapers looking for the big announcement: Nelson to Illinois. Zero. And when we got back home,
he told us he wasn't taking the job after all. I knew right
away he had something better going for him, but wasn't re-
leasing any secrets. We had confidence in him.

Then things began getting complicated for me. I heard
from Paul Dietzel, who had turned out a national championship team at Louisiana State in 1958, using our Wing-T.
He also had been elected Coach of the Year. Dietzel asked me
to come with him as backfield coach and offensive coordinator. I was to join Charley McClendon, the defensive
coach, as his top aides. I was tremendously interested.

A few years previously, Dave and I had done our act at a
clinic at the University of Florida. He fell in love with the
place. "This is the spot to be," he said. "The athletic director
also is the football coach, and I like that." So when he rejected Illinois, I had the feeling he was considering a juicy
offer from Florida. And he was.

I met with Dietzel in New York. By then, Nelson had told
us about the Florida setup. I turned down the shot at LSU.
Nelson then called the staffers together for what we all
thought would be the this-is-it switch to Florida. Forget it.
Dave said he had indeed gone to Gainesville to discuss their
offer, but had shut them off. Like he didn't want to go to
Illinois, he didn't want to go to Florida. This upset me for a
little while, because I had turned down Dietzel. I thought
about calling him to see if he still wanted me, but I didn't. So
we all went into another season at Delaware, the 1960 disas-
ter. I've never been bluer.

Dave now had discouraged half the NCAA, and had convinced himself that he would go all the way at Delaware —
but he also wanted to free himself of coaching to concentrate
on his ever-expanding responsibilities as director of athletics
and physical education. He told me at the coaches' conven-

tion in Pittsburgh in 1961 that he wanted to make the move as quickly as possible.

But I was ready to throw in the towel. I told Nelson I had apparently failed, because he never encouraged me, never complimented me; I would have to make it somewhere else. I was about to go shopping.

"That's ridiculous," he said. "I've tried to get you jobs at West Virginia, Iowa and Pennsylvania."

"Well, I don't know which way I'm going with you," I replied.

"This is the way you're going — I want you to succeed me."

I was startled. Dave is a reserved, conservative and quiet gentleman. Honest, sincere, solid. He is not demonstrative, not given to praise. His saying he wanted me to take over for him amounted to an impassioned speech, if you know the Admiral.

A step in his intended direction was to relieve me of coaching the baseball team. Now I was strictly football.

Still, it took a catalyst from the outside to convince the ivory tower at Delaware that the change had to be made. The catalyst was the University of Connecticut. I had been in that picture before, in 1964, but lost out to Rick Forzano in a photo finish for the head-coaching vacancy. Politics had been involved; the governor of Connecticut and some Washington types got into the appointment picture.

But two years later, the president of the university himself called me from Storrs. He said he needed a head coach. Rick Forzano had signed on with the Naval Academy. Was I interested? I told him I had been — a couple of years earlier, but now I wasn't so sure.

"Come on up and we'll talk," he said. "Bring your wife. Even if you are not interested now, perhaps you will be when you see what we're doing. You won't be dealing with any selection committee. The job is yours if you want it."

I laid it on Nelson.

"Don't go up there and mess it up like you did the last time," he said. Then he added, "Hey, maybe we can use this to demonstrate to our people that if we don't make you the coach now, we're going to lose you and destroy the basis of our program."

I came back from Connecticut without giving them an answer. They said they could wait.

"What am I going to do if they don't make a move here?" I asked Nelson.

"You're going to have to go to Connecticut," he said, a typical, unsmiling Nelsonism. "But let me get something started here."

He did. He went right to the university president, Dr. John A. Perkins, and told him he was about to lose Tubby Raymond. For five years, Dave had been talking about his coaching retirement plans to John DeLuca and Bob Carpenter. John Perkins was not one of the big spenders of history. Under the arrangement Nelson wanted, there would be both a director of athletics (him) and a football coach (me). Perkins loved the economy of the dual role Dave had been playing. He said Delaware couldn't afford a change in the setup. Carpenter said Delaware could. He and DeLuca stuck their necks out and insisted the move be made. President Perkins finally made the decision. That was the ball game.

This is how I remember Nelson as my boss: He would give you responsibility and go under with it rather than interfere.

He made switches that kept me from getting jaded in my twelve years as assistant. After my third season, he turned over the quarterback responsibilities to me, and now I had the whole backfield. After several more years, he put me in charge of almost the entire offense.

The Admiral took off his coach's hat in early 1966 and lost himself in his duties as director of the Division of Physical Education, Athletics and Recreation, overseeing what now is a total of twenty-one varsity sports, the recreation and intramural program and our first-class phys-ed and athletic plant. For fifteen years he had been both coach and athletic director. He had launched the Blue Hens into a new era of football excellence and become one of the most successful coaches in the country, his Wing-T offense generating an eventual battalion of copycats.

Connecticut or Delaware? No contest. An easy decision for me. I was where I really wanted to be — the coach of the Blue Hens, in charge of guarding and maintaining a tradition. Everything Nelson had been saying about the University of Delaware has turned out to be true: that all the thrills you want to get out of coaching can be yours, right here. It is a clean academic climate where you feel as though you are contributing to the entire university picture.

If it could keep Dave Nelson all those years, it must have something.

Thanks anyhow, Connecticut.

8

The Seasons Go Rolling Along

I feel like Phyllis Diller following Elke Sommer, or . . .

I feel as welcome as a hernia at a weight-lifting tournament.

One-liners. I dropped them when I was asked how it felt to follow the venerated Dave Nelson as football coach at the University of Delaware. Elke was the Bo Derek of the '60s. Phyllis and hernias are still around.

But seriously . . . I had no great feeling of "following" Dave. Delaware football had been such a great part of me for twelve years, and I had worked with Dave so closely, that the new job was more like a continuation. I had a sense of satisfaction and accomplishment, rather than apprehension. The apprehension came later — like when the season opened.

You have to remember that those weren't all 8-and-0 seasons the Blue Hens were having. If they were, then the spot I was on would have been passed along to my tailor. Of the six seasons before I became head coach, three were winners, two were losers, the other a break-even. We had won 30 out of 52. Not exactly the weight of the world on my shoulders.

Strange. With the appointment, I felt a great surge of relief. When I took over the squad, I didn't feel nearly the pressure I did when I was in the system. As an assistant, I had a terrible fear that I would do something wrong, that I would not be what Nelson wanted me to be, that I'd louse up my career. In retrospect, this was pretty silly stuff, because Dave and I worked together as well as any two men possibly could in a football situation. Still, I must confess I agonized quite a bit.

Now, as the head coach, all I had to worry about was winning. Does that make sense?

When we brought the football team in, I gave them a message to the effect that there would be no change — the only difference was that Dave Nelson wouldn't be here. (Could I really have said ONLY?).

I did do a few small things. One was to feed the entire squad prior to a game, as opposed to the forty-five who had been given this treatment in past years. This was a relatively simple thing to do, and the Bursar's Office had to be proud of me. All we did was cut down the menu and make sure everybody got to the groceries, for the same amount of money we had been spending on fewer personnel.

I also dropped back on "local lodging." For a home game, we always had made motel rooms available for players who ordinarily would be sleeping in a dormitory or a fraternity house where there might be a lot of noise. Now I took a page out of my Michigan experience. Fritz Crisler felt that his Michigan players would sleep better in their own beds than they would in a totally different atmosphere, even a motel's.

As great a coach as Dave Nelson was, he had his critics. And if HE had them, I know I couldn't miss developing my own. In a way, this understanding — or resignation — helped me make the big jump.

On my treks to the spotters' box before the games and at halftime, I'd hear fans putting the rap on Dave. That's when it dawned on me that for some people, it is always open season on the head coach, no matter what his record. I'd hear them charging Dave with conservatism, ripping him for his failure to open up an offense. I knew that some day, they would get on me, too. They did get on me, they are on me — and it doesn't annoy me.

For the ball players, they went from the reserve of Dave Nelson to the caustic, sarcastic, volatile, strident Tubby Raymond. I am all of those adjectives, and more, when I try to get an emotional effort from a team — especially in a big game. Dave had his means, I had mine.

My family probably got to see more of me as head coach than they did my last year as assistant. They couldn't have been any more neglected then. That was the year I completed a master's thesis and degree, helped the Phillies with a re-search program, recruited in both football and baseball and played a full baseball schedule, in addition to helping coach football. So the promotion gave me a little more time at home. But as we often say around our place, it's not the quantity of the time you spend at home, but the quality.

As head coach, I slept and ate no worse or no better than I had been doing. The most difficult section of the week is Sunday night through Tuesday, because that is when you are making your decisions for the upcoming game.

That first season was not without its apprehension, as I have indicated. I wasn't sure we were getting it all together, despite the confidence I had in my staff.

Once you get to a Thursday, most of the hay is in the barn and you are either going to play well or you aren't. The preparation is over. That's why I've always slept well on Thursday and Friday nights. No problem. The horror sets in when you wake up Saturday. Then it hits you that today is the day, and you must get yourself to the arena.

I have a rather substantial breakfast because I know I'm not going to eat again, or even want to eat again, for quite some time. After the last cup of coffee and the last handful of Maalox tablets, I take off to watch the ball players eat.

The first few seasons, I had the feeling that my sitting in on the squad breakfast might have been a mistake. They had to see I was all tied up in knots, and they definitely knew I was no ray of sunshine at that hour. I just didn't want to hear them talking on game morning. If they were babbling and laughing and joking, they were not concentrating on their assignments and the game plan and they were not going to be ready.

It was sort of a Captain Queeg operation. I would march in there and have another coffee and sit glaring at a player or an assistant. Nobody was allowed to say anything. Ed Maley and Ted Kempski always came over to have a cup with me because it was about this time I started looking for friends. The tension got to be pretty heavy, and it wasn't going to get any better until the release that comes with the kickoff.

I'm a bit more relaxed now and so, not surprisingly, is the atmosphere. If it's a game we are supposed to win, I am going to use every pressure method I can think of to make sure the players don't get carried away with over-confidence. No matter what club we are about to play, I never think it's going to be easy. How well I know that you can three-putt the green that is a football field.

If we're going into a toss-up game, or one in which we're the underdog, I change my style. I will let the players listen to music while they're eating. Don't say it, I know — I'm all heart.

My rookie year of 1966, I did not permit myself the luxury — or the fear — of speculating how many games we would win. I decided the best thing was to get the job done the best way I knew how. I had a reasonable amount of confidence, but at the same time I was concerned about whether or not we would be able to maintain the Nelson tradition of producing quality football. I had made the comment that I wasn't concerned about filling Dave's shoes as much as I was

about filling his hat — and I wasn't pulling a Henny Youngman. I meant it as a commentary on his intellect.

New coach, new team. I inherited only three interior
linemen, offense and defense combined. We didn't have
enough good players to go two-platoon all the way, so Ed
Sand, our captain; Herb Slattery and Lee Hackney, all linemen, were told they would go both ways.

I also inherited the same nine-game schedule, starting
with Hofstra. That summer, Sterling Brown of the Villanova
staff had warned me that Hofstra had the makings of a great
football team and might even go unbeaten. Thanks, Sterling.
But Hofstra came in 0-and-1, having lost its opener to Gettysburg, and we hung another one on them by 35-13 and out-
yardaged them 373 to 65 and I had my first ride off the field
on the shoulders of my warriors.

It was a coaching debut that was harder on Bob Carpenter, who was sort of my sponsor for the job, than it was on
me. He had forced the change that kept me at Delaware, and
now his stomach was doubting the wisdom of this decision
— so much so that he had to throw up behind the stadium
hedges before the game. Bob claims the day of MY first game
was the most pressure he has ever experienced.

I had decided to go with the basic Nelson offense, with
very little innovation. Somebody who had gone to living in a
cave and emerged not knowing the coaching change had
been made would not have noticed a bit of difference in the
field modus operandi of Dave's last team and my first one in
that Hofstra game.

My first road game took us, in the rain, to Gettysburg.
We won a 3-0 squeaker when Jeff Lippincott kicked a 43-yard
field goal through the downpour with a substantial wind
blowing sideways just before halftime. With three seconds to
go, I had nonchalantly said to Lippincott "Go kick a field
goal." After the game, Jeff told the reporters he hasn't been

nervous because "Coach Raymond wasn't nervous — he had confidence in me. He just told me to go in and kick it." Actually, I had no confidence at all in the move. I just figured that was the way they would have done it in the pros; besides, we had no alternative. Way to go, Jeff.

We won our third straight against Lafayette and then I discovered how it was to lose as a head coach. How it was, was awful. Villanova took a 6-0 lead at the half and we came back strong but not strong enough, losing 16-14, the first of many squeakers we were to have with the Wildcats. The good news: For the first time, we began to run with effectiveness a play called 1-21, which is a buck sweep in which the fullback fakes the buck up the middle and the quarterback instead hands to the tailback, who does the sweeping (running to the outside), led by two pulling guards. Stu Green and Brian Wright ran well. I thought we had the makings of a pretty good football play and, as it turned out, we did.

That very first defeat didn't send me into seclusion. I felt Villanova was probably the toughest team on our schedule — but Buffalo and Boston University were to prove tougher — and I saw progress. We had given them a battle.

One of the most exciting games I've ever been involved in happened that year when we knocked off Temple, which was unbeaten. It was so very important for me because it meant the Middle Atlantic Conference championship. I don't think I have ever had a football team that high. They really wanted to play well.

I can laugh at it now, but the one play that sticks in my mind gave me a great deal of frustration at the time. It was a tackle-eligible play we had designed for Harry Starrett, our left tackle and a converted running back. He caught a 25 yard pass from Frank Linzenbold which had been described to the officials before the game. But lo and behold, they called the play back because "somebody was in motion." But they couldn't tell me who had been in motion. "Somebody HAD to be in motion." I had the feeling the officials choked at the time. Anyhow, we pulled the game out by 20-14.

It was just a magnificent performance that Captain Sand and the troops can be extremely proud of. They weren't tired at halftime and they weren't tired after the game. Herb Slattery was the bulwark of the defense, a local Delaware boy who is one of the best linebackers we've ever had. He became the most-honored Blue Hen lineman in history after the season, with first-team Little All-American the big bauble.

The Hens had put so much of themselves into beating Temple that we lost the next two, badly, to superior forces from Buffalo and Boston U., giving up 78 points. We finished 6-and-3. A great record, considering inexperience, considering we were very thin after the first level. We had won the conference from some teams that had better personnel, which means our players made perfect use of their intangibles.

Frank Linzenbold, who came with the lease as my first quarterback, led the conference in total offense and passing and set a house record for completions.

The next year? Don't ask. The fast way to say it is that we won all but seven games, which meant we were 2-and-7, the only loser I've had. It was the ever-popular rebuilding year. I should have realized it was going to be a long one because of what happened in a pre-season scrimmage against our freshmen. Glenn Davis, who never made it with the varsity, threw four touchdown passes against us. But I was still optimistic — although, as usual, not in public. We were the defending champs in the MAC and I figured we really had things rolling.

We blew the opener to Rhode Island even though we led up to the final two minutes. After four games, Delaware was 0-and-4 and the new coach was suffering. You know, I have been described as being the perennial pessimist, and I think that bleak stretch had a lot to do with molding my general outlook. We kept moving the ball better than our opponents, but we could not win. We came from behind to tie Villanova 13-13 at halftime, then scored 11 first downs to their one in the second half and still lost 21-13. The next Saturday we lost a sluggers' duel to Hofstra 33-31 after leading 31-14. Lippincott missed a field goal at the tail-end that could have won it but our defense was really bad, especially against passing. Joe Purczyki, the key to our defensive backfield, was out with an injury and Hofstra picked on us for 19 points in the last quarter.

We had Temple down 17-0, and lost. Of our seven defeats, five came in the last two minutes because of our inability to guard against the thrown ball.

I still have scars from that season. We found a victim in Lehigh the next-to-last game, and now we were to face Bucknell. I had heard they were wracked with dissension, and I was hoping to leave everybody laughing with a victory. We might have made them laugh, but not with a victory. We were terrible. We couldn't block. We couldn't tackle. They beat us 35-6 and I was glad the year was over.

I was really gun-shy about going into another season. It was like my world had collapsed. Could I be that lousy a coach, an organizer? I've never really forgotten the autumn of '67.

We had Linzenbold throwing 242 times, a fantastic amount for a Delaware quarterback up to then, for almost 1,500 yards but we only scored four TDs that way.

It was a struggle to get myself together and plan for the 1968 season, which was to consist of the first ten-game schedule in Delaware history. But ah! What a delight that season turned out to be. I like to refer to it as the beginning of the 1971 and 1972 championship teams. We started eleven sophomores, and it was a brilliant crop — youngsters like

Yancy Phillips, Conway Hayman, Chuck Hall, Dick Kelley, Ron Klein, Ted Gregory, Chuck Avery, Sonny Merkel, Pat Walker.

We decided to go with them, to start all over again, from the bottom, and with a fundamental offense. I announced we were going to teach football again. They came along so well that they threw Delaware into the national limelight and as we won people began voting for us in the polls.

DiMuzio had been a left halfback with the also-rans of the previous year. Now we moved him to quarterback. He wasn't very good in the early going. Tom got booed a lot. The fans wanted Sonny Merkel, who had been an all-state Delaware schoolboy on fabulous teams at Middletown High, but we had changed Sonny from quarterback to defensive back.

This was Tom DiMuzio: Early in one game, he had thrown the ball into the ground on third down; he was upset with himself and the crowd was upset with his performance and started chanting for an appearance at quarterback by Merkel. I walked over to Tom and was going to say something encouraging, but before I could he put an arm around my shoulder and said "Don't worry about it, Coach, I'm going to be fine." It was then I knew that he really was going to be, and he did develop into a gutsy, winning quarterback.

At fullback, we had intended to start George Lacsny, who was a little faster than another soph, Chuck Hall. Hall couldn't understand this move. I explained to him that we were going to play both of them, but that Lacsny was going to get the first shot, with Hall as back-up, and if Chuck didn't like this setup, well, he could just take the job away from Lacsny — and this was a definite possibility because we were by no means set at the position.

Opening day against Hofstra, Lacsny twisted a knee in the first quarter and had to be helped off the field. He never played another minute. Hall did the old Broadway understudy bit. In fact, he overdid it. It was the first of his 100-yards-by-rushing games. For three seasons, Hall made 100 yards against everybody. He could have done it against a brick wall, too, this 5-foot-10, 200-pound building block.

We had found ourselves a great fullback. When he finished three varsity seasons, Chuck had set university rushing records for total carries, career yards and career game-average.

Chuck Hall of Delaware was the epitome of the indestructible fullback. He played his senior year with a shoulder brace. But the athlete who might have been the hardest running back we've ever had at Delaware later fell victim to Hodgkin's Disease, and he died in December of 1973. John Favero, who had been a teammate, said it for all of us: "Chuck always knew exactly where the first-down marker was, and he'd reach it and then some. And a lot of times when team morale was a little shakey, his hustle picked us up."

The first time we handled the ball since that horrendous previous season, we drove it 87 yards for a touchdown and went on to rout Hofstra, 35-0, with a total offense of almost 550 yards.

But we went from that giddy scene to a shutout at the hands of our old tormentors from Villanova, 16-0. After four games we were .500, but the two losses were to Villanova and Buffalo, which at that time were very superior to us athletically. Those were difficult games for Delaware. Then we won five of the next six, losing only to Rutgers, and by now DiMuzio, our diamond in the rough, was a very good football player. And this was the boy who looked so awkward to us as a high school quarterback that we thought he should be a running back or a defensive back.

Our finish set up the first of four eastern championship appearances in the Boardwalk Bowl, so named because the field was in Atlantic City's hardtop, the Convention Hall. Our opponent was Indiana (Pa.) State. This was the pairing that so disgusted a Wilmington sports editor whose initials were Al Cartwright that he wrote a scathing column about the "Cakewalk Bowl," declaring that the matchmaking was a letdown and that Delaware was going to play a bush-league team. As a punch line, he suggested that the Indiana guys tack the column on their locker-room bulletin board, and you can be assured that they did. It had to have a lot to do with an almost frightening emotional effort on the part of the Pennsylvanians, who had only won all nine of their regular-season games.

That Cakewalk stuff could have affected Delaware, too. Let us say that this implication of a stroll in the park for Delaware might have diluted the determination that brings great efforts. Too early in the game, we played as though we already had it won. We did run up a 10-0 lead on a 50-yard pass from DiMuzio to Dick Kelley and a field goal by Jeff Lippincott. The Cakewalk proponents were filling the hall with "I told you so's".

But then Indiana started coming at us. They zoomed ahead by 21-10 at halftime. We turned it on again in the third quarter, Kelley running 31 yards for a TD and DiMuzio passing 43 to split end Ron Withelder for another. But darned if Indiana didn't block a punt, for the second time, and then kick a field goal to lead 24-23 with one minute to go. This is a Cakewalk?

Jimmy Lazarski rallied us with a beautifully executed kickoff return almost to midfield. Like a master, DiMuzio ran a two-minute drill. He hit Withelder on an outcut, and Ron stepped out of bounds. He hit Pat Walker for 11 and Walker stopped the clock, too. Then Tom rolled to the sideline, came back to the middle and threw to Sam Brickley, who made a great catch inside their 15. Kelley kept us going to the 9.

There was a television timeout and it seemed as if the whole world was focused on a conversation between DiMuzio and me, waiting for me to decide whether to go for the touchdown or have Lippincott try another field goal. Irv Wisniewski in the spotters' box had called down during the last quarter that the "curl" was open, meaning the opportunity was there for the spread receiver to dash downfield, pivot and make a short buttonhook back for a pass.

DiMuzio spoke up. "Let me throw that curl pattern. We're not going to need any field goal." I figured that anybody who felt that strongly about it and looked that confident knew what he was doing, so I gave him the go-ahead, telling him that if the curl was covered to be sure and throw the ball out of bounds. That way, we could still kick the field goal to win. As it developed, there was an opening of about three feet in width, and he threw right in the middle of it and hit Withelder in the belly for the TD. Then he added insult to injury by passing to Mark Lipson for a two-point conversion.

Tom had led us 57 yards in 45 seconds, connecting with all of his four passes. He was simply a great athlete. The game ended with our captain, Bob Novotny, flattening the Indiana quarterback.

We went into the 1969 season with our sophomores older, wiser and better. Joe Purczyki, who had lived through the 1967 debacle, was the captain.

Those Blue Hens had a general maturing. We overpowered Gettysburg and then did another stumble against Villanova. We had them 33-7 going into the last quarter. Picture that. Then picture Villanova winning 36-33. There was no way we could lose that one, but the Villanova jinx lingered on. It seemed they could throw the ball to Mike Siani, their great receiver, any time they wanted.

Win or lose, I always went home and unwound by walking. Room to room, and then I hit the streets. This went on until early in the morning. I did a lot of walking after that Villanova game. Of recent seasons, Sue and I have been known to drive to our escape hatch in Rehoboth Beach, a condominium townhouse we bought, immediately after a home game. She meets me at the fieldhouse door as soon as the press conference is over and in my field clothes, I head for the change of pace of the seashore in the fall.

A funny thing happened to me the next game, at Massachusetts. The night before, by accident, I walked into their dressing room at the stadium, thinking I was in Delaware's. And there on the wall were all of our basic football plays and a listing for each Massachusetts defender on how to defense them. It looked as if they had read us very well. That prompted me to tell my staff "If we get out of this game alive, we'll never run the Wing-T again. We're going to use some new stuff. They're catching on to us."

Massachusetts scored on the first play of the game but we came back to win the thing 28-23 thanks to a low-level senior quarterback, Carmine Infante. DiMuzio had been hurt in the second quarter and Jim Colbert had broken a bone in his leg in the Villanova game. Bobby Buckley also was hurt. We were down to Infante. He was not very fast, but he knew what he was doing. Massachusetts took a 21-20 lead into the last period and was driving for more when Bruce Fad made a big interception. Infante took the winning touchdown over himself. The players voted him the game ball.

P.S. — I decided not to discard the Wing-T offense.

One of the most exciting stretches of my Delaware career was our back-to-back wins over Temple and Rutgers, the big guys. Both shutouts, by a combined 77-0, and over what were supposedly good teams that year.

Our offensive was rolling. Pat Walker was playing exceptionally well at tight end; he had great speed. DiMuzio was running and throwing well. He is one of the few quarterbacks

I've seen who would rather run over top of somebody than step out of bounds. Some of the things you see today — the quarterback doing a leg-under slide or diving out of bounds so he can't be hit — is not the DiMuzio style. He would turn back from the sideline and take everybody on. We were developing a strong attack with people who were going to be even better — Dick Kelley, Chuck Hall, Gardy Kahoe, Billy Armstrong, all learning how to play.

Rutgers came in with the leading passer in the country in Rick Policastro and ranked second in the East to Penn State. They were unbeaten after six games but we crushed them, 44-0, their only defeat of the season.

You do that well against teams like Temple and Rutgers, it means your defense is doing a job. Those two shutouts were just what we were looking for defensively.

But a 30-14 loss to Boston University hurt. I thought it would keep us out of a return to the Boardwalk Bowl. Boston U. hit us with a load of talent, including seven players who went into the NFL. One of these, Bruce Taylor, who became a defensive back for the San Francisco 49ers for a decade, dazzled us. We had trouble containing him.

We did get to go to Atlantic City and play North Carolina Central. They were so big that I thought our offense might have met its match, but we won the bowl again, 31-13. Those Boardwalk Bowls were exciting times for the Raymonds. We had a suite at the Dennis Hotel. The children were small and enjoyed their relationships with the players. Exciting for us and for Delaware football in general.

Our star sophomores of 1968 flowered into our seniors of 1970. They knew how to play. They were dedicated and physically strong. But I had experienced some sinking spells going into the season because I thought we'd never be able to find a quarterback like DiMuzio. Jim Colbert took over and ran a backfield that Wayne Hardin, the Temple coach, dubbed The Five Horsemen. It included Hall and Armstrong, and Kelley alternating with Kahoe. It was the year of the running back. We set a bunch of records.

Our third game out, we defeated New Hampshire by 53-12 and Jim Root, their coach, said after the game, "I'll never coach against that team again. They should be playing Ohio State; I've never seen anything like it." I think he had to be especially impressed, or depressed, with Gardy Kahoe, all 6-2 and 215 pounds of him.

For the second year in a row, we lost a three-pointer to Villanova and again we surrendered a lead in the last quarter. It was a game that provided an entry for My Most Embarrassing Moments.

On fourth-and-one, inside their 45, I chose not to punt and we didn't make it. They turned around and threw a scoring pass to Siani. It was a pass that would have gone 50 yards or 70 yards or 3½ miles — we just wouldn't have stopped it. I didn't second-guess myself. I would have made the same gamble again, but maybe not with the same fourth-down play.

So that wasn't the embarrassing moment. THAT came just before halftime. We were knocking on their door. With the ball on about their 6, I sent in a pass play and told Colbert to try and score with it and if he didn't, I was going to rush in the field-goal team. I figured that if we failed to score on the pass, the clock would be stopped by the incompletion.

Instead of passing, Colbert elected the option of keeping and ran to somewhere around the 1-yard line. I didn't know how close he was, and I didn't get any information from the spotters. There was just enough time to send in Marc Samonisky and his field goal team. Just as I sent them on their way, Colbert ran a hurried sneak and scored the touchdown. But while he was doing this, we had half the student body on the field and thus, had committed a foul.

The TD was wiped out and we had the small solace of kicking the field goal.

The natives weren't too kindly about my coaching that day. It was one of my all-time rocks.

We Boardwalk Bowled again and won from Morgan State, making us undefeated in Atlantic City and giving us another Eastern Regional championship. For a third consecutive Boardwalk game, Dick Kelley gained more than 100 yards rushing.

An interesting thing happened in that bowl game, if you're a sadist. Colbert was very sick the morning of the game; a flu bug had hit him. During the quarterback meeting, he had to excuse himself several times to throwup and his complexion kept switching colors, mostly green and white. He had been our offensive leader all year and I wanted to avoid arbitrarily making a switch to Sam Neff, although Neff was a talented young man.

The problem was that we were limited in the number of people we could dress for the game, and I hadn't wanted to dress any dead horses — people who did not figure to play. Our back-up list was small. But Dr. Roy Donoho, our team physician, and Roy Rylander, our trainer, told me as we got ready to leave for the game that they saw no reason why Colbert could not start and that we could get a half or even three quarters out of him; he could not hurt himself.

Jim quarterbacked us until deep in the second quarter, leading us to a 21-7 advantage. A tackler's head struck him in the belly. Down he went and down he stayed. It was one of the few times I've ever gone out on the field to check a player myself. Jim looked up at me weakly and said "Coach, I just can't wheel any more. This is it." We scraped Jim — now the head coach at C. W. Post — off the field and Neff gave us a good second half.

The 1971 Delawares had a tough act to follow — but they

improved on it. After winning 10 out of 11, we were voted
No. 1 in both the Associated Press and United Press International Polls. The Washington Touchdown Club also honored
us as the best College Division team in the country. Just as
our captain, Ralph Borgess, had predicted — when I wasn't
within hearing range — we had won the national championship. And here we had lost fifteen of the twenty-two starters from a team that had given Delaware its third straight
Lambert Cup, which is symbolic of the best College Division
team in the East.

Neff controlled a backfield that averaged 371 yards a
game on the ground. Gardy Kahoe, Billy Armstrong and
Glenn Covin were something to behold as running backs.
While the offense was getting itself straightened out early in
the season, the defense kept us in the ball games. Bob Depew,
Joe Carbone, Ralph Borgess and Dennis Johnson made us especially tough against the rush. During the regular season,
the opposition rushed for only 57 yards a game and then we
held C. W. Post to minus 55 in the Boardwalk Bowl.

We finally beat Villanova in a game marked by the defensive job our 5-foot-10 cornerback, John Bush, did on the
great Mike Siani. He limited Siani to five catches, all in the
first half.

Our only loss was to Temple by 32-27 in a classic that
drew a record crowd of 22,500 to our stadium. They long-
balled us with a TD run of 70 yards, a punt return of 72 and
an interception of 92. We had a 27-19 lead in the last period,
thanks to Kahoe's third touchdown.

We went up to Boston University and won 54-0. The
night before, I read in the papers that Larry Naviaux, the Boston coach, said he planned to stop our counter play, the
tackle-trap up the middle. It got me to thinking what he
might do, and for the first time ever I threw out our opening
sequence of plays.

"Let's run outside," I told my staff. "They can't do much fooling around with the defense on the outside. Apparently they've got something worked up in the middle."

Our first play, we shifted to the left with an unbalanced line and gave the ball to Glenn Covin. He ran 76 yards to score. Nobody touched him. The next time we got the ball, we shifted to the right and quarterback Neff sent Kahoe outside that way — 60 yards. So that was 136 yards on the first two plays.

When we made our annual appearance in the Boardwalk Bowl and scored 72 points against C. W. Post, there were mutterings that we had run up the score to impress somebody. I repeat that you could only dress so many people — 38 — for that game, and they all played and they all played hard and we just let them go. Every football game, bowl or whatever, is an opportunity for a team to get better in some way. And the sophomores and juniors of that year were playing as if they were auditioning for next season — which they were. You have to play football the way the game was meant to be played.

Gary Wichard, the C. W. Post quarterback, had come into the game with a suitcase full of rave notices. He had received the Time Magazine treatment. He was quoted as saying he was a better passer than contemporary Sonny Sixkiller of the University of Washington and even Fran Tarkenton of the New York Giants. Y. A. Tittle had worked with him and said he had the best young natural arm in the game.

Gary Wichard had a long day. We sacked him eight times and intercepted four of his 34 passes. "If pro football is like this," he said later in answer to a question about his future, "I don't want to have anything to do with it." But do you know we found a friend in him? Every season he calls me with a rating on certain prospects in the New York area.

That season meant a lot to me personally. The American

Football Coaches Association voted me Coach of the Year in my division, which opened up all sorts of fringe benefits and enabled me to go all around the country talking football to and with people I had admired from afar.

We had twenty-eight lettermen back in 1972, including nine defensive starters. With that nucleus, we should have been good and we were — Delaware swept all 10 games and won the Lambert Cup for an unprecedented fifth year. We had a defense that gave up an average of 64 yards and eight points a game. We intercepted 25 passes and John Bush ran one of them back, against Temple, for 100 yards. Dennis Johnson, our captain and a superlative tackle who went on to the NFL, was our big guy up front.

All you read about the tension of maintaining an undefeated season is correct. The scary part comes in playing teams you are SUPPOSED to beat. There is the gnawing possibility you will blow it. It is the upset potential that is frightening.

Lehigh almost turned us over on opening day, and they weren't that good. Glenn Covin, our leading running back of the previous year, tore up his leg on the fifth play of that game and went out for the season.

I have to admit that the 1972 schedule was more realistic than some we were to play later. We stepped above our division only to play Temple and Villanova — and beat them back-to-back, incidentally. We had a football team to match the schedule and we went all the way. It felt good to knock off Temple by 28-9 and get even for the only game we lost the previous year. It felt especially good to Roger Mason, who had made a juicy fumble in that loss. This time, Mason carried for a school-record 45 times, gaining more than 180 yards and scoring three touchdowns. It felt especially bad to Doug Shobert, the Temple quarterback, who the week of the game had announced "Delaware will never beat us again."

We didn't go to the Boardwalk Bowl, although we were invited there to play Massachusetts. We already had been voted No. 1 in both wire-service polls. Massachusetts had lost to Bucknell, a team we had beaten handily. The Delaware squad was unhappy with this pairing. So was I. I can get along without post-season games anyhow. It is an academic drain on the players. And a Boardwalk Bowl, even though one game, extended the season three weeks. You spend the interval practicing.

I told the ball players to make up their minds. They did. They voted not to go. They didn't like the idea of leaving so many men home because of the numerical limit the NCAA put on the squad for the game. They also issued a statement: "The University of Delaware team feels that the NCAA does not represent the interests of any top-ranked team in the current College Division bowl arrangement." By that, they indicated that our No. 1 rating entitled us to be paired with a potentially stronger opponent. Why should we play for the Eastern title when we were No. 1 nationally?

That statement drew no applause in Massachusetts and in some parts of Delaware, either. Dave Nelson, among others, was upset. But I told him we couldn't teach the players responsibility by giving them the opportunity to vote on something and then not hearing them out.

The NCAA drafted the University of California at Davis to play Massachusetts. We would have been delighted to play Davis.

The season of 1973 was one in which we were working on an undefeated streak that was to reach 20 games, over three years. Now THAT'S pressure. And the schedule got tougher. On successive weeks, we were to play three Division I schools — Rutgers, Temple and Villanova. Four years ago, they had discarded the "need" determination for financial aid, and their recruiting zeal was now paying off. Anybody in the East could have also discarded that determination, but these three schools in particular let it all hang out.

We won our first six that year. Rutgers put an end to the streak in a 24-7 game and it was almost a relief. We were emotionally shot. The heat on everybody, coaches and players, was intense. We lost to Temple and Villanova, too; it was not a very happy time. We had our first three-game losing streak since 1967.

But the Blue Hens regrouped to beat Maine and bury Bucknell and that made us 8-and-3 in our first 11-game season and put us in the NCAA's new post-season playoffs. We were eliminated in the first round by Grambling, the perennial powerhouse from Louisiana, by 17-8. That might have been the only game I ever lost — possibly excluding our scrappy match with Villanova my first year — that I was happy about. The score could have been 50 to 0. We couldn't move the ball at all; we couldn't sweat a drop of anything. Things kept happening to Grambling and they couldn't score as they should have.

We weren't geared for that kind of opposition, which was to have four first-round choices in the next NFL draft. We were lucky to get out alive. Three years later, when I was coaching in the College All-Star game, I ran into two of those Grambling guys in a hotel lobby in Skokie, Ill. I shook hands with Jimmy Hunter of the Detroit Lions and Sammy White of the Minnesota Vikings, and Hunter whipped out a photograph. It showed those two arm-in-arm with Scotty Reihm and Herky Billings after the Atlantic City game.

Ed Clark was elected captain of our 1974 team. Before the season, he told me that all they wanted was to be known as a great Delaware football team. He said he wasn't forecasting any national titles, as Ralph Borgess had done previously. Ed Clark got his wish, and I was the first to tell him in the ashes of our 54-14 loss to Central Michigan in the NCAA finals in Sacramento, Calif. We had won 12 out of 13 to get that far.

I never felt the Central Michigan game was a fair test of our strength. We had six regulars out. Nate Beasley, a great running back who rushed for almost 1,400 yards that season to get a school record, limped out after his first carry of the second half. Our team was but a shadow of itself, and the loss was the worst a Delaware team had suffered in more than forty years.

Central Michigan jolted us with a 68-yard touchdown on the first play. We never got over it. As I said on TV at halftime, everything had happened to us but an earthquake — and I wasn't sure that wasn't going to take place, either.

For the first time in history, a University of Delaware game was nationally televised. What timing! Thanks to the clout of Gov. Sherman Tribbitt and some other important persons, the finals went into the Philadelphia area on a channel that originally had intended to cover the city high school championship game. That gave me a line to use on the banquet circuit that winter: "Just think, without their help millions might not have known what happened."

When you reach the national finals, you have to assume that you will emerge as at least the No. 2 team in the country. But when they took the final wire polls, we were fourth. I still can't figure that one out.

We had played our best football of the year in the semifinals when we eliminated Nevada of Las Vegas, 49-11, at Baton Rouge, La. They had been 12-and-0. Vern Roberts had a phenomenal day carrying the ball and set six playoff records, including the scoring of four touchdowns.

That also was the year we played McNeese State of Louisiana, a consistent vote-getter in the annual polls. Hardly a traditional game, though, or a geographical natural. I had the feeling that now we were going to play anybody, any place, any time, any team that could knock the chip off my shoulder. When we swept the No. 1 poll ratings in 1971, McNeese was No. 2 the last three games and their coach and athletic director, Jack Doland, couldn't wait to get a game with us. Three years later, the $15,000 guarantee brought McNeese to Delaware Stadium and we won an exciting game, 29-24, by scoring three touchdowns — all by Vern Roberts — in less than six minutes of the last quarter. Doland later became president of his college. I saw him at a recent coaches' convention and told him that if he now was the guy who hired the football coach, I would like to apply for the job. He dismissed me with some fine expletives.

We went into the 1975 with a holdover quarterback in Bill Zwaan and a completely new offensive line. Ray Sweeney, a Little All-American guard, and Bill Cubit, a marvelous split end, were some of the talent we had to replace.

Opening up at Virginia Military, we turned a blocked field goal into the points that won a 10-9 squeaker. Lucky? Maybe. But we also practice what to do with blocked field goals. On any aborted field goal or point-after-touchdown attempt, we have a procedure. The holder of the ball yells "Fire!" and that is the signal for four receivers to head for the end zone and for the linemen not to cross the scrimmage line.

When Hank Kline's kick from the 10 was blocked with 10 minutes left in the game and the score tied at 3, Larry Wagner retrieved the ball on the 23, started running, made with the "Fire!" yell and threw to Cliff Ainsworth on the 8, Ainsworth scoring. VMI came back with a touchdown and went for a two-point conversion instead of playing for the tie and they missed because the ball was intercepted by Greg Galeone, capping a great day for this linebacker.

We finished 8-and-3 but it was an up-and-down year. We could have played better.

After VMI, we played Wittenberg at home on a hot day and deserved to lose, 14-18, in what was the one hundredth game of my head-coaching career. We lost to Lehigh and on the blackest of weekends, Temple scored 21 points before we could get on our feet and stomped us, 45-0. Zwaan, who was injured in the Lehigh game, couldn't play against Temple. Sue's mother was critically ill and right after the game, we flew to her home in Sarasota, Fla. She died several weeks later.

We did come back the next Saturday to edge Villanova, 14-13, after the Wildcats threw a 13-point first period at us. We held them to 95 rushing yards. Our playoff chances were pretty thin, and as it turned out, they were nil.

The Bicentennial season of 1976 brought us a sharp up-turn in the schedule, one of the toughest we have had. Eastern Kentucky, The Citadel and William and Mary were on there along with the usual toughies from Temple and Villanova. It also was the season that brought us Jeff Komlo — by the back door, sort of — the Komlo who was to become an all-timer for Delaware at quarterback. Ben Belicic opened the season at quarterback against Eastern Kentucky, although he was nursing a bad shoulder. When he pulled a Tony Franklin on me (Tony Franklin, class, is the Philadelphia Eagles placekicker who defied orders in a playoff game and booted an onsides kick) and threw the ball on third down from his own 20, I replaced him with Jimmy Castello and Belicic never played again.

Komlo spent the opener on the sidelines. His only claim to fame had been an excellent second half in the annual spring scrimmage, and he was our third-stringer. The next week, against The Citadel, he got his chance. Sent in to replace Castellino in a game we wound up losing, 17-15, he completed 5 of 10 passes and took us 63 yards for our final touchdown. He almost pulled it out for us, but it wasn't a good game for Delaware. A miscue on a kickoff by Ivory Sully inside their five set up the winning touchdown for The Citadel.

The coaching debate the next week centered on the quarterback to start against North Dakota: Castellino or Komlo? We decided to test Komlo. With the sophomore at the helm, we ran up and down the field for 519 yards and 59 points. Komlo had to throw only two passes.

Then we survived successive two-point-margin games with Temple and William and Mary, led by our now-prized sophomore. The 18-16 win over Temple at Franklin Field was a tremendous upset, for the Owls had come close to beating both Penn State and Pitt. Jeff was outstanding, completing 11 of 17 passes and scoring twice himself. That game is one of my fondest memories. I can see Larry Wagner making four catches for more than 100 yards. I can see Gary Bell, our captain and linebacker, and Bobby Pietuszka punishing Temple on defense and Pietuszka clinching the victory with an interception. David Raymond, My Son the Punter, had a hand — or a foot — in this big one. With this, I became Delaware's all-time winningest coach and definitely proved that I was our best since Dave Nelson.

We had a letdown at William and Mary but still won when Larry Wagner made a one-handed circus catch of a Komlo pass that had interception possibilities and thus gave me a dandy heart tremor.

We flattened out with a tie with Villanova (I remember when I would have SETTLED for a tie with Villanova) and a loss to VMI. It looked as if the fire was out, but we swept the last four and earned the right to lose to Northern Michigan in the playoff quarterfinals in our stadium. We led 17-7 midway in the third quarter, then 17-14.

That was the point of the infamous, or insidious, Sleeper Play. Gil Krueger, their coach, was giving the officials a lot of stormy weather; he had already drawn an unsportsmanlike-conduct penalty. I maintain that the officials were staying as far away from Krueger as possible. Northern Michigan was sending in two receivers on every play in the last period — two in, two out. Suddenly they sent in one and pulled two out, but it was a fake, as it turned out. One of the allegedly departing players didn't go to the bench. In the films, his feet seemed to be on the sideline and he was intermingled with coaches and players. His shoulders were perpendicular to the line of scrimmage, which is another no-no — and how many can you have on one play?

Northern Michigan came out over the ball with the receiver standing over there in a mob scene, and we didn't see him. We have a technique in which each cornerback describes what he sees as he cases the offense. Bob Slowik yelled "Weak tight end," meaning there was a tight end but no flanker on his side. Bob Pietuszka shouted "Weak spread end." So all of a sudden we realized they were short, but we didn't know where the guy was. When the ball was snapped, the Lonesome End just took off down the sideline and nobody was within 30 yards of him as he grabbed a pass and went 41 yards for the deciding touchdown. The officials looked at each other and then made the TD signal.

I understand that Krueger did alert the officials to this play before the game, and that they told him that what he was describing was legal with one possible exception: That if the substitution rule is used to deceive and confuse the opponents in any way, it is illegal. They DID use deception on the substitution procedure, and confused we were. Final score, 28-17. My Bicentennial season had closed with a 200-year-old sandlot play beating me.

The next season was made a success on the last day when we hung a 21-3 defeat on undefeated Colgate, a Division I team, turning their bowl dreams into a nightmare. I'll mention that one fast before I retreat to a defeat at the hands of Temple, of all people, that was my own personal nightmare.

The scenario: With less than a minute left, we were trailing 6-3 and had the ball on their 9, fourth down and four yards to go. No timeouts left. I went for the tie and sent in Brandt Kennedy and the field-goal team. It didn't work, and 20,000 people stood up in unison and booed to remind me that it hadn't worked and even if it had, they wouldn't have approved. The booing found its mark. It did not delight me.

Stubborn person that I am, I would call for the field goal again in the same situation. I thought we had a better chance of kicking it than we had of running or throwing for the score or the down. If we picked up the down, we would have had to waste another to set up a field goal, with time running out. It was too far out to risk a run, and they certainly would be looking for the pass.

Whether the American sports fan admits it or not, a tie is infinitely better than a defeat. Our tieing Temple, with our football team against what they had, would have been a substantial accomplishment. Strangely enough, not a fan derided me as I went to the fieldhouse via what Ted Kempski has christened "Parents' Walk," that area outside the locker room where the parents of the players gather right after the game to receive congratulations, or to act coolly towards the coach, their mood depending on their sons' fortunes that day. On a radio call-in program the next week, I explained my rationale and nobody called in to suggest that I be garroted. Or had I lost my radio audience along with the game?

The ball players didn't say anything, either, although I had the feeling some of them had wanted to go for the touchdown. "Let him who is without sin cast the first stone." Not one of my athletes was going to cast a stone at me. I have seen them in the worst possible situations, and they have seen me that way, too.

In 1978, we won the first three games big and then lost to Temple and Lehigh. That defeat by Lehigh stung. They had quit playing us for two years and in so doing, had won the national division title in '77. In my opinion, they had softened their schedule by ignoring us. I felt that our players would respond to this. They had said they wanted to be national champions, but I had reminded them that they couldn't be national champions unless they could control their own back yard — and Lehigh was in that back yard. Even though Lehigh now was in Division 1-AA, they had a comparable football program and we have to win these kind of matches.

Ours was sort of a struggling team, despite the fact we reached the national playoff finals. A football team never stays the same. It either gets better or gets worse; it seldom hangs right in there. For a while I didn't know which way the Hens were going to turn. They started to pick up steam late in the season with a little win streak that victimized Villanova and Colgate.

Winning our first two playoff games, we found ourselves in Longview, Tex., playing Eastern Illinois for the championship. Not exactly your ideal location. It wasn't a town big enough to handle the job, in terms of accommodations. We flipped a coin to see who would get the motel with the dining room, and we won. That was nice, but Eastern Illinois won the game, 10-9. I had a feeling they resented our getting "special" treatment and Coach Dale Mudra parlayed this situation and an underdog role into a victory.

Eastern Illinois had a fine team. Mudra, who had lost his job at Florida State, was determined to make a go of his new setup and had himself a rough, tough outfit, with something like twenty junior-college transfers. It looked like a mercenary army, and we didn't play ugly enough to conquer them in that dismal, cold, Astro-Turfed high-school stadium.

I did some second-guessing. With two and one-half minutes left we had third down and about six to go on their 45 and they threw Jeff Komlo for a loss of eight. Now it was fourth and fourteen from the middle of the field and I decided that if we punted, we would never get the ball back in time to drive for a score. So I let Komlo throw on the same pattern, which probably was over-used, and they knocked it down and took possession.

But Captain Jim Brandimarte's defense played well enough to turn the ball over to us again, and we did have another shot, after all. Komlo drove us to field-goal range by passing to Pete Ravettine. Brandt Kennedy's kick from the 40 with the clock ticking off gave my insides one of my all-time roller-coaster rides. I felt sure it was on its way to being good, but it missed by inches. We were held to 135 yards rushing, our lowest total of the year, and lost four fumbles.

We were going to have to wait some more for our first on-the-field national championship, after coming away empty two times. But we didn't have to wait long. Just a year.

9

Dropping Names

Make the dateline Lubbock, Texas. The time, June of 1972. I was there as one of three coaches for the East team in the Kodak All-American Game. Paul Bryant of Alabama, old walk-on-water Bear himself, was the head coach. His trusty assistants were Bo Schembechler of Michigan and me.

You have to figure that of that trio, I am going to be the one who winds up driving the staff car. You are correct. The evening of the game, an extremely hot one, we piled into the car and I pointed it in the direction of the stadium across town. As I slowed down on the highway to make my usual left turn into the stadium lot, we could see that the entrance we had been using for ten days of practice was barricaded. What's more, it was guarded by three well-nourished Texas troopers.

I stopped on the four-lane, two-way pike, but what to do? The Bear, riding shotgun, growled at me to go in there the way we always did. So I waited for the traffic to pass and made my turn. When I reached the barricade, the car was still sticking out on the highway. Rolling down the window and letting in some good Lubbock heat, I told an officer that we were the East coaching staff for tonight's game, and we would like to go in here and get to our team quarters.

"No way, Buddy" replied the trooper, not realizing my

name was Tubby. The Bear poked me in the ribs. He was wearing that famous hounds-tooth hat. The hat is a trademark, like Rex Harrison's, and Tennille's Captain's before the Captain took it off and became a sex symbol. It was tilted down on Bryant's nose.

Getting his message, I tried this tack: "Officer, this is Coach Bryant of the University of Alabama, who is the head coach of the East team."

The officer started looking a little uglier. "I don't care who he is, or you are. You are not going in here."

With that, the Bear grumbled "Run over the son of a bitch, Shorty." That was all the encouragement I needed — to send me into retreat. I backed out of there, across traffic, and all the while my head coach was cussing me.

"Godammit, Shorty, when I tell you to run over somebody, you are supposed to run over them!" he barked. You know what? I'm not absolutely sure he wasn't serious.

One of the great fringe benefits of being Coach of the Year is the opportunity to breathe the same air as the Bryants and the Schembechlers of football. I first won this award in the College Division after the 1971 season. Bear Bryant won in the University Division. The voting is done by the membership of the American Football Coaches Association. We were honored at its annual banquet, which at that time was held in Hollywood, Fla. It was a great evening. I got a tingle out of Anita Bryant's singing "The Delaware Fight Song." This was back when Anita was noted only for her singing voice.

The election meant the Bryant, who in 1973 was to be chosen by the ACFA for a third time, was automatically a head coach in the All-American Game and it also moved me in as an assistant. Schembechler, who had gone undefeated in eleven games at Michigan and then lost a squeaker in the Rose Bowl to Stanford, was a geographical choice.

I wasn't so sure I wanted to be involved — because of Bear Bryant, — and I discussed this with Sue when I got home. I had read quite a bit about him in the newspapers and magazines, and he didn't appeal to me for one reason or another. The rough old cuss who had bounced from Maryland to Kentucky to Texas A. & M. and finally to immortality at Alabama didn't seem my type of person. He had some recruiting and training raps against him. Maybe it was the eastern egg-head influence working on me. I also told Sue I'd feel out of place mixing with those headline coaches and players. For another thing, I suspected the game would come up a little short in organization.

Soon after the announcement was made, I got a call from the Bear, and my opinion of him started to change immediately.

"This is the way it is goin' to work," he said, after telling me he was glad he was going to get to be associated with me. "You are goin' to coach the defense and Schembechler is goin' to coach the offense and I am goin' to take my golf clubs. You bring your clubs, too. We've had enough struggle with football. Let's have some fun out of it."

I had to like this approach. We went.

In the coaches' suite at the hotel, we met the opposition. Chuck Fairbanks of Colorado was in charge of the West. His assistants were Jim Sweeney of Washington State, now with the New York Giants, and Tony Knapp of Boise State. The Bear was there, of course. He came over and hugged Sue and gave her a kiss on the cheek and that was the beginning of a love affair. I cannot say a bad word around the house about Bear Bryant.

I hadn't realized how much of a gas this Lubbock thing was going to be. Bear knighted me instantly as his chauffeur. He always rode beside me, with Schembechler in the back seat. Schembechler had been Coach of the Year himself in 1969.

At our first meeting, the Bear gave me my marching orders. "Shorty, I want to tell you something: There's one thing I really admire in football and that's winnin', and anybody who wins can do anything they want. I'm here to find out how you been winnin' up there at Delaware. So you go ahead and do whatever you would like to do with the defense."

He also told me I was to take over the stretching and exercise period for the athletes before each workout. The first day, I started warming them up, and it looked as if I were doing a single. It was awful. They were just kind of staggering around, completely indifferent, taking up a lot of time we really didn't have — we coaches had to get to the golf course after the practice, remember. I got a little testy.

"OK," I shouted. "I want to get this done and we are going to GET it done. If you want to fool around, you fool around when Coach Bryant has you. You are not about to waste MY time."

With that, the Bear looked at Schembechler, popping his eyes. "My God," he said. "We've got Napoleon on our side." And ever since, he has called me Napoleon.

I also saw the soft side of Bear Bryant, one I never knew existed. Billy Taylor, a great running back from Michigan, was on our club. He was an All-American who had eclipsed many of Tom Harmon's records at Ann Arbor.

Taylor had been raised by an aunt and uncle; in Cleveland, I believe. We found out early one morning that his guardians had been victims of a murder-suicide. Taylor was not aware of the tragedy. Three coaches stared into their breakfast coffee, wondering how to handle this. Bo spoke up. He said Billy was his man from Michigan, so he would go tell him and make arrangements for him to leave camp.

"Hold on," the Bear said. "I know you are close to him,

but this is my squad, my responsibility." So Bear broke the shocking news to Taylor. He also put his own Lear Jet at Billy's disposal. "You do whatever needs to be done at home," he said, "and don't worry about a little old exhibition football game. If you don't want to come back, we will understand." Billy was back in three days and played well.

We also had a lineman who learned that his three-year-old son back home had swallowed some rat poison and was in critical condition. Again, Bear flew him home to be with his family.

Bear, Bo and Napoleon had some good times. Schembechler is a tough nut who is sort of a professional complainer. One day when we were driving home from a workout, he started to get on Dave Nelson, my boss, with words to the effect that Dave was a problem for the coaches in general because he was in a position of authority on the rules committee, talked about things he didn't know anything about, was not involved in recruiting, and so on into the beef.

I stopped the car and went into my tongue-and-cheek number, although I was truly annoyed. "Get out, Bo," I said. "I'm going to clean up the street with you. There's no way you can talk about Dave Nelson like that."

That cracked the Bear up. "Napoleon is right, Bo," he said when he stopped laughing. "There's no reason to carry on like that."

Through clever scheduling and pacing, we managed to get in a lot of golf. Chuck Fairbanks, the West head coach, struck me as an aloof gentleman and a fine golfer.

We all had to make a number of personal appearances in and about Lubbock to promote the game. It was obvious that there would be parking problems downtown, the same as you would encounter anywhere and leading to a lot of frustration — unless you were Bear Bryant.

"Park it right here," he would say to me when we were in the block of the building we wanted.

"That's no parking space," I would point out. "The hell it ain't," he shot back. "There's room." To Bear, if there was room, it was legal. To this day in our family, that kind of spot is known as a Bear Bryant Parking Space.

And now meet Bear Bryant, the strategist. The night of the game, while the West squad was warming up, he sauntered over to me. "Watch this, Napoleon — come with me." We walked to the general vicinity of the West punter. The Bear took out a stopwatch and we watched the kicker. The kid had to recognize the guy in the hat who was checking him out as he kept on booting the ball.

"What's going on?" I asked. "Are you timing him?" The Bear told me to be quiet. The kid also figured he was being clocked on how long it took him to get the ball off after he took the snap. He started to hurry his kicks. His timing suffered. After a minute of this, the Bear led me away. "I wasn't timing him," he said, "but did you see how nervous I made him? By the way, do you have a punt-block in, Napoleon?"

I did. And sure enough, we blocked a kick the first time they tried it and turned it into a touchdown. No wonder the Bear walks on water.

Going over our personnel the second day we were there, the Bear found out we needed an outside linebacker and a strong safety, or someone who might be able to handle either position. Bo couldn't conscript any more Michigan players. He already had the maximum four, and he said he didn't know of anybody else who might be able to help us. Bryant then asked me.

"Yes — I've got one at Delaware," I said. "His name is Billy Armstrong."

That took some guts. Billy Armstrong had been a running back for us for three years — rushing for better than

2,300 yards — and hadn't played any defense at all. But I
knew he could play, period. He covered kicks for us. I knew
he could tackle. One spring he helped out on defense. For
flat-out football ability, he is one of the greatest players we've
ever had at Delaware. He could do it all, if you asked him.

"Give him a call," the Bear said. "Get him out here."

Billy showed up the next day and we threw him in with
the All-Americans. By the time the ball game rolled around,
the player who was supposed to start at outside linebacker
had pulled a hamstring. He was done. And so in front of
55,000 people, and on national television, Billy Armstrong of
Delaware went out to play a new position he had been re-
hearsing for all of a week, facing Chuck Fairbanks' Wishbone
offense.

Jack Mildren had been one of the top quarterbacks in the
country, a big reason why Oklahoma was rated No. 3 the previous season. In the Sooners' 35-31 victory over Auburn in
the Sugar Bowl, he scored three times himself on short runs.
He was as swift a quarterback as you'll find. Mildren had
killed the opposition with a triple option, using the fullback
ride with revolting success.

On the first series of downs, Mildren came down the line
on the option and Armstrong stuck him. Mildren coughed
the ball up right there on the 10. We of the Golden East recovered and went in to score.

Billy played well all night. I don't know who glowed the
most, Billy or me. He made me a star. What's more, we won
the game — big.

"A great kid," Bryant agreed. "He could play on any
team I've ever had."

We had been to a number of functions during Game
Week — just about every night. And at each dinner, without
fail, they served some form of beef. What else, deep in the
heart of Texas? We had sirloin, we had filet, we had T-bone,

we had rump roast, fried, broiled, parched, every way you could fix beef. And always accompanied by baked potato and peas. Even at its best, which it was, a relentless diet of beef can get to you.

For our post-game feast, we had been promised the best breakfast in all of Texas, a midnight buffet of fruit, scrambled eggs, sausage, bacon, toast. Not a steer in sight. All this for the game coaches, the trustees of the American Football Coaches Association and important Lubbock people.

I couldn't wait to dive into the buffet, and took my place in the chow line. But Bryant intercepted me. He grabbed me by the arm and he also had a grip on Bo Schembechler.

"Come back here," he demanded. "No coaches of mine are going to eat that garbage after a ball game." And with that, he plunked us down at a corner table and told the waiter, "Bring us the three biggest steaks in the house." I suppressed a groan. The fruits of victory. Oh, well.

By the time the Board of Trustees of the coaches convened in Shreveport, La., in 1973, Bryant and John Underwood of *Sports Illustrated* had come out with a book called *Bear, The Hard Life And Good Times Of Alabama's Coach Bryant*. Also by this time, the Raymonds and the Bryants had become close.

Sue and Bear's wife, Mary Harmon, have a lot in common. They are deeply religious and they are true ladies and they enjoy shopping binges. Mary Harmon has a presence, a star quality. She walks in a store and people take care of her.

She had promised Sue an autographed copy of BEAR, but when the day came for us to leave, the book had not arrived. Mary Harmon went into action. The previous day, her husband had promoted and autographed books in a department store. She got on the phone and called not the head of the book department, nor the branch manager, but the president of the entire Lubbock chain.

"Papa wants a book sent out here to the motel right away," she said. "He wants to sign it for Tubby Raymond."

Apparently the store executive hesitated. I could just picture him thinking, "Tubby what?"

"It is for Tubby Raymond," Mama Bear repeated, and then she hit him with the punch line. "He is one of the best SMALL-TIME coaches there ever was."

We've had many a laugh rehashing that story.

I repeated as Coach of the Year in 1972, and here we go again with the All-American Game, which was held over in Lubbock. The East head coach was the late Shug Jordan of Auburn. My fellow assistant was Lou Holtz of North Carolina State, now very big at Arkansas. Jordan was a very calm person, Holtz a special kind of guy: extremely funny, very energetic, with good stand-up material.

Things weren't wrapped as tightly as in the game of the year before. Holtz kept wanting to know when we were going to have a coaches' meeting, but Jordan never gave him any satisfaction and instead would suggest that we eat. We finally had a meeting — about an hour before the first practice. I quickly structured a workout plan and we put the troops through it.

When the drill was over, Holtz asked, "When are we going to have another meeting?"

Jordan shrugged. "There ain't no sense in screwin' this up. Let's keep it like it is." And we never had another meeting — but we won the game.

After the 1973 season, it was announced that I would be an assistant coach in the very traditional Shrine East-West game in San Francisco, the one they play for the benefit of the Shriners' Crippled Children Hospital. Charley McLendon of Louisiana State was picked as the East coach, but he eventually had to withdraw because his team got into a bowl game. Paul Dietzel, then of South Carolina, took over. John Jardine of Wisconsin and I were Paul's helpers.

That was a most rewarding experience. The very first full day, the coaches and players of both squads visited the kids in the hospital. I remembered a marvelous column Jim Murray of the Los Angeles Times had written about these kids. He described them as "broken dolls." They were so beautiful, the way they greeted us and talked with us. It was something that made the game personnel feel like family, and the only time before the game we all saw each other. Unlike the All-American Game in Texas, the Shrine game put up the teams in different hotels. We were in Palo Alto; the West was somewhere else. I didn't like that scattered arrangement, but the fact that we lost the ball game had nothing to do with that.

Before McLendon had to bow out, our coaching staff had a Saturday night on the town with him in New Orleans, his home grounds. We did the Al Hirt scene and checked out a few more spots. Charley is a live one; he'll stay up with you.

My mingling with the biggies, with successful coaches I had developed such admiration for without knowing them, began when I was an assistant at Delaware. The Du Pont Company sponsored a Football Play of the Year contest as a promotion for its film department, and Dave Nelson put it together for them and generously got me involved. Entry blanks were made available to high school coaches all over the country. We asked them to give us things like the first play on first-and-10 from the middle of the field in a certain situation, or what play they would use when they were on the four-yard line, trailing by five points, with time for only one play remaining.

It was a lot of fun judging the entries, but the big kick was the chance to be with the other members of the panel.

Darrell Royal of Texas. The rough, gregarious Frank Howard of Clemson. And Ara Parseghian. The one and only Ara.

I first met Parseghian several years before, at a clinic during the coaches' convention. We enjoyed talking football and became friends — which always isn't the case when coaches get together. Sometimes the shop talk is a bore. Sometimes you want to get away from it for a spell, no matter who your companion. But I never tired of talking the game with Ara.

The Du Pont promotion took us to the New York World's Fair for a press luncheon. Eddie Bracken, the actor, was there, for some reason that escapes me now. Just a small gathering; maybe fifteen people.

Ara and I sat next to each other. Between courses, he began drawing a new formation, which happened to be the Power-I, and showed it to me. He asked me what I thought of it. I told him it just wouldn't work; in fact, I added, it was terrible. I had no idea there were people eavesdropping. You can imagine the feelings of some of the newspaper guys when they saw this anonymous assistant coach from Delaware, a total stranger to them, telling the great Parseghian his formation was from hunger. Believe it or not, the friendship survived.

If I were in a position of hiring a football coach, and had the pick of the land, there is no question who my man would be: Ara Parseghian. He is the best I have ever encountered. He has a measure of everything. A forceful but warm personality. Articulate, intelligent, sensitive. Inspiring, just to be near him.

All coaches know the basic game, the book. That's the easy part. Anyone can learn this, thanks to clinics. We all know the formations, the techniques. But it takes something extra. And to me, No. 1 in the something-extra is the ability to communicate. A lot of coaches talk about "motivation" as the key to success. Parseghian communicates. He communicates at the players' level — he brings them on. He gets across to them what needs to be done.

For several seasons after I became head coach, there wasn't a football week that went by in which we weren't on the phone with each other. What a thrill it was to have Ara call for my offensive advice. (Make that for my advice on offensive football).

It was the winter of 1973 when Ara telephoned from Notre Dame to ask if I would send him a film that would show what we were running offensively. We had come off an 8-and-4 season in which we did a lot of scoring. I shipped him the film of our opening game against Akron — which is Ara's home town, by the way. We had won it by 45-24, and Vernon Roberts had a great day as a running back.

Ara checked in again a few days later. He said he was impressed with our attack and mentioned that "that guy Roberts" looked as if he could play with anybody. He said he wanted to talk some more, in person. We arranged to meet at the Philadelphia International Airport — I would defy anyone to find us then in that madhouse. We huddled for several hours, and Ara took a Delaware playbook back to South Bend.

During his spring practice, he called rather frequently to tell me how our offense was doing under the Golden Dome. When we got into the season, he would call on Monday and again on Wednesday. We swapped what problems we expected to face the upcoming Saturday, and what we intended to do about them. It was an exchange of ideas.

We both started to win. That season, 1974, was the year the Blue Hens were 12-and-2. Now it got to be a superstitious thing: He HAD to call. After the season — the Fighting Irish were 9-and-2 and went on to knock off Alabama in the Orange Bowl — he sent me a couple of films to critique and in spite of my objections, insisted on paying for my time. What he was doing was paying me for MY education.

One of the problems I felt the Irish were having in running the Wing-T involved the quarterback. He didn't seem to call the plays the way they were intended to be called. He wasn't using the series theory — one series setting up another, and another, and another. I wrote this in a report to Ara.

He read it and got on the phone: "What do you mean my quarterback isn't calling the plays right?" he said with a laugh. "I'M the one who calls the plays."

Ara was a help to me one time by reputation. We have our quarterback meetings on Wednesdays. Jimmy Maskas thought he, not Bill Zwaan, should be the starting quarterback in 1974, and he wasn't bashful about telling me. During one meeting, my phone rang and my secretary, Kathy McKittrick, answered it in the outer office. Kathy knew a great deal about what was going on with the team, including the Maskas intrigue.

"Excuse me, Coach Raymond," she said, stepping into our meeting. "Ara Parseghian is on the line. He says he needs your help right away."

Kathy knew that would make an impression on Maskas, who had to be doubting my coaching credentials, and I think it did. Somebody dropped a name for me, for a change.

A couple of years later, Ara asked me if I would assist him as coach in the College All-Star Game in Chicago, the game in which the college stars of the previous year take on — or are thrown to — a team from the National Football League. He didn't have to repeat the invitation. His staff also included Dick Nolan and Sid Gillman, former NFL coaches; Dave Levy, the defensive coach for John McKay at Southern California, and the state of Delaware's own Ron Waller, the former University of Maryland and Los Angeles Rams' halfback who now is with the Kansas City Chiefs organization.

I coached the linebackers, Waller the special teams. The College All-Stars, most of them taking time out from their rookie camps in NFL, had Archie Griffin, the two-time Heisman Trophy winner from Ohio State; Chuck Muncie, California's All-American runner, and Leroy and Dewey Selmon, the ponderous brothers from Oklahoma's defensive line. But we were to play the Pittsburgh Steelers on relatively short notice. Need I say more? I will say only the final score was 24-0, in favor of the overdogs.

But the game gave me the opportunity to get closer to Ara — on and off the field. We relaxed on the golf course.

I was surprised when Ara quit coaching after that 1974 season. So was everybody else. His answer to inquiries was that he hadn't retired, but had resigned from coaching. I had not sensed the incredible pressure that was on him to win at Notre Dame. Ara just decided he just didn't need that punishment any more. He once told me he envied my setup at Delaware because I had time to coach. The time he had to spend with alumni, press and promotion cut deeply into his coaching hours.

I'll lay a little Woody Hayes on you while I'm at it. This was while I was assisting at Delaware. We had missed out on a good high-school running back in northern New Jersey because, by our computation, he could not meet the national 1.6 rule, which had to be the academic minimum of any football player entering college.

When Dave Nelson read that this kid had been recruited by Ohio State, he had me call Larry Catuzzi, our former quarterback who was the backfield coach at Ohio State, to find out the story.

As I placed the call, I was browsing through Woody Hayes' new book. Woody himself answered the phone. He said Larry wasn't around, but that he'd have him call me. (Incidentally, by Ohio State standards, the North Jersey kid was fair game). I mentioned that I was reading his book.

"Turn to Page 83 right now," Woody said. "There are some plays there I don't want you to miss, but they don't have the right dope on them."

So there was Woody Hayes correcting the book for me, over the phone. He wanted to make sure I had the right information. I was amazed at the enthusiasm of a guy who had been around that long, and who still was meticulous for detail.

I had the good fortune to be on the same bill with Joe Paterno at a clinic in Wildwood, N.J., in the late '60s. Sue went with me, and seemed awed just to be in the same county with Paterno, who had just been named Coach of the Year. She insisted he had flown in, and had not driven like us peasants from Delaware. When I mentioned this to Joe, he got a belt out of it, and he kept it alive at Sue's expense after he met her.

"By the way, Sue," he said. "Would you like to go home with us in our private plane? We just never bother with our car."

Paterno operates outside the American Football Coaches Association, and that doesn't set well with me. I think he could make a better contribution to the game by making his opinions known through the association, rather than criticizing coaches for some of their alleged wrongdoings. But he seems to prefer being on his own. He relinquished his position on the Board of Trustees and while he still is an AFCA member, he is not active. You don't see him at the meetings.

I believe it all started with a book — which should be a lesson to me, maybe. Gordon White of the New York Times did the writing for him. Paterno was very critical of some of the top coaches like Ara Parseghian and Darrell Royal, fellow trustees. He suggested that neither the Notre Dame nor Texas programs were operating on the same high plane as Penn State's. Ara and Darrell naturally had a few words to say about this. One thing led to another and Joe, feeling he just couldn't be part of the association, quit the board.

The name of his book was *Football, My Way*.

When you are elected Coach of the Year, even in the College Division, there is a material gain, too. Including the Chevrolet they let you have for a year, with an option to buy for a substantial discount — the car deal since has been discontinued —I would say the award brings you an extra $10,000. You hear from more clinics, more banquets. You lecture at a clinic for two hours and the check is for anywhere from $150 to $500. Bear Bryant went all-out and gave me $1,000 to speak at his clinic at Alabama.

But it was a priceless honor for me to be elected to the Board of Trustees of the Coaches Association in 1975. When you are a trustee, you move up through the ranks to the eventual presidency. This will happen to me this winter in Hollywood, Fla. I am now the first vice-president to Jerry Clairborne of Maryland. I will preside at the 1982 convention in Houston, and my first vice-president will be Michigan's Bo Schembechler.

I'm already practicing my "The meeting will come to order-s." I wonder if they will pay any attention to Mrs. Bear Bryant's small-time coach?

10

The Offers to Jump

The grass is greener on THIS side — Delaware's. That's why I'm still here. I do not mean green as in money. I have been offered a lot more to coach elsewhere, but I would be paying a price. I would be compromising.

I am convinced that mostly it is the bad jobs that are open in the college football coaching profession. Maybe "bad" is too strong a word. How about "unattractive"? I like the way Bear Bryant, in all his cotton-country logic, puts it: "You rarely inherit a warm bed in this business." A coach jumps to another college, he inherits a bed made cold by a losing program.

But it is gratifying to be wanted by others, and I've been tempted to make the jump to those "others" a few times. However, I have always looked before I leaped, sooner or later, and that accounts for the fact that I haven't leaped.

First, let me try to explain what it is about coaching at the University of Delaware that makes it such a fine place to practice a profession. It is the kind of coaching I like because for the players, football is part of the total picture of education. Football is not the only reason they are attending Delaware. Also, what we are doing is recognized by the faculty, the students and the community, and that is of great importance to me.

I am not claiming that the Delaware situation is unique. There are colleges and universities with the same approach. You might ask, isn't a football program recognized by the faculty, the students and the community everywhere? And please do, because I have the answer.

The answer is "No." One recent year I spent two weeks at Princeton, as a member of an advisory board studying their football program. They were searching for a coach — Jake McAndless had quit — but I wasn't there as a candidate, and nobody told me I was a prospect. I went up to help make recommendations that would lead to Princeton's filling the vacancy.

When we had finished evaluating, I was told that the university president, William G. Bowen, was going to host a cocktail party for the advisory board, sort of a thank-you deal, I guessed. I said I'd be there. But when I showed up, I was all alone with President Bowen. No cocktail party.

He came to the point right away. "We'd like YOU to be the coach."

We talked eye-to-eye. I was on a "Bill" basis with the prexy. He said he did not want his football coach to be a member of the faculty. That disturbed me. I told him so. "Before you say no," he said, "I wish you would go to New York with Royce Flippin" (the director of athletics) and meet some of our outstanding alumni, some very successful businessmen."

I went. Royce took me to a couple of imposing brokerage houses that might have thought I was a messenger boy. I met the big alumni in their executive suites, and they started talking some pretty impressive figures. Salary, I mean. But by now I definitely realized what had been gnawing at me on the Princeton campus — that I would not be happy in the job because football really wasn't WANTED there. Oh, the players obviously wanted it, and the coaches — past and future — did. But I felt the students could not care less and that many administrators merely tolerated the sport. I had the definite impression that it was the alumni that really pushed Princeton football. It just wasn't my idea of a healthy situation. I'd be coaching to try and improve the morale at Princeton Clubs throughout the East.

And I certainly couldn't put myself in a place where I would not be a member of the faculty. I would immediately know the university itself did not consider what I was doing to be of academic value, that they would have me in the same category as the recreation director or, in its most menial terms, the people who maintain the stadium. Talking with Princeton, I sensed that my effect on the ball players and my inter-action with the faculty would be a great deal less than I have at Delaware.

At the risk of being accused of knocking the Ivy League, it is my opinion that there is a sophistication among its students that causes them to consider football to be perhaps just a slight bit below them. I am sure they could never see a relationship between football and learning. I went back to an old conclusion of mine: that if it was just football I wanted — practice, play the games, forget the academic world of the student, forget them from one season to the next, don't-come-to-me-with-your-problems — then I'd go into the National Football League, or maybe professional wrestling.

Princeton turned to Bob Casciola of the University of Connecticut, who had my recommendation, and gave him a five-year contract. When it expired they fired him. By the way, Delaware and Princeton will be opponents in 1981 and 1982.

Another Ivy Leaguer, Cornell, also was interested in what passes for my body. That was four years ago, and I stopped that with the first phone call from Ithaca. They said it was definitely an offer. They were going to make Cornell one of the finer football programs in the league and were quite anxious for me to orchestrate the reconstruction, etc. It was a simple decision for me: I just would rather have the coaching job at Delaware than I would at Cornell, primarily because our university family and the people in our state LIKE football. You can tell that by the response from the students, the citizens. It is a response that makes me quite happy.

Some of these job approaches and interviews get to be on the cloak-and-dagger side. They amused me then and they do now. The West Point Story, for example. No, not the old movie that starred James Cagney and Doris Day.

Army called and asked if I would be interested in the head coaching job. They had just fired Homer Smith, who then charged Army with illegal recruiting practices and an attempted coverup. Homer also said he was fired three days after he resigned.

My answer was "Not really." But then I got another call, a local one, from Art Vanderpool, who was a National Guard officer in Delaware. He said he had been approached indirectly by the Military Academy to see if he could convince me to talk with them.

It was a time when things had to happen fast at West Point. It was after the season of 1978, and they wanted to hire a head coach rather quickly and announce it before the cadets left for Christmas vacation. Timing was important, because the cadets themselves are a salient part of their football recruiting. They go home and tell their town high-school phenom that we just hired so-and-so as head football coach and you really should consider going to the Point. That makes sense.

If you are still with me, shift the scene to a runway of the Greater Wilmington Airport. There I was waiting for a helicopter to arrive from West Point. That's right: we had agreed to meet at the airport. Sure enough, here comes the chopper right on the dot at 11:30 a.m. Major Gen. Ray P. Murphy, the athletics director, stepped out as advertised. He didn't want anybody to see him and I didn't want anybody to see me, and it was kind of James Bond-ish.

We jumped in my car and headed for lunch in a nearby restaurant on the Du Pont Highway. It was at a back table that we talked. Much to my chagrin, the waitress didn't recognize me. Nobody paid any attention to us. I listened to what the General had to say. Then I told him my feelings: that while West Point sounded exciting, and that their schedule was certainly exciting, I did not feel that I would have enough time there to coach. The cadets' schedule is so demanding that only an hour and a half each day is allotted for football — and that includes transportation and some of the dressing time.

Still, I felt embarrassed saying "No thanks" to the U.S. Military Academy and its great tradition, where the immortal Red Blaik had coached and where the coaching line also had included Paul Dietzel. There I was, a little guy from the north end of Flint, Mich., saying "Gee, I don't think this is what I want to do." But say it I did. They hired Lou Saban, the old NFL coach, coaxing him away from the University of Miami. Army won two games last year and Saban wound up complaining in print about alleged renegings on promises made and agreements entered. He quit the following July.

I think that even before Major Gen. R. P. Murphy (how I'd love to have his initials) boarded his helicopter in West Point, he suspected we would be speaking two different languages. I am convinced the Military Academy would like to go back to pre-World War II days when it was a national power. But it's not going to happen. It is going to be very difficult for the service academies to play the kind of football they want, not only because of the restrictions their curriculums put on the program but because Viet Nam turned off a lot of kids and their parents from anything to do with the military. I would not like to be recruiting for West Point, or Annapolis.

Ten years ago, the pitch was from the University of Maryland. Dim Montero, who had been an almost unbeatable coach at Salesianum School in Wilmington, was on the Terrapins' staff, and I have to believe he was the instigator. Jim Kehoe, the athletics director, didn't fool around when he got me on the phone. He said I could have the job, but I would have to show up right away. That was impossible. We were getting ready to play North Carolina Central in the Boardwalk Bowl. I also had several off-the-field commitments: to speak at the Wilmington Touchdown Club and the Newark Touchdown Club, and to do a program with WHYY-TV in Wilmington. Those were no big deals, but I had promised to do them in the name of the University of Delaware and I didn't feel I could cancel out to talk about a job somewhere else.

"But I will see you right after the ball game in Atlantic City," I told Kehoe.

"You don't sound like you want the job," he said.

"It sounds like something I might want," I said, "and I definitely would like to hear what you have to say. But put it this way: if I were your football coach, and we were getting ready for a bowl game, would you like me to be out soliciting another job?"

"Definitely not, and you sound like the kind of guy I want," Kehoe said. I told him that was the kind of guy I was. We agreed to get together after the game, and I went back to the business of preparing for it. The morning of the game in Atlantic City, I picked up the paper and read that Maryland had hired Jerry Clairborne as head football coach.

Ara Parseghian
. . . the greatest of all coaches.

Joe Paterno
. . . he deactivated himself in the coaches association.

Hal Bodley
Sports Editor, News-Journal Papers

Bob Kelley

. . . before broadcasting our games grayed him up a bit. He's one of the best play-by-players around and has done it for us now for twenty-five years.

Two men you want on your side in a department of athletics: Dave Nelson (left) and Bob Carpenter.

Delaware Stadium – Home of the Fightin' Blue Hens.

Some of the hardware we've collected: Left to right: "Timmie" the Washington Touchdown Club trophy symbolic of the national small-college championship, the Lambert Cup, the UPI National Championship Trophy, the AP National Championship Trophy, the NCAA Eastern Championship Plaque.

Lawrence Welk's back-up group? No, the coaching staff in the Kodak All-American Game the summer of 1972. Left to right: Tony Knapp, Boise State; Tim Sweeney, Washington State; Chuck Fairbanks, Oklahoma; Bear Bryant, Alabama; Bo Schembechler, Michigan, and the Bear's chauffeur, Delaware. Judging from the fit, the three guys on the right got to the jackets last.

You go 10-and-0, you can spend the winter laughing. This was when Delaware was presented with the "Timmie" award at the Washington Touchdown Club's 1973 banquet. In the huddle, from left, are: Earl Weaver, the Baltimore Orioles manager; Sen. Caleb Boggs of Delaware; Rep. Emanuel Celler of New York, and Hal Bodley, Wilmington News-Journal sports editor.

The Many Faces of

Tubby Raymond

Go ahead and ask: Who's the big guy with Tubby Raymond and Bob Blackman? In January 1974, John Wayne received the Great American Award from the American Football Coaches Association and Blackman was its president.

When you're short, you'll try anything. Here is one way I check out the over-all scene at our pre-season practice.

Me and my blackboard. No, I'm not predicting we'll be No. 1. That'll be the day.

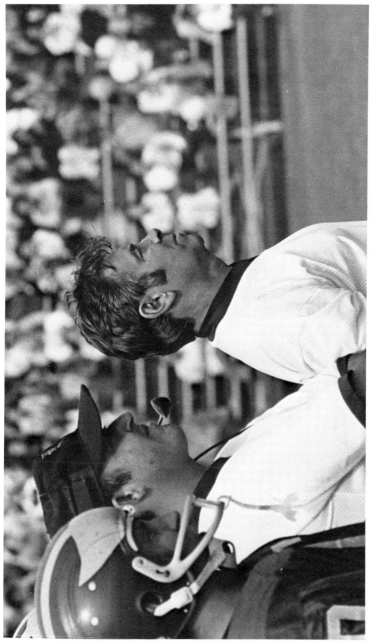

Ted Kempski is the man on the phone. He is our offensive coordinator and one of the few persons who can make me laugh during the heat of a season.

A lot of linebackers saw the late Chuck Hall, 1968-1970, when he burst through the line this way. The angle didn't do them much good, though, for Delaware's No. 1 career rusher amassed 3,157 career yards. He is my all-time power runner.

*Conway Hayman lettered as an offensive lineman, 1968-1970. He's now
with the Houston Oilers. Conway and I had our little differences when he
was a sophomore.*

On the sidelines with Sam Neff during the 1971 Boardwalk Bowl. Sam steered us to a one-sided victory over C. W. Post in what was a belated "Cakewalk Bowl."

Just as well. If that's the way they operated, I don't think I would have fit in very well well at College Park.

Generally speaking, any college that contacts a coach to talk employment should do so through that coach's director of athletics, in my case Dave Nelson. They should have his permission to discuss the position with me.

But in the case of an offer from the University of Iowa, it was only natural that Bump Elliott should contact me directly. We are old buddies — baseball and football teammates at Michigan, even roommates. Since he became Iowa athletics director, he has had to hire several head coaches and each time he has buzzed me.

The first time, I just couldn't see going to a doormat situation and building from the bottom. Who needed that, with the setup I had at Delaware? A few years went by when for the third time in the Elliott regime Iowa was in the market for a coach. This was late in 1978, when we had qualified for the playoffs again. There was no way I could get to Iowa.

"Don't worry about it," Bump said. "I'll come to you."

That he did. And he brought along a university vice president. At midnight, we talked in a room of the Iron Hill Inn, just down the road from Delaware Stadium. I think the Iron Hill Inn introduced water beds to the hotel industry in Delaware. I thought I'd throw in that bit of vital information in case you were getting the opinion I didn't know what was happening outside of my little sphere of football.

Iowa hit me with some goodies. A television program on the side, with a lot of money involved. But to me, a TV program is just another detraction from your ability to coach. It takes time to do a TV show well; a lot of big-time coaches go on cold, but I would prefer to spend some time with it. And then where would I be — part Howard Cosell, part coach?

I told them I didn't believe I would fit into a place, Iowa

or wherever, at which I couldn't develop an educational experience for my players.

"No problem," Bump said. "you take care of the football players. You see that their experience is educational. Now . . . we would like you to get us to the .500 level within three years and be in contention for a championship within five years."

I had to smile at this, because these objectives weren't exactly compatible with my taking care of the young men or developing an educational atmosphere. Bump checked out of the Iron Hill Inn and went on to hire Hayden Fry, who probably was much more qualified for a rebuilding job than I am. He is an exceptional coach who has that wide-open Texas flare, a come-from-behind offensive. I guess I have had my last professional visit from my old roomie, Bump Elliott.

I would prefer that a job I might accept not depend upon how many people come to the ball park, which I suspected was a requisite at Iowa. When you get to that stage, changes are made for commercial purposes. Those are really professional programs, and in that kind of setup the pressure goes right on through the coaches directly to the players. It's why a lot of major-league baseball managers get fired: the box office comes first.

There are too many college football coaches whose approach is: 1, we're gonna put people in the stands; 2, we're gonna win; 3, if you have time to go to school, that's nice, and 4, if you get time to graduate, that's even nicer — but remember, we are in a business.

The National Football League definitely is a business — forget my educational rah-rah philosophy there. And I came close to joining the pros two years ago, but not as a head coach. This one got into the newspapers. Hal Bodley, sports editor of the Wilmington News-Journal, had his ear to the ground — or wall — at a meeting of newspaper people in

Chicago and picked up the flash that I had been talking with the Kansas City Chiefs.

The Chiefs' coach, Marv Levy, is a long-time friend. When he went to the University of California in 1960, he tried to hire me as his backfield coach. It didn't tempt me, although it would have been fun working with Levy and his quarterback, who happened to be Craig Morton. For one major reason, my wife Sue was in the hospital with her hearing problem. I recommended Rocky Carzo, a fellow staffer at Delaware and a former fullback for us. He took the job.

Jump ahead some years. December of 1978, I was in Atlanta for a coaches' convention and over a cup of coffee, Marv Levy told me he had just signed to coach the Chiefs. He also told me he wanted to introduce our Wing-T into the National Football League — with my help. What he was doing was offering me the job as his offensive coordinator. He thought the Wing-T would be extremely unique in the NFL.

Marv knew our Delaware act pretty good. Before he went up to coach the Montreal Alouettes in the Canadian Football League for five seasons, he spent four days at Delaware picking our alleged brains. He took much of our offensive philosophy with him to Montreal. Marv was extremely successful there, although the aspect of ball control on the ground is not exactly hand-made for Canadian football with its three-down restriction and defensive linemen playing a yard or so from the ball. But he made a whole series of adjustments and now, as the new man at Kansas City, he was interested in doing much the same.

The night after our morning cup of coffee in Atlanta, Marv and I went at it again over bacon and eggs — one of those 1 a.m. sessions. He sold me. I couldn't wait to get up to the room and phone Sue.

"Get ready," I announced. "We're moving to Kansas

City. I'm going to help Marv Levy with the Chiefs and there is a deaf program out there you could be happy with."

What would I do without Sue? "Have another cup of coffee," she said. "Go to bed and call me back in the morning."

For several hours I had been fantasizing what it would be like coaching in the NFL, and Sue was telling me to slow down. Cool it. She was right. I awoke with the conviction I would be getting myself into a bunch of changes, probably the most difficult of which would be my own decline from head coach to assistant coach.

I've always considered the job of assistant coach as the most difficult in football, because any creativity you do express has to be either accepted or rejected by the head coach, and you find yourself trying to act within his image. It's tough on Saturdays to try and make contributions and keep them within someone else's intellectual framework.

I turned down that opportunity to go pro, but still wound up with the cake. Shortly afterward, I spent four days with Marv in Kansas City, talking about our offensive approach — for a fee. I've done it several times since, every time I go west and have a chance to stop off in K.C.

I think the Chiefs were second in rushing that first year of Levy in 1978, even though they won only four games. In 1979, Marv had to abandon much of the Wing-T the last third of the season because of injuries. He could get by with two running backs, instead of three. The Chiefs have a particular interest in our waggle play, where the quarterback stays away from the play action and you end up with five receivers, which is really a professional concept of the passing game. I don't want to lose you with blackboard stuff, but the most important thing about that kind of passing is that the quarterback is not throwing from the same spot all the time. He is moving around.

I got a kick out of Jeff Komlo's comment during his first

year in the NFL, with the Detroit Lions. Our ace quarterback of 1978 said the pass rush was unbelievable . . . "they come at you from all angles because they know where you are going to set up; if it's third-and-15, they know where you're gonna be and they meet you at the pass." What Levy has in mind, with the Wing-T, is busting up that NFL stereotype.

One more backward look at the Chiefs' offer: "offensive coordinator" is a pretty fancy title, but it still boils down to being somebody's helper. There is a horribly insecure ring to that. In the NFL, the head coaches might have contracts running into years, but the assistants' contracts are from season to season, and if something happens and the owner wants to blow the head coach out of there, they pay him off and blow the assistants away, too. I never really wanted to do what Bob Hollway, my Michigan buddy and fellow assistant coach, wound up doing as a coach. He had a great career, but at the same time he lived in about nine places in fifteen years.

The University of Arizona didn't offer me the job, but did a little trolling. Dave Strack, the athletics director and a former Michigan basketball star and coach, got in touch. He said he was looking for a football coach, one whose major responsibility would be fund-raising for the Department of Athletics. He listed some twenty-five golf outings the coach would have to show up for, playing with specific people, and said I would have to be at Arizona "at least half the time." Whatever interest I might have had in Arizona died right there. I didn't want to be a fund-raiser. If I did, I'd go out and raise funds for myself.

I must sound pretty picky, pretty demanding. I am. If ever I would leave Delaware, it would be for an opportunity to keep on coaching football the way I want to coach it, to run a program that is not totally dependent upon gate receipts to stay alive. Certainly it is important to bring fans into Delaware Stadium, but it is not the dominant reason for our program. That's the kind of job I like and maybe there aren't any more around. That's OK with me.

People ask me if I could stand the "pressure" of an Iowa, or an Army, or a Cornell. I don't think I could be any more pressured than I am now, in my own mind, to do a quality job.

In my discussions with Ara Parseghian, he said that one of the things that really bothered him about coaching in the college majors was that he couldn't get to the field on time, or get to it adequately prepared. There were always so many things in his way, things that did not involve football. He actually felt he wasn't coaching.

What my staying boils down to is that I have never been offered a better position than the one I have. I am a full professor and I have faculty status and tenure, which means I cannot be fired. (All our coaches have faculty status). My appointment as football coach is an administrative one. I could be removed from that position and be given other responsibilities, the same as any one else on tenure.

The administration regards my work as contributing to the academic community, which pleases me. I am surrounded with outstanding people and have enjoyed my association with players, coaches, faculty and friends like the Carpenters and John DeLuca, who not only actively support our football program but have played a great part in creating forty years of athletic stability at Delware.

The job hasn't made me rich in terms of money, but I have been able to provide a good standard of living for my family and have seen my three children be graduated from college.

Ergo, sports fans of Delaware, you are currently stuck with me — but that doesn't mean I have isolated myself from the possibilities of a move.

I went along operating on the Fritz Crisler theory: That

you should't go knocking on doors. Let them come to you. If you ask for a job, then you have nothing to say about it, and you will find a lot of things you don't like that probably will make it impossible.

But you know what, Coach Crisler? I might have made a mistake. Your theory isn't necessarily the right one in these times. There have been good jobs open. If you don't express an interest in something you might like, people figure you are settled for life and won't approach you. I never have applied for a job, but sometimes I think I should have sent out some feelers. If my son Chris would tell me about a coaching job that was open, and which looked promising to him, I would encourage him to apply, to make it known that he was aggressively interested. Sorry about that, Fritz, but I now believe you shouldn't wait to be asked.

11

Goin' Fishin' . . . The Recruiting Trail

The boy's name was Steve Orsini, and he was an outstanding halfback for Lower Dauphin High School in the
Harrisburg, Pa., area.

The recruiters had given him his best shot, and he had
boiled his choices down to Notre Dame, Villanova and Delaware.

He decided on Villanova. All I could say was "Good
luck. We're sorry you're not going to be with us, but we hope
things work out for you."

Three days later, his high-school coach called. "Steve is
still confused. He doesn't know whether he's afoot or horse-
back. Would you come up and talk to him again?"

It was an emergency call, but we are open all night at
Delaware when it comes to recruiting. Ed Maley and I hit the
highways, picking up a couple of Gino's along the way.

At the Orsini household, we could see that the young
man was truly upset. He wasn't sure he wanted to go to Villanova, after all. He didn't know WHERE he wanted to go.

Naturally, I had to ask him if he still had an interest in
Delaware. He said he thought he did, but he wanted to talk to
me about his chances of making it big-time, meaning Notre
Dame. The Irish wanted him, but he wondered if he was
good enough.

That was my cue. I reeled out some line. "If I thought you weren't good enough for Notre Dame, do you think I'd be here talking to you? I wouldn't even want you."

"You mean that?" he said.

"I mean it so much that if I were you, I'd GO to Notre Dame. Why would you not want to go, if you have this great opportunity?"

That should have been HIS cue to say "If you have that much confidence in me, then I should be playing for you. I'm going to Delaware." I truly wanted him in a Blue Hens uniform. He sounded so skeptical about his chances of making it at Notre Dame that I thought he's forget that and go back to his original choice, Villanova, and I knew I could convince him we had more to offer than Villanova. Thus, we would have him at Delaware. Mal and I left his house with that feeling, although nothing had been resolved.

Orsini telephoned me the next morning. "Coach, I'm truly grateful for the time you spent with me and for your advice. You talked me into it. I'm going to Notre Dame."

And he did. And he became a regular. And Ara Parseghian would tell me how much he appreciated my sending the boy his way. Arrggh! Orsini went on to tri-captain the national championship team that Ara's successor, Dan Devine, coached.

Every coach must have a million recruiting stories — the ones he landed, the ones that got away.

You plan but you lose a Steve Orsini. You stumble into a Jeff Komlo, who came in out of the cold and became our Little All-American quarterback.

I had gone a-callin' to Fork Union Military Academy in Virginia for so many seasons that I developed a nice relationship with the coach, Red Pulliam. He has sent us a number of good people. Mike Donnalley, the center on our 1979 championship team, was one.

"I've got a quarterback nobody has really made a move on," Pulliam told me on one of my visits. That's when I first met Jeff Komlo. I invited him to check out Delaware, and his parents came with him. They left rather non-committal. A short time later, Jeff phoned and said he would like to come to Delaware.

There was no financial inducement. Not a bit of aid, although there was some later in his college career when his family's economic situation changed. (The parents' application for aid is filed every year).

It was a while before anybody even knew Jeff was around. He never started for the freshman team — and in lieu of what he was to become, we've given Jimmy Flynn, who was then the frosh coach, some good rips about that. The next spring, Jeff was our fourth-stringer. We had a quarterback and didn't know it. But he won the job after two games of his sophomore season and away he went, taking us with him for three great years.

And he had been at Fork Union for the taking. Komlo was an all-around athlete in high school in New Jersey, and his reputation was strongest in baseball and basketball. He went to prep school to attract some attention in football, his favorite sport, but he never really came off with it. His coach recommended him to me with the amendment that he thought Ben Belicic was a better quarterback. Belicic was there earlier, and he was at Delaware when Komlo arrived, and Jeff beat him out of the job with us.

What happened was that Jeff got caught in the numbers game when it came time for him to go to college, and I'm talking of the possibility of a major school taking him. There is a lot of arithmetic involved in the distribution of scholarships. Jeff was sitting there for us to pluck.

Scott Brunner, who sat on the bench for two seasons waiting for Komlo to get out of town, and then quarterbacked us all the way to the national title in 1979, was another interesting recruiting case.

His father, John, was a member of the Temple coaching staff and because of that, of course, he never spoke to us and the feeling was mutual. At that time, it would have been gross disloyalty for either John or me to attempt hellos. We were involved in what is known as a grudge rivalry.

But when John switched to the Princeton staff, we said hello and then some.

"How would you like to have a 6-foot-4 quarterback who weighs 190 pounds and likes to play?" he asked me.

"I'll take him — where is he?" I replied.

"Over at my house," John said. "He's my son."

I hit the house immediately. I found a tall, undeveloped young man who had grown too fast for his skills, but he had been a championship, all-star quarterback in Lawrenceville, N.J.

We talked. Irv Wisniewski did a follow-up number for us, and so we landed Scott Brunner. In the meantime, the Princeton staff dissolved and John, the old man, went back to Temple — faced with the prospect of having his son oppose him. I think that family situation has had much to do with the improvement in our relations with the Owls. John never wanted to be in a position of coaching his own boy, and that's why he recommended him to us. That had to make me feel good.

Let me explain our recruiting policy. We do not go out in the field armed with full scholarships for the asking. We can offer aid to a player only on the basis of a confidential financial statement filed by the parents. Our financial-aid officer checks this statement and decides whether the player is entitled to full aid, partial aid or no aid.

Sure, we get hurt. There justifiably are parents who are not interested in sending their young men to Delaware because there is no financial inducement. These are families we think can afford to pick up the tab.

Full aid means room, board and tuition. No books, although some athletes qualify for the books, too, under academic aid.

Temple, to use a for-example opponent, has a no-need policy: It can offer room, board, tuition and books without requiring the parents to fill out an application. And they can do it immediately. The prospects we are interested in have to wait for the aid application to be filed and wait some more to have it processed.

Ours is not the easiest way to attract football talent, but it is the healthiest, in my opinion. People read that we are one of the wealthiest state-related colleges in the country, and wonder why we don't spend some of that money to flat-out pay for football players. This is why: It is a philosophical thing. While aid based on need appears socialistic and is, in a sense, it keeps us from paying young men to play. It keeps us as far away from professionalism as we can be and still be competitive. Eastern schools long have had a background of grants-in-aid. Not all have continued with it. We have. We like it. There are no money-under-the-table deals at the University of Delaware.

But why would a high school boy want to come to Delaware when he might be able to do better financially elsewhere? Pull up a chair.

I would tell him about our excellent academic rating. I would mention our over-all fiscal stability, which means that our physical facilities and educational opportunities are superior to many schools. I would tell him about our tradition of excellence in football, about the excitement that surrounds Delaware football, with a fine stadium filled every home game.

We feel we have designed a football program that is

better than most. We don't want to be Penn State, or Michigan, or Texas. We don't feel we could compete at that level without making academic concessions. Ours is not a three hundred and sixty-five day football program. We have established priorities we feel will produce the best football and academic experiences for our people. Don't compare us with the Penn States, the Notre Dames. They play another game.

We are better than the alternatives, which are the total-football majors or those colleges where the student body, in effect, doesn't know the football team exists. Delaware has a measure of it all: national status and community interest and none of the negative accoutrements.

Our self-imposed restriction of aid based on need is an advantage, in the long run. We are permitted to have the equivalence of sixty full scholarships in school at any one time, but these may be spread among as many as eighty-five people. If we did not have the aid policy, we'd have to pay everybody. We would never get a player for free. We would never get a Jeff Cannon or Curt Morgan, who became team captains, or an Ivory Sully, all of whom paid their own way. If you want to call them walk-ons, that's what they were, and they walked on with enthusiasm because they knew they weren't going to be surrounded with free-ride players.

We never look at a roster in terms of how much money we have in financial aid, but rather in how many helmets we are filling. There is safety in numbers. The more people you have, the more chance there is of finding an outstanding player. In our spring practice, 1980, we had one hundred and forty players. Temple, Maryland, Villanova had about seventy-five — all on full scholarships. If you are going to throw full scholarships around, you had better know exactly what you are getting because you are going to be stuck with them for four years.

Over a long period of time, we have found that the boys

who really want an education are the best bets. I am looking for such a boy who feels he just cannot go to school without playing football.

If everyone knew who the football players were, we wouldn't get any of them They would all go to the big leagues. And so in reality it is the mistakes other recruiters make that help us get talent.

We do not use freshman players on the varsity — another seemingly negative factor that also is a positive. That turns off a lot of young men who want action as soon as they hit the campus. But it appeals to many parents who want their sons to get their feet on the ground educationally and socially before tackling the responsibility of trying to make the football team. By the time a Delaware freshman reports for his first spring practice, he is pretty well adjusted to his whole new world.

Our freshman rule has some sound financial reasoning to it, too. If you permit frosh to play with the varsity, you must bring them to school early for pre-season practice and this would mean an expense of about $10,000 a year. And if you select twenty to come in early, you probably are going to upset the other fifty freshman players — and who knows if we are picking the right twenty in the first place?

As of the 1980 season, we will have advanced from Division II to I-AA on the NCAA competitive ladder and this entitles us to give a maximum seventy-five full-scholarship equivalencies. However, we have no plans to do this. We are sticking with sixty.

If a Delaware player on aid is injured so severely he no longer can play, his aid will be renewed each year. If a player who is getting help decides he wants to quit football, his application is turned over to the financial-aid officer to see if he qualifies as a non-football-playing student. We could interrupt the aid in February if the boy quits during the fall, but we have never done this. We have allowed him to stay the full school year.

Recruiting is a long and tedious trail. We begin our initial contacts in March. Our area is all of Delaware and Maryland, Washington, a large part of Pennsylvania, a share of New York and the northern tip of Virginia, which gives us a mailing list of about two thousand five hundred schools. We're in continuous communication with them. The coaches try to identify their oustanding prospects for us. Recent legislation makes it difficult for us to obtain academic information, but we manage to get a pretty good idea of whether or not the boy can cut it with the books.

Then we build our list. Each of our coaches is assigned an area. We send questionnaires to boys in the summer preceding their senior years — and this can serve as an elimination process. Right after each University of Delaware season, the coaches hit the road. We meet the boys personally and invite them to campus. Throughout the winter, we have an open house on Monday afternoons, Friday afternoons and Saturday mornings. Between thirty and seventy-five prospects will call on us each week.

We don't usually bring them in overnight. They pay their own transportation, and we spring for lunch. We cannot work them out — physical testing in any form is illegal. All we can go on is the material we have compiled. During the interview, we ask them to file applications for admission and financial aid. When we put them together, we discover who we can talk to with some kind of a financial offer, those we can encourage to come on their own and those we can encourage to seek federal or state aid.

Our area of operations is our own idea, based on practicality — how far we can go and how far we can operate efficiently. It wouldn't make much sense for us to scout the state of Michigan, or Ohio, and ask those athletes to fly in on their own. The real hangup is transportation. Ed Maley goes to the Pittsburgh area once a year, and that's a far-flung outpost for us. Again, a negative is a positive: The boys who go to a college relatively close to their homes are generally happier and most likely to play better.

I believe in recruiting, and I love to do it. I accept it as part of coaching. Dave Nelson, my predecessor, abhorred recruiting and refused to do it. He called himself the world's worst salesman — he would tell the boys "This is what we have at Delaware," and if it didn't appeal to them, so be it. He let his assistants make all contacts.

What I do not like are the occasional brush-offs you get, the looks-down-the-nose as the high-school hot-shot says "Delaware? You're kidding. I'm gonna play for Alabama, or LSU, or Ohio State." A quarterback at Cherry Hill East High in New Jersey pulled that on me. He was a tall one, so he literally looked down on me. I told him that was nice and gave him my best wishes. I also could not resist the temptation to tell him that at best, he would be third-string with us because it was a time when we had both Jeff Komlo and Scott Brunner.

It bugs me to read in our local press about boys accepting full scholarships to Division I football schools, because even a partial scholarship at Delaware may open up a far better opportunity. His chances of playing for us are so much better. I can understand a boy getting stars in his eyes and succumbing to the alleged glamour of the big-time, but so many of them would be so much better off in a familiar environment.

We have a very saleable item at this university. Of all those where the classroom comes first and the football field second, this is the best. There are no academic concessions. If a boy tells me, say, he wants to be a doctor, I will tell him

Delaware is the place for him; his chances of getting into medical school from here are as good as any place.

As head coach, I no longer knock on high-school doors. In the state of Delaware, I make many of the initial contacts. Out of state, the assistants have done their work. Excluding interviews on campus, my role really is to go into the home and talk to the parents and give them either good or bad news concerning financial aid.

I used to think that getting into post-season games put us at a disadvantage in the recruiting whirl because it took away the time we could be doing our selling job. But it has turned out to be a plus in this field. When we won the national championship in 1979, the reaction from the interscholastic front was amazing. Within a week, I had a deskfull of questionnaire answers. Those boys had seen us play on TV and wanted to make themselves known as soon as possible. Thus, the exposure was a recruiting arm in itself.

We try not to waste our time by reaching for the moon. Usually a high-school coach will tell us to hold off if his star player has his heart set on going to the majors. I remind my assistants that they should try to recognize these situations as soon as possible. There was a time when we drew up a "Utopia" list, a No. 1 list and a No. 2 list. We never got any of the Utopians — they were All-Americans in high school and went somewhere else.

There is only so much time and energy we can spend on recruiting, and we should be spending it on those we have a chance of getting. The stars they call the blue-chippers, we still spray them to let them know we are alive. We'll say hello just to see if there is any interest.

Dennis Johnson was a big one that didn't get away. He became a Little All-American defensive tackle for us in 1972 and went on to play in the National Football League. He is from Passaic, N.J., and his coach was John Federici, whose son, Mark, later played for us.

"I have this great lineman, and everybody seems to be after him," Federici told me. "Ohio State, the whole schmear. Why don't you introduce yourself?"

We did. It seemed that Johnson was as loving as he was large. He was saying hello to everybody. There was no limitation at the time as to how many colleges a prospect could visit, so Dennis was going everywhere. On his travels, he came to see us. Then he took off again.

Early in July of 1969, I got a phone call. "This is Dennis. Can I still come?"

He sure could. His mother, Lucille, later would call me: "How is Dennis doing?" Couldn't be better, Lucille. Why would Dennis Johnson pick Delaware over Ohio State? Ask him and I think he'll tell you that he liked our approach, he liked our physical plant and he wanted to be closer to the old homestead.

The traditional "everybody" also was after Tom Di-Muzio, who became a great quarterback for us. Gampy Pellegrini, a Delaware quarterback of the past, was his high-school coach in Philadelphia and brought him down. Big, strapping Tom. Our first king-sized quarterback. In the old days, we might have made him a tackle.

Tom told us he had promised to visit several other schools. Every week, we would call him. He would say "Yes, I did enjoy Yale (or Maryland, or Army), but I did like Delaware, too." And his choice was Delaware. He just fell in love with the place, and decided it was where he wanted to be.

I took a good shot at Franco Harris. Yes, THAT Franco Harris, who wound up starring for Penn State and then helping to make the Pittsburgh Steelers a dynasty. I spent more time at his home in New Jersey than I ordinarily would. Even the family dog got to know me. His mother still remembers me. I see her at banquets in the area.

Tell you how smart I was: I was ready to make a tight end, or a defensive end, out of Harris if I got my clutches on him. I saw him play fullback for his high school on film and decided he never would be a running back because he was too clumsy.

I logged a lot of hours with Lydell Mitchell, who also was to choose Penn State. The next time I saw him, he was an established back with the Baltimore Colts and we were in the same foursome in a charity golf tournament at Cavaliers Country Club outside of Wilmington. We were playing five dollar Nassau with automatic presses, and Lydell was on the other team. I knew I was a better golfer than the other three and it looked as if I was going to come out of it with a pretty good piece of change. But I really didn't want to take Lydell's money — I still looked on him as a kid from Salem, N.J., I had tried to recruit. So I was relieved when a thunderstorm washed us out after seven holes.

We had dinner in the clubhouse and continued to have a pleasant time. When we all went to get our cars, Lydell jumped into a Lincoln Continental that seemed as long as a par-three fairway. I jumped into my Ford. So much for charity.

Films of the high-school boys in action are of great value to a recruiter. Any of our coaches who looks at a film files an evaluation sheet and tosses it into our file. I try to see the movies of the quarterbacks.

I like to think I can read a boy's intensity and his interest in football just by talking to him. These conversations are most important. When I see him with his family, it helps me decide whether he is in the process of breaking away from home, is already independent or is terribly dependent on his parents. Going to college requires a psychological adjustment that is greater than most of them realize. They are first-level in high school, but when they report as college freshmen they are on the bottom of an organization, just one of a bunch of ex-first-levels. Some are not happy at the prospect of digging themselves out of such a hole, and they leave. Every year, there are two or three who disappoint you.

I do not encourage Delaware alumni to bird-dog for us, unless they are in the coaching profession. You can get yourself into a pit listening to the old grads. As head coach, I have to make the selection of who we want to take a chance on, and I cannot let an alumnus, or an alumnae, make that decision for me.

But I am not writing off the old grads. Once you find somebody you want, then the alumni in his area can be of tremendous help. They can talk to the boy, they can write to him.

Speaking of writing, let me drop a letterhead on you. Bob Carpenter and Ruly Carpenter of the Phillies have been of great assistance to our recruiting program — and I don't mean with their zillions. Over the years, they have had such a strong interest in our athletics program and the university as a whole that they send a letter to all the young men we are interested in, disclosing this interest and expressing the hope that the player at least will go down and take a look at the university before making his final decision. The letter is on Phillies stationery, and it has to be impressive. Robin Roberts, the Phillies' old mealticket pitcher who has a son who is a Delaware graduate, also has done a lot of indirect contact work for us.

I just thought of something: I wonder if the Carpenters enclose a copy of the Phillies' home schedule, along with a season-ticket order form? Just kidding, men.

The old-fashioned walk-on, the unknown boy who enrolls on his own and then comes out of the woodwork to make the team, is a rarity. If he has any potential at all, chances are we have heard from his high-school coach and know he is on campus even though we had not made an effort to recruit him.

We will have between seventeen and twenty-three people in a freshman group whom we have helped in a financial sense, but we will have as many as eighty on that squad. So that means that three-quarters of them have, in a sense, walked on.

The banquet circuit is part of the fishing expedition. It gives you another chance to sell yourself and your university. I feel that I have attracted some boys this way. Speaking at banquets gives me the same feeling I get when I cut commercials for Boots Campbell and his Ford agency (now I'm dropping show business on you). The more the young athletes know I exist, the stronger are my chances of getting to talk with them.

Banquet season, I'm out there four nights a week. It has reached the point that whenever I see a fruit cup, I get up and start speaking. But I can do a better job of recruiting this way than I can ringing doorbells.

There are so many former Delaware players now coaching high schools in our tri-state area that it has given us a feeder system. Johnny Oberg of Delsea Regional in Franklinville, N.J., has sent us a number of players, including John Jr. Oberg played for us in the fifties, and seeing his boy in that blue and gold uniform does nothing for my ego.

I hope the Delaware football program is ever-improving. What I do know is that the Delaware football players are ever-increasing in size. Sometimes the old grads forget this. They're still recommending one hundred and seventy-five pound guards, the kind we used to have. Joe Carbone, who was a Little All-American defensive end for us in 1972, now an insurance salesman on Long Island, wrote me recently and touted a six-foot, two hundred and ten-pound tackle. I had to remind Joe that we haven't had a two hundred and ten-pound anything play up front for a long time.

I also hear the argument "Yeah, but he's going to grow up." So I have to whisper in the tout's ear that the boy will have to grow up on his own time, and when he does, let me see him — because at the level we are competing, we need comparable people. Young men are getting bigger, and there are more of them.

The way to be sure that you have a football team is to select a battalion of players; that way, your selection process does not become nearly as critical. Johnny Majors won that national championship at Pitt in 1966 with volumes of people. But with the advent of the ninety-five limitation on scholarships, and no more than thirty a year, places like Pitt and Temple that used to have between one hundred and fifty and one hundred and sixty people on scholarship no longer can reach those numbers. This leaves a lot of boys available for places like Delaware. During the last several years, we have encountered boys we were told were on the list at Maryland or Penn State or West Virginia, but those schools ran out of numbers and the young men were washed down to our plateau.

I am not one for standing in line at a high school, waiting for four or five other coaches to see a particular prospect, waiting your turn. When I see this, I leave. I don't want to be part of a waiting game. I personally feel they should bar coaches from the schools and let us visit the boys only in their homes.

I'll include tranfers in this section on recruiting, although we don't go trolling for transfers. The NCAA has definite ground rules on this. If a player at another college tells us he is interested in switching to Delaware, I am obligated to write to his athletics director and ask permission to discuss the transfer with the player. After I write the letter, I also make it a point to call the coach.

Garry Kuhlman, who had been a two-time All-Stater at Glasgow High School near our university, was a boy we wanted badly, but he decided on Penn State. He was there only two weeks when he called us and said he wanted to come home and play. I told him he should talk to his coach, Joe Paterno, and discuss whatever problems he thought he had and make an effort to stay there. I also spoke to his parents.

Garry did finish his freshman year at Penn State before he transferred. Why didn't I encourage him to jump to us immediately? I wanted him to be very sure he knew what he was doing, and not to be making such an important decision just because of something that might have happened in that day's practice. I told him to show me some maturity. When his year was up, he and his parents and Joe Paterno, too, had accepted the fact that he would he happier at Delaware. I went through the proper procedure. Kuhlman was a superb offensive tackle for us in 1979.

By the way, here is an NCAA transfer law most fans do not know: If a college does not want to release a transfer-minded freshman, then the college of the second part cannot offer him any financial aid of any kind for one full year.

Herb Beck came to us by way of the University of Georgia and became our first four-year starter since Don Miller was Dave Nelson's first quarterback. An NCAA adjustment in eligibility rules gave him that fourth year with us.

Beck spent only three days at Georgia. He was a long way from home and was sort of overwhelmed by the whole big-league scene. Vince Dooley, the Georgia coach, wouldn't give him his release. That meant we could not offer Herb any aid for a year. But he came anyway, with money his grandfather provided. And, of course, he turned out to be a University of Delaware all-timer, a Little All-American on our championship team.

Dutch Hoffman, who came to us a year ago and figures prominently in our 1980 quarterback picture, spent two seasons in the West Virginia line-up, and when he became unhappy with his playing situation, he was automatically free to do whatever he wanted. As a resident of the state of Delaware, it was easier for him to get full financial aid. Dutch was an All-Stater at Newark High who played there for his late father, Bob. I delivered the eulogy at Bob Hoffman's funeral service.

The endless search for talent is a fascinating, sometimes heartbreaking part of coaching. The old story: Many are called, few are chosen. Sometimes they don't choose Delaware. We have had to give up on some prospects when we discovered they could do everything with a football but sign their names on it. And the next thing we know we're playing against them.

The Delaware-Temple Series

1979	Temple 31	DELAWARE 14
1978	Temple 38	DELAWARE 7
1977	Temple 6	DELAWARE 3
1976	DELAWARE 18	Temple 16
1975	Temple 45	DELAWARE 0
1974	Temple 21	DELAWARE 17
1973	Temple 31	DELAWARE 8
1972	DELAWARE 28	Temple 9
1971	Temple 32	DELAWARE 27
1970	DELAWARE 15	Temple 13
1969	DELAWARE 33	Temple 0
1968	DELAWARE 50	Temple 27
1967	Temple 26	DELAWARE 17
1966	DELAWARE 20	Temple 14
1965	Temple 31	DELAWARE 22
1964	Temple 21	DELAWARE 0
1963	DELAWARE 32	Temple 23
1962	DELAWARE 20	Temple 8
1961	DELAWARE 28	Temple 0
1960	DELAWARE 26	Temple 12
1959	DELAWARE 62	Temple 0
1958	DELAWARE 35	Temple 14
1957	DELAWARE 71	Temple 7
1956	DELAWARE 14	Temple 7
1955	DELAWARE 46	Temple 0
1954	DELAWARE 51	Temple 13
1951	Temple 13	DELAWARE 7
1950	Temple 39	DELAWARE 0
1914	DELAWARE 20	Temple 7
1913	DELAWARE 28	Temple 4

TOTAL
DELAWARE 18, Temple 12

12

Why We Hated Temple

Enough of this Mr. Nice Guy stuff. Let's change the subject to Temple University and the Delaware-Temple series.

My dictionary defines hate as "to have strong dislike, or ill will for."

I had strong dislike for Temple. In my opinion, they were Eastern-college football's ambassadors of ill will. It took some doing, but my strong dislike/hatred has changed to respect.

When we first came to Delaware, and by "we" I mean the Dave Nelson era, Temple had a rather poor football program and had reached the frustrating point where they would lose the ball game but win the fight. We would win the game by some enormous scores and when things started to get out of the Owls' control, they started losing control of themselves. They would reflect their lack of discipline by going into their dirty-tricks routine. Dirty tricks, as in punching. The big-city kids from the concrete campus inevitably blew their cool when they found themselves losing to the "small college" from the Delaware sticks.

I got a flash of this my second year as Dave's assistant. We had buried Temple by 51-13 the previous season. The next time around, up in Temple Stadium, we did it again by

46-0. And from that game we still have a great piece of film. It isn't so great to Bob Hooper, though.

Hooper was our quarterback that year. Filling the huge brogans of Don Miller, our Little All-American, Hooper led us to an 8-1 record.

However, Bob never was one of Nelson's favorites. Dave thought he was a hot dog; Hooper's fussiness annoyed him. Bob was the guy with the shower clogs, the deodorant, the shampoo before all this paraphernalia became standard equipment. I always had to suppress a laugh at the look on Dave's face when Hooper would clatter by him in the locker room. This scenario starring his quarterback, his field leader, bothered the Admiral.

Also, Hooper threw the ball a little too much to suit Dave. "If he was in the ocean, struggling, and somebody threw him a life preserver," Dave once said, "Hooper would throw it back."

In this game at Temple, Hooper was bootlegging the ball (concealing it against his thigh) on a pass rollout when a defensive end slammed into him and knocked him down. When everybody unwound, Hooper was still horizontal.

"Get him out of there," Dave snapped to me. "He's hot-dogging again."

Trainer Roy Rylander led a groggy Hooper off the field — once Bob revived.

"What are you fooling around for at a time like this?" I asked as I intercepted him on the sidelines.

"Fooling around hell," said Bob, and now I could see the glass in his eyes. "Didn't you see what happened? That guy slugged me, knocked me cold. Wait till you catch the films."

He was right. The game movies clearly showed the Temple end punching him on the jaw as Hooper lay prone.

That's when I realized Temple wasn't in the same universe with us with their approach to football. They played with sandlot abandon — once they were beyond recall on the scoreboard. The Owls had plenty of opportunity to do this against us. We licked them 12 times in a row, including a series record 71-7 score.

But they succeeded in irritating us even deeper when they began trying to catch up by financial methods. Prior to 1965, financial aid in the Eastern College Athletic Conference was awarded on the basis of a confidential statement filed by the parents. That was our bag; we were proud of the players we were able to recruit on a need basis. All but a few colleges followed the rule to the letter, but generally we were all alike. Penn State, for one maverick, claimed it was giving football scholarships on the basis of academic rating.

When the rule was dropped in 1965, Temple had to be delighted. Now they could go out and underwrite the un-needy, too. And they did. We stuck with the aid rule, but now we were in a different world. We felt Temple was trying to catch up by buying talent. The games became closer, al-though we cut loose for 50 and 33 points against them in successive games in the late '60s; it eventually became dif-ficult to compete with them and their major-league illusions.

Their aspirations to be big-time broke up the Middle At-lantic Conference. It's hard to forgive them for that. They de-cided they were worthy of better opposition and scheduled around the MAC. What was upsetting to the Delaware or-ganization was that the Owls had never won the conference championship — and here they were pulling out and de-stroying the league. My first team managed to win the con-ference in 1966, and we repeated in 1968 and 1969 and each time we defeated Temple. That had to be hard for them to swallow.

So here was Temple attempting to catch us by throwing free-ride scholarships around, firing a couple of coaches along the way, instead of doing it with hard work and tradition and some of the other things we put into our program. They were claiming "big time" before they really made it.

This difference in philosophy only heated up the rivalry, as far as we were concerned. We were determined to show them it was going to take more than money to field a respectable and respected football team. I felt our players would always be ready for Temple. Playing them arouses the patriotism in us. The old Fritz Crisler approach: Fritz always reminded his Michigan squads that the Prussians licked the mercenaries every time. It hasn't worked out that way — going into the 1980 season, they had won the last three encounters — but we take great delight in making it difficult for Temple and those 95 scholarships.

We've had some great games with the alleged big-timers. You'll never see a better one than the 1974 renewal at Veterans Stadium in Philadelphia — and I'm saying this even though we lost. They best us 21-17 in a real groaner. We scored a touchdown that would have won it for us, but Ray Sweeney was detected pulling early at right guard and the TD was nullified. We couldn't get it in again.

Beating Temple by 18-16 in 1976, on a rainy night in spooky Franklin Field, was a great accomplishment. The Owls had come within a point of tying Penn State and had lost to Pittsburgh, which went on to win the national championship, by only 10.

Since Wayne Hardin came along to coach Temple, a number of things have changed — for the better. Wayne inherited a residue of arrogance, but has eliminated much of this. Now we find the Owls a disciplined bunch, as opposed to their barnyard-football teams. The rivalry is just as intense, but Temple's pugnacity against us has turned to respect. I no longer hate. I can say sincerely that the Temple program is a credit to eastern football.

Still, a victory over the Owls is the sweetest of them all

for us. For one thing, the game gives us a measuring stick for our program: How good are we? We have talked about dropping Temple from our schedule, because they now definitely are out of our league and are doing things far beyond our power. But it is a healthy rivalry. It used to be a nasty one.

I know our fans don't want to hear anything about differences in philosophy, and why Temple can give complete aid and in some cases we cannot. They just want to see us win a big football game, and Temple is a big one. It is getting to the point in the series where our ambitions might be exceeding our grasp, but I still think the rivalry is good for Delaware. There isn't a better series in the Philadelphia area. I can't work up any ill will against Wayne Hardin, even though he does have me down seven games to four.

The recruiting war adds fuel to the fire. They come down to our state for talent. For instance, we could not give aid to Dave Chapman, a fine linebacker and guard at Newark High, on the basis of his parents' confidential statement. He went to Temple. Bruce Gordon, a linebacker from Ridley Park, Pa., we liked very much, was a similar case. His father is a physician. There are any number of boys we really can't reach, and Temple can. Steve Watson, an exceptional athlete for St. Mark's High in Wilmington, wound up playing and starring for Temple while the fans — and the sports writers — wondered why we didn't get this hot kid from our own back yard. I am not faulting Steve. He thought he would have a better chance to play pro football if he had a Temple background. To each his own. Steve indeed did go on into the NFL. In some cases, Delaware loses players to Temple — and others — because they do not meet our academic requirements.

When we played Temple in 1979, we faced them with about a 37-35 NCAA equivalency against their 95, when you consider that we are not using freshmen on the varsity and they are. They have more firepower than we are capable of assembling. An equivalency is the amount of aid that amounts to a full scholarship. An equivalency could be split among several players.

Jim Barniak, then of the Philadelphia Bulletin, wrote a pre-game column in which, using an Early Hyperbole style, he said that Temple gets its football players at truck stops and Delaware finds theirs in the nooks of the college library, or words to that effect. I guess that line was inspired by Joe Klecko, who played defensive tackle for the Owls for four years and now is with the New York Jets.

Big Joe, a free spirit, gave Temple that truck-driver image. I will settle for the library image, however inaccurate it may be, that Barniak, tongue-in-typewriter, hung on us.

Joe Klecko was quite a story, if you like those kind of stories associated with your favorite college football team. By his own admission, he never was interested in going to college. Academically inclined he wasn't. Coming out of St. James High School in Chester, Pa., he got a job driving a truck and took to playing semi-pro football with the legendary Aston Knights in Pennsylvania's Delaware County. In the light of his later enrolling at Temple, you have to question his athletic eligibility. You had to wonder if the Knights paid him.

Anyhow, to me, it was a great meeting of the minds — the semi-pro and the Temple football program. He was to be quoted in the newspapers that the principal things he learned on the semi-pro front were (a) how to drink beer and (b) how to punch in the pileups.

Let us say there was a question of inequity in Temple's recruiting Joe. Suddenly he is a freshman who is going to start against us; it was another one of those things that spur your imagination as to what is going on in the enemy camp. They got a large one in Klecko, I'll say that. Six-feet-four and

260 pounds of uninhibited Aston Knight. Help us make it through the Knight.

I had said a few published words about Klecko's preparatory school days with the semi-pros. After his first meeting with us — and they won it by 31-8 — Joe came by to see me. I knew there would be no physical confrontation. I could get lost in one of the cleat holes he had left on the field. He shook hands and gave me the "Nice game — see you next year" ritual and I had the feeling he was kind and considerate. Up close, you had to like the guy.

Joe was on the winning side against us three years in a row. Then we won that 18-16 thriller his senior year — and here came Joe to see me again as we walked off the field, saying nice things. Now he is doing well with the Jets — still no academician, but enjoying the game of football, which is his life.

We never needed any help to get up for a Temple game, but one of their players gave us a boost with a crack he made after they beat us by five points in 1971 — the only time we lost that year.

"Delaware will never beat Temple again!" Doug Shobert, their quarterback, declared in trying to make the point that Temple had arrived in the majors, at last, and no longer would be bothered by their somewhat rustic neighbors to the south. We had been wearing Temple out. Beat them 16 out of 19, including the three seasons previous to '71.

We didn't forget that crack. Our troops took a rather serious approach to the statement that Delaware would never do it again. We did it again the very next time we played them, 28-9, in a big ball game in Philadelphia. Big? Any time we play Temple, it is big.

We get along with the big-city Temples much better now. We keep trying to upset them and they go on trying to keep us where they think we belong — out of their league. I no longer consider Temple a truck stop on our schedule.

Temple vs. Delaware is no place for a faint-hearted football player, but Bob Hooper will be glad to know we no longer have to work on a defense against dirty tricks.

13

An Assist from the Staff

If somebody on our staff ever drops dead on the field, I hope it is the head coach — because I am convinced everything will continue to go smoothly. That's how much I think of the people around me.

There are fans who wonder why top men like Ed Maley and Ted Kempski are still with Delaware, apparently contented with their roles as assistant coaches. Twenty years ago, I would have been wondering the same thing about aides of their ability.

Young coaches somehow associate mobility with success, and vice versa. In other words, you have to be moving, occupationally, to be successful. I have learned this is a bad theory.

Another misconception among younger aides in college football is that every good assistant coach is going to become a head coach, without fail. They don't realize the odds.

There are some 600 intercollegiate football programs in America, and they probably average out to five assistants apiece. That means the assistants are outnumbering the head coaches 5 to 1. So there just aren't that many jobs open to take care of all the ambitious assistants.

You get a man like Ted Kempski, who has been with us thirteen years and is my offensive coordinator, and you are indeed a fortunate head coach. He is widely sought for clinics, and I know he has had chances to go elsewhere. But there are not that many positions that are better than what he has. He likes the responsibility, we love him, we respect him, he is part of our family — and besides, I couldn't get along without his sense of humor. He loosens me up when I need it, even if I don't think I need it.

Ted went through a couple of disturbing situations before he came to us in 1968 as offensive backfield coach. He was an assistant coach at George Washington University when they dropped football. He was an assistant at Marshall College when the head coach was fired. He has told us many times, "I don't want to go through those scenes again."

Kempski, who had been an All-Stater for Wilmington's Salesianum School, was our starting quarterback in 1961 and 1962. His senior year, we won the Middle Atlantic Conference title and also the Lambert Cup as the best in our division in the East. That was the year he won the university's scholar-athlete award. Ted went on to get a master's degree.

It bothers me that the contributions of the Kempskis and the Maleys of our organization do not get more recognition from the news media. Maley is about as "Delaware" as you can get, even though he is a native of the Pittsburgh area. He played tackle for us for three years in the '50s and after serving in the Army for two years, came back in 1959 as Dave Nelson's offensive and defensive line coach. He was able to concentrate on the defensive line in 1968 with the adoption of platoon football. He married Pat Lyons, who captained our cheerleaders. For twenty-six years, counting his playing career, Mal has been all Blue and Gold.

Mal is our defensive coordinator, is coordinator of admissions and is in charge of recruiting. He is really administrative assistant. He works with Scotty Duncan and Judy DuRoss of our Department of Athletics — and I can't say enough about that team — on travel preparations and all administrative aspects of the football program.

Ed reminds me of Bennie Oosterbaan, who played at the University of Michigan, stayed there as a graduate assistant, assisted Fritz Crisler and then became the head coach. He never left until he retired, never coached anywhere else.

Young coaches seek out Ed Maley, for good reason — and I'm talking about young coaches from all over the country. I hope I don't sound smug, but it doesn't surprise me that Mal hasn't left. Like Kempski, he has the respect and the admiration of the players, the profession and the community. He has a good job, he does a great job and he is well paid. (You are, aren't you, Mal?)

We have a nice mesh of personalities. Mal has an intellectual approach to the game and although you could describe him as quiet, he is forceful and very demanding from a technical standpoint. Very, very detail minded.

He and Paul Billy, our interior line coach, are a study in contrasts. They are almost an act. I enjoy seeing them work together with a defensive front. There will be Paul, whom we call "Bear" and who also coaches the varsity wrestling team with great results, being very vocal, yelling things like "That's terrible . . . What's going on? . . . Strike a blow . . . Move!" and there will be Mal trailing him, softly advising a player to move his left foot six inches or to carry his right arm differently.

So you have the innate hardness, the emotional drive of Paul Billy mixed with the cool technical command of Ed Maley, who just about instinctively knows what we're doing and why we're doing it. The ball players get the advantages of both sides. While Billy is gruff and oftimes abrasive at work, I have it on good authority he is a real soft touch at home.

I was fortunate to come up with Joe Purzycki as a

member of my cabinet, the coach of the defensive backs, from the high-school ranks. Here is a young man who is an exceptional football coach; I hope we can hold on to him. He has it all. He is inspirational, he is aggressive, he is technically superior to his counterparts with the opposition. And like all of us, he is dedicated.

Bear Bryant says that if you can give up football coaching, you should do it; get away as fast as you can, get into business and make some money. I don't believe Joe can give up football. He was a great defensive back and our team captain in 1969, when he set a team record of nine interceptions that still stands. He went away to coach, but, fortunately, not very far. In three years at Caesar Rodney High School in Camden-Wyoming, Del., he won thirty-three games and lost only two and won a state championship. I couldn't go to a banquet in lower Delaware without stumbling over Joe. Every time you turned around, he was receiving another award.

Bob Depew, who coaches the defensive ends, joined us a couple of years ago and we kind of tolerate him as the intellectual of our group. Can you believe a guy who was Academic All-American two years running? We've put that brain to work off the field, too, in working out recruiting procedures. Bob also is our propaganda man — he's in charge of poring over newspapers and looking for inflammatory remarks by the enemy that we can both display on our bulletin board and file in each locker.

One year, we decided we needed a light touch to our bulletin board. Thus, Don Harnum, the late (as in departed) basketball coach at Delaware and then our offensive end coach, was appointed the mixed-metaphor man. He would hang up a big sign in the locker room that would disclose something like "It isn't the fuzz on the peach, but the rungs on the ladder." Not exactly Shecky Greene at his finest, but it did loosen up the squad. It also puzzled a few defensive tackles, who spent days trying to figure out the message.

It seems as though Ron Rogerson has been all over the field for us in his eight years at Newark. He came in as defensive end coach when Don Harnum left to take the Juniata College basketball coaching job. Ron moved to the defensive secondary for three years, but his first love always was the offensive line. We of course had the gentlemanly Irv Wisniewski running that department for many fruitful years, but personal problems forced him to retire and Jim Grube, who had been coaching the ends, took over Wiz's responsibilities. When Jim left to go to Middlebury College as Mickey Heinecken's assistant, Ron, who had been waiting in the wings, got the job he really wanted.

Rogerson is an old Maine Black Bear. After receiving his degree there, he went out to Colorado State as a graduate assistant, helping Mike Lude. Then he switched to Lebanon Valley College, where he was assistant coach and coordinator of recruiting. We knew all about Ron Rogerson. He showed up at a lot of our spring practices, and we liked his style. He gives us more than just a touch of class as a recruiter.

Getting back to Ted Kempski, he's pretty good with lines, too — the funny kind. I especially remember one he came up with during our widely heralded game with Colgate, the one that closed the 1977 season. Colgate came into the game as one of two major teams in the country that had won them all. Texas was the other.

So the Red Raiders were starting to wonder, and announce, in print just how good they really were. They were talking about possible bowl invitations, and it sounded as if they just might be one of the greatest college football teams of all time.

Even though we disillusioned them by the relatively low score of 21 to 3, there was no comparison in the quality of the hitting of the two teams. It soon became apparent that we were superior physically. We were a lot harder and more aggressive. The score didn't reflect that difference.

By the third quarter, Colgate had begun to succumb to our contact. They completed a pass to a tight end. There was nobody around him, but he grimaced as he took off, took about three drunken steps and, obviously expecting to be hit at any moment, fell down.

"This," said Kempski, nudging me, "has to be the greatest humanitarian act of all time."

I scowled. I am not much for humor at any point in any ball game. "What do you mean?"

"What I mean is, can you imagine that garbage in the Sugar Bowl?" Ted said. Even I had to admit, in the heat of battle, that it was a zinger.

Kempski and Mal make it especially easy for me during the practice week. We have the defense led by Mal on one field, Kempski's offensive players on another. I ramble back and forth. Every play we have is listed by number and the way our practice is planned, I can go from one field to another and know exactly what is happening and where everybody is stationed.

Game days, Kempski is on my right with the offensive telephone and Maley on my left with the defensive phone, both hooked up to the spotters' perch. The respective platoons are sitting behind their coaches. The starting players are in the first row of seats, so that they can come off the field and sit down with no confusion, catch their breath and still be able to see as much as possible. Behind them are the substitutes.

Upstairs in the booth, Joe Purzycki is on the defensive phone and Ron Rogerson is on the other end of Kempski's line. When we have the ball, the offensive phone is the hot line. On the sidelines, we have the worst seats in the house.

The field is unbelievably turtled, the better to drain. Thus, we depend on Rogerson to give us the true location of the ball, the yardage situation and any adjustments the opposition is making on defense. We get a continuous run of information offensively.

At that time, our defensive players can get on the phone and talk to Purzycki. Mal, of course, also will be discussing problems with Joe. When we turn the ball over, the defensive phone becomes the hot one. Now, also, Kempski and his quarterbacks can discuss suggestions for offensive plays, and the direction of our offense, with spotter Rogerson.

We have a clipboard for both offense and defense. When we go on the attack, or if we are doing well defensively, I check our "short list," the six or seven plays our quarterback takes into a game — even though we have at our disposal more than a hundred. I go over it before he goes back into action. Defensively, I can check the clipboard against any problems we may be having.

Ed Maley flashes signals to the defense, just like a third-base coach signals a batter. Mal telegraphs the middle linebacker and the three safeties, using hands to face, chest, ears, belt. Bringing his hands together in a certain way would denote certain stunts (a last-second, snap-of-the-ball change in positioning by the linebacker or the deep men). He has input from both Purzycki and me.

My function is to control the level of risk. I might want to take a chance, for instance, on pressuring the opposing quarterback — just taking off and stampeding him. Then again, I might not — because if the guy with the ball runs past this pressure, it is goodbye. Temple got off a breakaway run in our 1979 game because I asked for pressure.

I'm also available to say a few words to Kempski about the offense. This usually is done during a punting situation, when we're about to get the ball. I make a quick check with

Ted to see what he and the quarterback have been talking about. I talk with the quarterback myself, to get a feel for what we're about to do. So, you see, my assistants form a four-man upstairs-downstairs team, with me in the middle.

I'll mention here that while Mal signals his defenders, we do not throw signs to our quarterback. We would rather he call his own plays because he has access to information, a grasp of the game that we do not have. We also like him to be on his own for his own good, to develop his leadership qual-ities. I tell my offensive players not to look at me — I'm too small, I can't block or tackle and I can't throw the ball very well. So take yourselves to your leader, your quarterback.

Sure, we send in plays. We will interrupt a quarterback to that degree. But it has been my experience that he will execute a play of his choosing much more effectively than he would one that is imposed on him, particularly a pass play. When we do send in a substitute with a pass play, we will in a sense try to sell the quarterback on the idea that this is a shot that could get us a touchdown.

Speaking of sidelines, please don't remind me of the in-door one at Atlantic City's Convention Hall, site of the old Boardwalk Bowl. It was all of three-and-one-half feet wide. During our 1969 victory there over North Carolina Central, you never saw such a sideline mess. Besides the chain gang working the downs, there was a television crew of four people with cameras, sound equipment and wires trailing all over the place.

Mickey Heinecken, then of our staff, had the telephone head set on and thus had wires of his own leading to the press-box level. The TV gang was going back and forth and the officials were moving the chains and I happened to look Mickey's way once during a timeout, and there he was en-snarled in chains and wires as though Dr. Frankenstein was about to work on him. He had them all around his legs. He had the head linesman's gang fouled up. He had a TV guy tied up. His own phone lines were in there somewhere. It looked for a while as if we might have to stop the game so we could spring Mickey.

That sounds funny, and I guess it looked funny — if you didn't have the concentration on the game that the coaches and the players did. We've had many games where the communications system failed and the team got stuck. We since have come up with some techniques that allow us to stay alive down there on the sideline without any help from above.

I've often felt that my responsibility as a head coach is really coaching the coaches. When we have a new man taking over on our staff, the superficial aspect of the change is immediately taken care of — he knows the assignment, the teaching progression. But he needs help in interpretation of those assignments against defenses, particularly those defenses that are changing rapidly. He has to have an interpretation of the assignment on the tip of his tongue; for example: How are we going to block this particular spacing in the defense's line?

There must be a common terminology so that there is no breakdown in communications. Mal and I have been together so long we speak the same football language; we know exactly what the other means. When we talk about assigning defensive "seams," for instance, we mean the spaces between linemen. A "disguising" of defenses would be the change in the spacing just prior to the snap of the ball.

Now when some one leaves, there is a break in the communication, and also the lubrication, and the newcomer is going to have to learn our terminology. It is going to take time to get back the flow we had with the previous setup.

That's why Ron Rogerson fit in so well as Grube's successor. He had coached the defensive ends and the defensive backs. Now he has the offensive line. His Delaware football lexicon is complete.

On the positive side of a break in the staff ranks, I once read a psychological piece that claimed that if a group is doing the same thing together for five years, it is going downhill, and that change is really necessary to maintain an aggressive, dynamic group. I try to accept this, because losing a coach is like losing a member of the family.

As I mentioned, Irv Wisniewski had to leave us as offensive coordinator and offensive line coach. I had to do an awful lot of rationalizing to weather this. I had gone to school with Irv, we were friends practically a lifetime and suddenly after nearly twenty years together at Delaware, he decided to get out of coaching.

Jim Grube had been an offensive lineman in college and there was no great transition on his part when he joined us to take over the offensive line, but it fell on Ted Kempski to pick up the slack left by Wisniewski's departure.

Ron Rogerson is so conscientious, and was so determined to make a smooth switch from defense to offense, that he often would stick around an hour or so after staff meetings broke up to make sure he was tuned in to our philosophy. He and Kempski work well together. They have to — Ted's backs have to be coordinated with the interpretation the line is making, and vice versa.

Over the last few years, we have used a graduate-assistant type to help with the ends and be the third member of that coaching team. I was pleased that my son Chris filled that spot for us for two years in a rather critical time in our camp. Believe it or not, but it was a total accident that brought Chris to our staff. You probably won't buy this, but dear old dad did not exercise any clout.

Chris had been a placekicker at the University of Virginia under Coach Sonny Randle, the former NFL pass-catching star. A placekicker's life is a lonely one; they do a lot of standing around during practice. So Chris did his running with the Virginia ends to stay in shape.

He graduated in 1973 with a degree in architecture and spent that summer working as an architectural draftsman in Wilmington. During that time, he lived at home again with the old folks.

We were eating dinner one evening when I mentioned to Sue that Donnie Miller had called me from Trinity College in New England. He wondered if I had any young people, graduate assistants, who might be able to go up to Hartford and coach the ends for him. I no sooner said it than Chris blurted, "I'll go."

I told him he had to be kidding, that I couldn't send Miller someone who knew nothing about the job. Chris got very indignant at this rap at his football experience. He said he had been close to the ends' situation at Virginia, and hadn't just been standing around with his foot in his shoe when he wasn't practicing kicking.

Well, he went to Trinity. The next year he came to Delaware and worked on his master's degree. During spring practice, when we were evaluating players, we drafted Chris to help because the end coach, Jim Grube, was busy coaching the lacrosse team. Chris jumped into the breach with the understanding that he would assist the freshman coach in the fall.

When the spring workouts were over, both Kempski and Rogerson came to me and said they enjoyed working with Chris so much, and were so impressed with the job he did, that they wanted him to stay with the varsity.

Our staff has such an objective outlook that I really did not believe Ted and Ron spoke up because I was Chris' father. They made a strong pitch to keep him. And so it turned out Chris coached our offensive ends for two years.

Herky Billings jumped in there for us in 1979 and he was a winner at the job, too. Chris now is the backfield coach and offensive coordinator for Vic Gatty at Tufts University.

Many head coaches operate on the theory that you should not make your assistants into your own image. What's more, they say, don't even try to do this. I agree that an assistant coach should be himself, but at the same time, we expect all of them to coach within a particular image. I prefer that we do not scream and shout at the players, and that we definitely do not resort to profanity.

The use of profanity in a teaching situation is not only distracting, but it suggests a lack of discipline. The educational backbone of football is discipline. You won't even hear me say "hell" to a player.

A newspaperman once asked me what advice I would give to an assistant coach who was about to go out into a head-coaching job. As a prologue to my answer, I mentioned that I have heard a lot of veteran coaches say they didn't realize how little they knew about football as a part of the university picture until they were thrust into the top job.

I recently went through an advisory session with Jim Colbert, who played for us a decade ago and who last winter was appointed coach at C. W. Post University on Long Island. He had been assisting at Davidson, and before that was a fine high school coach at Smyrna, Del.

I wasn't about to tell Jim how to coach football. My advice to him was brief, and it concerned off-the-field situations. As the Music Man chanted, you gotta know the territory. Find out where the fires are, where the holes are, and move slowly. Stay with the status quo as long as you can until you really know what moves you should be making.

Translation: By fires and holes, I meant problems that are particular to a football program and not to the school itself. Problems to an unsuspecting head coach could be a rigid admissions office, an inflexible financial-aid officer, a hard-nosed and one-way provost, who is the man who rides herd on the faculty. I don't think I had to tell Jim to surround himself with top-caliber assistants. Maybe I should have made that the Number One tip. Look what it has done for me. My personal twenty-one-gun salute goes to Maley and Kempski and Billy and Purzycki and Depew and Rogerson.

Don't any one of you dare drop dead on me.

It's impossible to tell the story of University of Delaware football and not dwell on Roy Rylander, our trainer.

Dr. Curtis R. Rylander, Ph.D.: He has to be one of the best in the business. He is superior. He is outstanding. And he is a presence. He could walk up to a train wreck and look at the bodies and say "Well, well. What do we have here?" He is not the panicky type. A trainer has to build up some scar tissue himself because he deals with so much misery. Roy is Mr. Calm.

The decision on when and if an injured athlete should play is his. I never question his judgment, although many times he doesn't exactly cheer me up.

One of the palace jokes has Roy telling an injured player, "Please don't scream — it upsets the coaches."

Counting war service, Roy Rylander has been a member of the staff for almost four decades. Countless people in the trade have come in to study his techniques. Don Seger, the Phillies' highly rated trainer, was one of them. He spent four months in the doctor's office. And both the Phillies and Eagles have assistant trainers who literally studied under Roy. He and Keith Handling, the assistant whom we refer to as Roy's interpreter, are invaluable. You cannot make plans without a skilled trainer.

14

The Delaware Wing-T

Read this chapter and you'll recognize a discernible uplift in literary quality. Step aside, Al — the coach is writing this one all by himself.

It's about coaching, working with people and the offensive football system known as the Wing-T.

I consider myself a very fortunate man. I like my work. There have been few times that I wasn't anxious to get to the office and even fewer times that I haven't been enthused about going to practice. I like people.

Football players are people. Like everyone else, they all began with a mother and father. They're all very special to someone. Even the defensive tackles have girl friends, some more than one. I have always considered it a special privilege to coach someone's son and to be in a position to assist him with an experience that can be very important to him in many ways.

I know this chapter is supposed to be about the Wing-T and its X's and O's, but I just can't help speaking first about what I feel is so important to our program. I would like to talk about motivation and teaching techniques, because they probably are more important aspects of coaching than the formations from which we run our offensive or defensive alignments.

I have referred several times to inspirational situations and dismissed them with what was done or said at the time. I have not mentioned our approach. The term "motivation" has a certain connotation that disturbs me because it implies pressure on a person or human manipulation. No one wants to be manipulated. He doesn't want to be made to laugh, or to be sold, or to be motivated. But everyone wants to be entertained, inspired and certainly wants to buy. The ticket is "have what they want to buy — give them what they want," and you are home free.

If you want to motivate or inspire someone to extend himself beyond what would normally be expected, it is necessary that he knows exactly what is expected of him and why. This is the format for not only motivation, but for the discipline which is so necessary in a sport that depends so much upon it. No one enjoys being disciplined, but self-discipline can be a great source of pride and extremely educational. That's right — we try to create an atmosphere where our players want to discipline themselves. I am not talking about wrist slaps. I am talking about the kind of discipline that makes beautiful music. It also makes a team beautiful, and is really the first reason for having football supported by an educational institution.

I will talk with every player in an effort to find out why he's out for football. If his objectives can be reached without compromising team goals, we will help him get what he wants. To me, this is the secret of success, winning, selling or whatever. I really believe we can all be successful if we spend enough time helping others get what they want.

If I feel that a boy just wants to be part of a team so he can dress on Saturday, I will get rid of him. He's wasting his time and should be doing something else. But if he wants to work at something, a particular skill, or if I find that he just has a great need to succeed, a drive for being special, I will join him fast. That's the kind I enjoy being around. They are productive. And don't be mislead: That kind of drive is infectious and you don't have to have many around before the whole team catches the disease.

We have our players in mind with every drill on the practice field, with each second spent creating a team. We never use exercise or overwork as punishment. When we run "gassers" (four 50-yard shuttle sprints in 35 seconds, repeated four times) we tell them, "This is not punishment. It is an exercise that will enable you to play well even when you experience fatigue on Saturday." And to those who don't run, we say, "Don't worry — I won't embarrass you in front of your family and friends during the game. You can stand real close to me on the sidelines." I never run 'em. Good players run hard and practice hard — only those who are out of shape stand and watch.

Let's go to the blackboard. Subject: What is the Wing-T?

The Wing-T is not a bird, nor a car model. Although we talk about them, it doesn't have anything to do with mirrors. The Wing-T is the Delaware offensive style of moving the ball or not moving it, depending on the particular day or who we happen to be playing. It's what the guys in blue are doing when Delaware has the ball at Delaware Stadium. Unlike most offenses which are labeled to describe their formations — I, Veer, Wishbone or Pro — the Delaware Wing-T is a system of moving the ball. It is a philosophy which employs many formations.

It has been suggested that the Indians were using it when Columbus dropped in as the first spectator. That Knute Rockne used it when the ball was square. Not quite true. However, its principles have stood the test of time, and glowed with the reflected glory of copy as the system has repeatedly demonstrated its effectiveness. Even though its face is continually changing, and like old wine getting better, much of the basic philosophy of the Wing-T is still in style.

Offensive systems labeled Wing-T are as old as the date on which the quarterback took the snap from center in the T-formation. Rip Engle used what he called the Wing-T at Penn State in the late '40s. Around the same time, Buff Donnelli called his offense the Wing-T at Boston University. Col. Red Blaik of Army made a reputation with it.

Dave Nelson's style of Wing-T was first put together in the fall of 1951 at the University of Maine. Like so many other football innovations, it was brought about by a reality requiring a change. It began with the realization that the single wing which we had used at the University of Michigan under Coach Fritz Crisler was an asymmetrical formation. That is, there were few similarities between the assignments on one side of the formation to those on the other. The halfbacks' responsibilities didn't resemble one another at all. The tailback was a runner, a passer and sometimes punter, giving rise to the term, "triple threat". The wingback was a running back or a blocking back, and a potential pass receiver.

When Nelson got to Maine, he realized that he just did not have the ability and depth that we had at the University of Michigan and that an injury to a specific player could easily cripple the entire offense. He needed an offense that was symmetrical so that the assignments of one position were the mirror of the other. This gave rise to the "Third-Man Theme" where a third man could replace his position on either side of the formation. A third guard, for example, was the back-up at both right and left guard. This meant, of course, that rather than having four guards you could get by with three. This Third Man Theme also applied to the backfield. The only true singular positions were those in the middle of the formations — at center, quarterback and fullback.

This offensive structure answered personnel problems for Dave at Maine. Now the "skill" responsibilities could be shared and consequently reduced. The primary running could be done by the fullbacks and halfbacks while the quarterback could be a passer or a runner, but not necessarily both. Now Dave was getting away from the Jack Armstrong requirement of the single-wing tailback.

The imagination of Dave Nelson, inspired by the necessity of change, combined proven principles of the Michigan single-wing offense with those of the basic T-formation of the day to form the Delaware Wing-T. Not only did this new system provide much needed depth and spread skill requirements, but it took the heat off individuals in other ways. Coaches have referred to the Wing-T as a misdirection offense. Several points of attack are threatened at the same time. This was a carryover from the single wing in which, for example, in a particular series, the fullback threatened the middle of the line as both halfbacks moved towards one flank. However, unlike the single wing, we didn't need to depend upon the center's pass to the tailback. Our quarterback took the ball directly from the center, and then faked after handing off. Now there are three points of attack being threatened at the same time: the fullback up the middle, halfbacks toward one flank and the quarterback faking a keep.

The Wing-T is series or sequence football. There is little "grab-bagging" of plays (use of specials) that really do nothing for you except the effect that they have at the moment they are being run. The Wing-T series aspect demonstrates that one play may add to the effectiveness of several companion plays. The fellow in the stands yelling "Turn the page, we've seen that play before!" may not realize that even an uninspiring play run into the middle of the line may be setting up a host of other plays by imposing pressure to a par-

ticular area of the defense. That one play will probably con-
tribute to the success of moving the ball before the day is
over.

There is an important principle involved that differs
from other offensive philosophies that are used today. We
have three pass receivers within a yard of the line of scrimmage: the tight end, a spread receiver and a wingback. Thus,
there are always three deep passing threats. We create the
spread receiver prior to the snap of the ball by splitting the
end from the rest of the line rather than removing a running
back from the formation and making him a flanker, as they
do in pro football. When you see a flanker and spread end,
whether they are on one or opposite sides of the formation,
there are only two running backs remaining. One back blocks
and the other one carries the ball. This is really the pro approach to offensive football or as we call it "two-back offense." In the Wing-T, all three backs — the halfbacks and
the fullbacks — are within reach of the ball. One can block
and one can fake while the other carries the ball.

What's the difference, then, between the Wing-T and the
Wishbone or the Power-I formation, which are also three-back
formations? The answer is simple — they do not have three
receivers near the line and really have only their ends as
deep passing threats. Most of the defenses against these formations use some form of a nine-man front, leaving only two
men deep — in other words, they gang up on the run. We
don't think you can successfully gang up on the running aspect of the Wing-T.

Another aspect of the Wing-T is the action of the quarterback, who in our system never uses the pro style "good
luck" hand-off. That's where the quarterback hands the ball
off and watches the ball-carrier while backing away from the
bad guys so as not to be hit. You often see this in pro football.

A Delaware quarterback is always faking either away

from or with the original play action and adds a dimension that makes an incredible difference in hiding the ball. This again takes heat from the ball-carrier by distracting the defense. Another thing that happens in our offense is something that won't grab the average guy in the stands: The blocking schemes are all subtly related even if the backfield technique differs. This relationship between blocking creates conflicts for defensive players. Specifically, I mean when a defensive player reacts to the blocking in front of him to stop a particular play he automatically makes himself vulnerable for a companion play.

I'm often asked what is the difference between the Wing-T that we ran in 1979 or what we are planning in 1980 that's different from Dave Nelson's offense which was run in the early '50s. It's a legitimate question. I'll precede the answer by saying that fear of embarrassment is probably the greatest inducement to creative offensive thinking. I am not a registered psychologist but I know that no one wants to be embarrassed. I also know that you don't want to stand on the sidelines yelling "Hold 'em!" all day. You want to move the ball, which means that the offense must adjust to defensive trends. We have seen an awful lot of defensive changes in the last thirty years, and consequently our football has changed. There's also been some embarrassment, but fortunately we have kept it to a minimum.

First of all, our blocking schemes are considerably different from those thirty years ago. We have gone to "one-on-one" blocking as opposed to the traditional style of creating openings by the double-team trap method, which was a carryover from the single wing. Another significant change is the use of the wide receiver or a spread end. We've smiled about the time in Maine when we sent Woody Carville out as a spread receiver and didn't know what to do with him. We really didn't know how to use the spread receiver thirty years ago. Today, we have a sophisticated spread-end game with both our rushing and passing.

We have added the option as an important part of our offense. That is, the quarterback has the option of either keeping the ball or pitching it outside. At one time, we seldom considered the option as an aspect of our running game. Today we use it outside more than any other play, and we're using three different backfield patterns with it. The "trap option" which has become popular nationally was first run at Delaware by quarterback Jim Colbert in 1971. I'll never forget Bob Kelley's comment on the radio. He was surprised by the new play and remarked, "There's a broken play that made ten yards."

We are now shifting a great deal. We change formations about a third of the time once we get on the ball.

Probably the greatest change of all is the number of passes we are throwing. I won't bore you with statistics, but I point out that last year Scott Brunner and the year before, Jeff Komlo probably threw five times as many passes in the season as did their counterparts in the late '50s.

We think we are more balanced today — balanced between running and passing. In 1978, we led Division II nationally in total offense and we were not in the top ten in either running or passing. We thought this was the ultimate in balance. In 1979, we again led the country in total offense and at the same time we were fourth in rushing and eleventh in passing. We are simply throwing a lot more than we used to and it has become a really important part of our offense. Maybe this change has been brought about by some folks in the stands yelling, "Throw the ball once in a while!"

We have a framed plaque on our family-room wall which says "God Bless Our Home Games." I love it because it summarizes my affection for Delaware in general and our fans in particular. They help us win. I love Saturday in Delaware

Stadium and our followers — even though I know there are many with "suggestions."

I'll go on record: If you're one of those guys who enjoys coming to the ball park and yelling at me or throwing aspersions at our players, our offense, or our football, I want you to know I encourage it. Come on down to the stadium and have a good time; that's all part of the game.

The boss has kicked you around all week, the little lady at home isn't giving you a bit of freedom — come, release your frustration on us in general or me in particular. Tell 'em how you used to run over 'em when you played. I understand. But I remind you that those boys are people, and our assistant coaches are among the best in football.

And I have never heard you! I have never heard you yell anything good or bad. I have never seen a Golden Girl, a cheerleader or any of the other frills. Saturday is a business day for me.

15

A Coach and His Players

To be a football coach is to be part psychiatrist, part chaplain, part psychologist. There almost isn't enough of you to go around.

There was the player who came into my office to talk about his domestic problems. Pretty soon he had collapsed in a heap on the floor, sobbing. His wife, he said, didn't love him, and had asked him to move out.

I don't need these scenes to remind me that I am dealing with human beings, not faceless and heartless and bloodless machines in football uniforms, but they help me not to forget it.

I have had to break the news to too many young men that their mother, or father, or another member of the family, has passed away. When the family cannot locate the boy, they usually call me to say they want him home right away; I just happen to be the one who has to tell him why. For some reason or other, they think it will be relatively easy for me to do, maybe because I am on the scene with him every day. That doesn't make it easy. But it is a duty I accept as going with the office.

What could I tell the heart-broken football player with marriage problems? I had no solution but to calm him down and sit with him and tell him these are the ways of the world, and he must try and find his own answer.

As in any other group, a college football squad has its share of those with severe personality problems that have nothing at all to do with the sport they are playing. Several years ago, a player began describing his problems to me as though they were not happening to him but to someone else — and he was observing the someone else. Relaxed and smiling, he really did give me the impression he was outside a room looking in on the things that were happening to him. He needed professional help, and I got him to a staff psychologist quickly.

I have had my share of Campus Lovers in uniform. I would be concerned about such a player possibly not getting enough sleep and whether or not his amorous activities were affecting his ability. And I have seen such a guy suddenly marry and become a bear-down, knock-down player any coach would welcome. Others fall in love and it isn't with a football; their affections go elsewhere and, like the old song, they have lost all ambition for wordly acclaim; their interest in football hits the skids.

It is a sad day for me when a boy tells me he does not want to play football any more for anything other than a physical reason, except in special cases. What he is really saying is that it doesn't look as if he is going to make the team, that he is not going to meet his own expectations.

The first week of June, every candidate signs a commitment card. It reads that he agrees to join the football team without reservation and to accept any responsibility given him, regardless of what it means from a personal standpoint. We hold him to it. He is commiting himself to being a part of the first team, the second team or the third team or whatever status he is given. Ours is a team concept. We stress that the game is not designed only for those who start. We have had a few walk out on this commitment. But for every one of those, there have been many more admirable cases of players sticking it out with very little reward in playing time.

Every man who leaves the squad is not a quitter. I can understand that new interests can get in the way of the football ambitions they brought with them to Delaware. Jim Kacersis was a good example. He came to us as an all-state end in Pennsylvania. He was a very fine high-school player, but leveled off in a couple of seasons with us. One day he told me he wanted to study medicine.

"I would like to get involved in medical research," he said, "and it is going to take a lot of my time. I don't think football is going to be for me."

I had to agree, and we parted on good terms.

Football at Delaware is an elective, not a compulsory activity. Nobody is making a living here playing football. Nobody is supporting his education this way. Each spring, we have an extended period of evaluation when we ask each player to make up his mind whether or not he wants to represent Delaware on the football field.

Once a player makes a commitment, we feel he should give it a ride for a full year. I do not like to see them walk off.

The pre-season practice in 1978 produced a disturbing situation. Chris Cosgrove had been with us for two varsity seasons, and had not played a great deal. But he had some ability and was hard and strong and he came to camp committed and ready to go. In retrospect, I have to say he had decided he was the first-string fullback and if that wasn't to be the case, then he wasn't going to compete.

In the first scrimmage, we alternated Cosgrove with Bo Dennis. Chris felt that he was above Dennis. We knew Cosgrove could play somewhere for us. He had been the defensive end as a sophomore. Now we thought that in his senior year he could help us best at either fullback, where he had earned a letter, or tight end. We had to find out quickly.

Chris obviously believed he was above all this, and just walked off. I was disturbed; I felt that somewhere along the line, his parents or his friends or someone had talked him out of his commitment. I think he was a young man who needed to play football, and I also think that had he stayed he would have been a great player.

You've heard of Little League fathers and/or mothers, and stage mothers. We have them in college football, too. A most unpleasant situation for me is dealing with the parent who thinks the son is a better player than he really is, and who has put a great deal of pressure on the boy. I wish somebody would write a book telling coaches how to deal with them.

I recently encountered the father of a boy we had tried to recruit some years back, but who decided to go to an Ivy League school. He wasn't able to play there, so he transferred to Delaware. He had taken on some unhealthy weight — some of these young athletes can get old fast. This one simply could not play because he just wasn't good enough. And he did not play for us.

However, his parents still envisioned him as a great athlete and decided it was my fault he had not actually received this recognition.

The old man approached me in a restaurant in Rehoboth Beach. I was with a group of people, but that didn't faze him.

"Well, Coach," he said. "We meet again. And now you are going to tell me how you handled my son and how you ruined his life."

I told him I obviously had more respect for his son than he did, because I wasn't about to discuss him in public. A small crowd started to gather and the father was getting louder and more accusatory. He not only blamed me for the fact that his son did not play football, but said I was the reason the boy went through two marriages within a few years after leaving college.

I had a great deal of sympathy for the boy, mostly because he was saddled with such a father. The latter had to help create the boy's losing situation, and here he was charging me with destroying the boy. I had worked hard to do just the opposite, to give him every chance to make good. I told the old man this, sharply. He finally walked away, muttering.

There is a similar story involving a player with starting possibilities who got hurt in our first pre-season contact drill. In the first game, he disobeyed an order and I replaced him and told him — firmly — why, and sat him down. He never showed up again.

A year later, I received a rather hysterical ten-page letter from his father, listing all the things I had not done for his injured son. He insisted — demanded, rather — on talking to me. "You are going to see me," he wrote, "whether it's at the Newark Country Club, the supermarket, on Main Street or on campus. You are going to see me because you are no busier than I am, and I am not going to make an appointment."

You could say he was a little wound up. I answered his letter. I told him I would certainly talk with him, but if he did not care to make an appointment he might not find me available. I was not about to discuss his son's problems anywhere but in private. I recommended that he both make the appointment and bring the boy with him as a third party.

They showed up. I had the injury documented. The boy had in fact received the proper medical treatment; the father had accused us of ignoring the injury. His son, in his embarrassment in leaving the team, had not come back for additional treatment, and we just do not make house calls.

Somehow, we had missed getting through to the boy

about the foundation of our team that is discipline. It troubles me not what the father thinks of me, but what the boy does.

Every Delaware player, very early in his career, learns what we expect of him as an individual and as a team member. We quickly turn the squad over to senior leadership. Not to do this would rob them of a feeling of accomplishment. If we have a good year, it is their good year — not the coaches'. I think that in 1979, the team really felt it won the national championship and that the coaches were just along for the ride. This really is the basis of discipline. Self-discipline. If we don't have any disciplinary problems, it is because the player leadership takes care of them — they are all wiped out before they have a chance to reach us.

I went through the long hair-and-beard era, and there is a cute story attached to it.

Call me square, but for people to try and be "outstanding" in a superficial way, by wearing ridiculous clothes, or overdoing it with the hair, is a bothersome thing to me.

There is plenty of room at the top if you want to be recognized. Just do something special. You don't have to let your hair grow forever to be recognized. The same goes for the player who shows up wearing yellow wrist bands, or adhesive tape around his thigh pads, or with "Killer" printed on his helmet or with his number on a towel tucked in his waistband. He is an individual trying to play a team game.

"Look," I have told the wrist-band set. "If you want to do something special out there, just knock somebody down and everybody will look up your name in the program. The uniform number is the only identity you need."

This individualism could get carried away to what I called the Purple Plume scene. ("Look for me, Mom; you can't miss me. I'll be the one with the purple plume stuck in my helmet").

And that thinking was the basis for my concern about

long hair on college football players, although I'm a bit embarrassed to be reminded of it. We had a no-facial-hair, no-
hair-below-the-helmet rule in the early '70s. It sounds
ridiculous now. And I admit it was.

Larry Washington, of the Cape May, N.J., Washingtons
and now an executive with General Motors, was a running
back for us. A black man, he loved to wear a mustache. I
wouldn't let him during football season. He came to me in
spring practice of 1972.

"I think you'll agree, Coach," he said, "that I don't look
too bad with that mustache. Every year I've shaved it off just
like you've asked and I never said a thing. Now I'd really like
to grow it for my senior season."

I concurred that Larry indeed did look handsome with
his mustache.

"I'd like you to grow it," I said, "but I don't know how to
handle it. I certainly can't let the black players wear mustaches and make everyone else shave them off. That's really a
form of racism. I don't know what to do."

Larry reminded me that I always said the team belongs to
the seniors. "Now I'm a senior. Let me handle it."

I told him to go ahead, and never gave it another
thought. When he came back for pre-season practice, Larry
had his mustache — and so did a number of other players.
Others had beards and long sideburns. The hair was a bit
long in places.

I called Larry in. "I thought you were going to handle
the mustache bit?"

"I did, Coach," he said. "I just told them it was all right
if they wore them."

And that was that. I realized how narrow-minded I had
been. Since then, of course, the football players have cleaned
up their hair acts on their own and they look good to me.

But I now realize I had been an inconsistent defender of

Square City. In 1971, Ralph Borgess, a defensive tackle, was our captain. He had a great deal of influence on the ball players, who referred to him as Captain Midnight.

Borgess and Jan Millon, a linebacker, didn't show up with long hair that season. They showed up with no hair at all. They had shaved it down to the bone except for a little pony tail with a rubber band around it. I took one look and told them to shave off the pony tail, too. Borgess' excuse was "The uglier you look, the uglier you play." While he was at it, he said we were going to win the national championship. He was right.

So my captain and his teammate went into the season bald, "recognized" not by adding something but by taking something away — their tresses. It was against my principles, but I couldn't make them grow hair any faster than it did naturally. By the time we won our No. 1 poll positions, they had hair again.

With or without hair, those teams were two great ones. Borgess captained a 10-and-1 club that won the Boardwalk Bowl. Washington and his fellow mustaches won them all, 10-and-0, the next year.

I have been known to get angry at a player. Pete Ravettine comes to mind. A spread receiver, he didn't play much for us in 1976. He had a problem with a wrist that had been fractured, and he lacked speed.

Every year, we pass out forms in which the players get a chance to evaluate the coaches. I usually don't pay much attention to the evaluations except for suggestions the players might have, but one — Ravettine's — caught my eye and generated some blood in it. This was with two games to go in the regular season. The evaluations are filed anonymously, but by positions, and I had no trouble figuring out this particular one was written by my substitute spread end.

He had given me just about a zero as a coach. A sophomore, yet. I called him in for a discussion.

"Pete," I said, with a grip on myself, "It's all right with
me if you think I am a poor football coach and it's all right
with me if you feel I cannot evaluate talent. But when you
tell me that I don't KNOW football and that I can't coach at
all and that I have no enthusiasm for the game and no ability
whatsoever, that cuts me."

I told Ravettine he was flagged. "You will never play
football for me again because I don't trust you. I don't believe
in you. If you want to stick around and be on the demonstration team, suit yourself — but that's it."

Pete looked me right in the eye and walked out — but he
didn't quit. He played on the demonstration team the rest of
the year, including the preparations for one playoff game.

I had reservations about bringing him back for his junior
season in 1977 because he just didn't seem to be part of the
team. But I did, and he signed a commitment card and came
in to see me.

"I'll do exactly what you want me to," he declared. "I'll
be a demonstration player till I'm through, if that's the
story."

He acted as cannon fodder in scrimmages at the start of
the season, taking the part of an opposing player to test our
defense. The fourth game of the season, we played Temple at
Veterans Stadium and had trouble running pass patterns. In
fact, we were having trouble running anything. I was ready
to try something new. I tried Ravettine, and he played extremely well. The next year, he became Jeff Komlo's favorite
passing target, setting a bunch of Delaware records as a receiver.

Maybe my wigging out woke Ravettine up. We patched
up our differences during his junior year and I needled him
about the rating he gave me as a coach. I kept telling him my

rating of him as a football player was still the same — that he wasn't any good but that he wanted to play so badly that he was making it anyhow. And who knows? Maybe Ravettine's scorecard of my ability woke me up, too.

Those young people with a certain spunk in their personalities are exciting and pleasant to be around. I push for people to extend themselves and to use every bit of talent they possess. Al Hirt, the great trumpet player, inspires me as I would like my players to be inspired. He plays every note as if it is going to be the very last of his career.

It is a delight to be the coach of someone like Yancy Phillips. He came to us from Carlisle, Pa., High School without a class rank his last semester, when he went into a self-study program. Yet all the time he was playing tackle for us, for three seasons, he was second or third in his class — the Class of '70. He took his degree as a chemical engineer into a responsible position with an oil company, then decided he didn't like that field. So he switched to a career in medicine, went through med school in record-breaking time and now, of all enviable positions, is a doctor in Hawaii.

You can sense that the Yancy Phillipses are going to be successful. I have the same feeling about Jaime Young and Pete Bistrian, for example, of our '79 champions. They have so much going for them, disregarding their ability to play football.

This is what I try to get a football player to do: to play to the very best of his ability. By doing the very best he can with what he has, by recognizing that his own particular situation is unique and that no one is exactly like him, by achieving in spite of limitations — that's what makes winners. Don't ask me if it is easier to inspire a player with ability or one with lesser talent, because I'm really working at having everyone extending himself beyond what would normally be considered a usual effort.

A football coach works with an army of young men, but you have to get through to some of them individually. I think the fastest way is to hit them at a personal level — by telling them that if they do not do this particular job, they will not play, which means to the boy that his parents and his girl friend will not see him play unless he does something about it.

We had some concern about Al Minite in our championship season last year. He reminded me that although he was a senior, he still was being forced into competing for a linebacker job with a junior, K. C. Keeler. He felt the job really should be his, because he had earned it. The tradeoff made him unhappy.

"OK, you'll get a chance to show your claim to the job," I told him. "Outplay the other guy." And it turned out the more pressure we put on him, the better he played.

In the final game in Albuquerque, Ara Parseghian asked me who I thought he should look at defensively on our club in his role as the TV commentator. I told him Al Minite backing the line and Vince Hyland in the secondary. Both had particular reasons to be inspired. Minite had been pressured into a position of self-defense, and Hyland wanted to be a professional football player and realized he was in a showcase game.

Sometimes you have to pull your punches, or your pushes. In 1967 we had a fullback, John Spangler, who simply could not run wind sprints. It took me a while to realize this. It was the first time I was ever confronted with a stamina problem. We did not use him in 1966 because I thought he was in poor shape, and I went through the whole psychological ploy trying to inspire him to better things before I realized I wasn't getting anywhere because he had a stamina shortage. We cut down on his practice work, and he played better.

Our training rules say there will be no use of tobacco or alcohol in any form. No marijuana. No non-therapeutic drugs. I insist on this. It is now an athletic governing board rule at Delaware that all the athletic teams conform to these rules, but we have had them in football for some time.

"Don't you think you're a little strict in these times?" a young opposing coach asked me. "At our place, we let them drink beer through Wednesday. After that, we get into serious training for the weekend."

I told him I didn't think that was too clever a policy.

"The only team in our program that trains like your football squad," he said, "is our crew. They don't drink and they don't smoke. They're national champions."

"That," I told him, "is exactly why we stay with what we're doing." I don't know how faithfully my football players follow the rules, but they know I won't tolerate a violation. I'll remind them to be on their guard with a comment like "I'm getting along in years now, men, and I missed a lot of things in my day. So I may take up drinking beer and may just drop into the Stone Balloon (Newark's nationally ranked — for total beer quaffed — oasis) or some other joint at any time. So stay loose."

But in all sincerity I have told them over and over that if they want to be part of a great football team and if they want their parents and their friends to have a great regard for this team, the best way is to demonstrate by their conduct off the field how much the game means to them. "Even if you have a beer with your father in your house after a game," I say, "he's going to think less of your effort than if you tell him we have a no-drinking rule during the season, and that you're going by the rules."

I've got a disciplinary story involving Conway Hayman, our Little All-American offensive guard of 1970 who has been playing in the National Football League ever since.

I'm not really sure Conway wanted to stay here his first couple of years. We were going through an integration era, and the young black athletes were restless and exhibiting a lack of confidence in the administration. I don't think we had a problem with it on the football team, but we knew — and certainly Conway knew — what was in the air.

One of our pre-season requirements for the big men at the time was for them to run a mile in six and a half minutes. The backs had to do it in an even six.

Hayman, then a sophomore, could not make the time. And so he, along with the others who failed, had to run a mile every morning after practice until he either cried "uncle" or the team leadership came to me and said "He's had enough; we accept him." It was a tough assignment, because we started our workouts at 6:15 a.m.

About the third day of Hayman's extra duty, I checked him out on the track and saw him trudging around in his stockinged feet. After two laps, he turned towards the locker room and I asked him where he was going.

"To the showers," he said. "I'm finished — I'm not running any more."

"Well, I'm glad you quit the team so early," I said. "Now we know where we stand."

"I'm not quitting," Hayman said. I told him he surely was quitting, unless he ran those miles. He returned to the track, but he was missing when we began the afternoon practice and I had his equipment picked up.

"You quit again," I told him when he finally showed up and asked where his gear was. "You missed the meeting. It's all over."

Conway asked if he could talk to me in my office. "I just have to play," he said. "I'm asking for another chance. I want to be part of the team."

"OK — then let's stop playing yo-yo," I said. "You're in

and you're out and I don't know where you are. If you want to play, make up your mind."

I told him he had the chance he requested, providing he fully understood and accepted what was expected of him. He thanked me and asked me what he could do for me. "Just bear down in football and in the classroom and get your degree," I answered.

The giant young prospect returned to the running grind, and for twelve days he battled that mile after the morning workout. He never did make it in six and a half minutes. The seniors on the club got him off the rack; it was agreed that for Conway Hayman to meet that requirement was an anatomical impossibility but that he had given it his best shot. And for the next three seasons, he gave it his best shot as a first-level player. Conway Hayman at his best was something to behold.

If you want to go through a classic experience of mixed emotions, you should be a college football coach whose son is a member of the squad. It is a pressure thing for both parties.

David Raymond, bless him, put us in that position when he was our punter in the 1976 and '77 seasons. I was proud that he was good enough to make the grade but at the same time uncomfortable because I knew there had to be charges of nepotism in the air, even though they were completely unfounded. I went out of my way not to be complimentary to David either in private or in public. That might not have been fair to him, but I thought it was the best way to handle it. In effect, he didn't have a father during the football seasons. Ours was a coach-player relationship, a bit more severe, from my side, than the usual kind.

I was against his enrolling at Delaware, and tried to talk him out of it by telling him he wasn't good enough to play. I struck out. David's life had been the university football scene ever since he was our thirteen-year-old ball boy. And his mother was on his side. She told me that I gave everybody else a chance, so why not David? And she threatened to station herself on "Parents' Walk" outside the stadium after every game and harass me.

In pre-season his junior year, my assistants told me David was our best kicker and should have the job. I steered clear of the kicking department and took no part in the evaluating. He did a decent job for us as a junior. He kicked left-footed, which means the safety men had an unusual spin to handle, and he created a lot of fumbles to help us beat Temple and William and Mary on successive Saturdays.

The first two games of his senior year, he was just plain poor as a kicker. It bothered me, more as a parent than as a coach. I seriously thought about replacing him but Ron Rogerson of our staff talked me out of it. He told me I wasn't that jumpy with others, so why should I make David an exception? We stuck with him and he regained his rhythm the next game.

Now he's famous, and I can't even claim I made him a star. He did it himself, as the Phillie Phanatic. And I am best known as the Phillie Phanatic's father.

The tragedy of my career was the case of a spiritually and physically beautiful young man named Len Perfetti, of Roxbury, N.J.

A senior, he started the first two games at offensive guard in 1977. The following Friday, he underwent a tonsillectomy that was to reveal malignant tissue. He was forced to leave school. A year later, Len was dead, the victim of a cancer of the lymphatic system known as lymphona.

Because the cancer was inoperable, he took chemotherapy treatments. But he came back to join us on the sidelines and for the final game, against Colgate, he dressed and shared the pre-game captaincy duties with fullback Dave

Bachkosky, whose season also ended early because of an infected knee.

I wondered how I would break the news of the malignancy to the squad, and I called his mother for advice. "Let Len do it," she said. And he did, also talking to reporters on his next trip down to see us. Some of the things he said stick with me: "You can't sit home and cry every night. You just have to try and go on. . .I feel that God plans everything and He has a good reason for everything and that reason is good enough for me, whatever it may be."

My all-time determination team would have to include Peter Good, of that same team. He was deaf — his hearing loss was sixty-five per cent — but he became our starting fullback late in the 1977 season and was our third leading rusher. He had one run of 52 yards against Middle Tennessee that was our longest of the year.

Pete read our quarterback's lips in the huddle. He and I also communicated by the sign language I have learned over the years since my wife suddenly lost her hearing.

The Newark Touchdown Club, at its annual season-ending banquet, honored Len Perfetti and Peter Good with special achievement awards for determination in the face of adversity.

16

Meet The Press

Some of my coaching colleagues across the country look upon the press as a necessary evil. They've told me this — the coaches, that is.

When I first began coaching, I considered the press to be an unnecessary evil.

I simply could not comprehend how someone could walk in off the street — and that really is what the press does — and editorialize ponderously and/or sarcastically on whether we threw the ball too much, or not enough, or on other alleged felonies. I felt — and still do — that many reporters are swayed by the crowd. As the spectators' reactions go, so do theirs; their feelings and their stories are dictated by the ups and downs of people who pay to get in the park.

Now that I've been around a while, I am convinced the press is necessary, and is not evil. I can understand why they have to go beyond bare, chronological game happenings, which is the type of coverage I grew up reading. They need something more than the score, and the play-by-play, although I sure do wish they would put the score a little closer to their by-lines, even in those psychiatric numbers some of them do on coaches and players after a game.

The important thing is that the newspapers are a source of recognition for your players. Coaches can attempt to motivate and inspire all they want, but a young man gets much more inspiration from reading in the paper that he played well on Saturday. That is much more effective than any oration I could aim at him.

We respect the press as an organization that helps fill our stadiums and informs the tens of thousands of others, those who cannot get to the games, how we are faring. The latter's impression of our team, of the ball games, is going to be dictated by how the sports writers feel about same. This puts the reporters in a very responsible position; one, that in my opinion, some of them abuse.

The angle guy bothers me. Ray Finocchiaro of the Wilmington News-Journal wrote some very aggravating stuff when he was covering us. His stories were pointed; there was no real attempt to describe what was taking place on the field. I had the feeling that the hard angle was the premeditated basis of his pre- and post-game stories. The Finocchiaro situation got to the point where we flagged him, but I must confess now this was a case of over-reaction. I apologized, and he didn't stay flagged very long.

In 1971, we were coming up to a game with Villanova, one of our major opponents; it's always a hot one. They had Mike Siani, a remarkable and vociferous pass-catching end who went on being remarkable in the National Football League. The Tuesday before the game, Finocchiaro came out with a story in the Morning News, quoting an unnamed Delaware defender as saying "I'd like to take a shot at him (Siani) every time he comes off the line. Then we'll see how many passes he catches. He's got a big mouth."

It was my impression that Ray had overheard that comment the previous Saturday on the team bus, after we had won at New Hampshire. The quote was picked up by the Philadelphia papers and drew angry criticism from the Villanova players, including, naturally, Mike Siani.

I thought Finocchiaro had violated a confidence by printing anything that was said on the team bus. We allow the writers to ride with us as a courtesy.

We knocked off Villanova 23-15. Now here comes Finocchiaro to do the regular post-game interviews. The senior players had approached me and told me they didn't want him in the locker room. I didn't either, and I told Ray this. We had a shouting match. Ray maintained he had not eavesdropped on the bus, but was sitting at the same motel dining-room table with safety Jim O'Brien, Gardy Kahoe and Billy Armstrong when O'Brien made the crack about Siani. He pointed out that they all knew he was a newspaperman.

But he didn't get in the locker room. In retrospect, it was a hilarious situation — and even Ray appreciated the humor of it — because he first had gone over to the Villanova quarters and THEY wouldn't let him in because of the same Siani story he had written. It was sort of an unprecedented grand slam. If Ray had been covering a triangular track meet, he might have broken a world record for having the door slammed on him.

Naturally, Ray's press-box associates rallied to his cause. Frank Dolson, sports editor and columnist of the Philadelphia Inquirer, came to the point right away: "This is really a violation of what you say are your ethics and principles, and of the University of Delaware's, too. It looks like you are taking a big step towards professionalism."

My answer was that my concern was for my ball players, that I had to respond to them if they felt that strongly about a reporter.

The next week, Jim O'Brien came to me and disclosed that he indeed had made the statement while he was sitting with Finocchiaro after the New Hampshire game — and not on the bus. I apologized to Ray and told him I had made a mistake in going along with my players' reaction, that it had been a case of over-sensitivity on my part. Ray was back in our midst immediately and a couple of years later, as acting coach in our spring game, he was a 20-0 winner over his boss, Hal Bodley, when his Blues beat Bodley's Whites.

Incidentally, the winter after the Villanova game, Finocchiaro also managed to get thrown out of our basketball locker room by Ken Helfand, acting as spokesman for the senior players, but Don Harnum, the coach, threw him right back in again.

I am not going to let Finocchiaro off scot-free here. The Siani incident, even though it was a bad rap against Ray, was the culmination of ill feeling he had instilled in our camp. New on the beat, he had written his way into our spleens. He had gone to Villanova the week of our game to talk to some former Delaware high-school players on the Wildcats' team. He wrote several articles about them in a way that never has been used to publicize our people. This is a policy I still cannot understand. The same thing happens when we are about to play Temple.

It is particularly disturbing when a Philadelphia college player he happens to be writing about is one who could not have gone to Delaware from an academic standpoint, or could not have obtained the financial aid he wanted because of our need rule, or had some other grudge against us. Finocchiaro would give this player a voice, a weapon to fire back at us.

I'm not asking reporters to lead cheers for us. But I think they have a responsibility to understand the emotion that is involved when a team is working towards a particular goal — to win within the bounds of recruiting propriety. Their printed comments are tremendously important. Sometimes they miss just how important they can be; they get blinded in their search for controversy.

The reporter who shows up with the intention of creating something that isn't there is doing a great injustice to the player and the reader. I have heard this type of writing referred to as the New Journalism. If it is, bring back the old kind. Tom Tomashek, who currently covers us for the News-Journal, strikes me as a first-class reporter. He writes very factually and makes an effort to limit his editorial comments.

Hal Bodley, the sports editor of the News-Journal papers, has seen more of our games than any other newspaper person and, I have to believe, shows up each Saturday with an open mind. His columns augment Tomashek's factual coverage of the game and if we're good or if we're dull, to use one of his favorite adjectives, he calls it, and I can't question his batting average.

We have made some big strides in press relations. We annually invite the reporters to our pre-season orientation luncheon. This not only gives them an idea of what we are trying to do technically, but gives them the chance to meet the players they will be interviewing during the course of the season.

I always explain to the squad that the writers have a job to do, and it is not to go out of their way to make the coaches and the players look good. As a result of these sessions, I have recognized more warmth, more understanding between press and player. When I first showed up twenty-five years ago, the writers did not have access to the players after a game because it was a physical impossibility. Our facilities were not set up for it. They had access to the coach, and that was it. There was a time when the coaches would get together and agree to an approach on a defeat and everybody would spout the same story.

Now it's a much better scene. After a home game, I talk briefly to the players in the stadium locker room, which is on the spartan side. Then they head for the fieldhouse locker room, where the press has immediate access to them. That's fine. I grab a Diet Pepsi and face the press in the office of Ben Sherman, our sports information director. I stay there until they run out of questions.

There have been times, after a bitter loss, when I might have been a little late for the press conference. That's because I have taken the time to throw a fit. I try and be honest with the writers. If I think they are out of line, if I think their questions are not appropriate, I will say so. But generally I enjoy the relationship. I like the exchange with the guys from Dover and Wilmington and Philadelphia. We are pleased that the Inquirer and the Bulletin have seen fit to cover us, because of our tremendous following. Now even more people know what and how we're doing.

Oh, yes. We took care of Mike Siani, or little Johnny Bush, our defensive back who stuck to him like a tattoo, did. Maybe we should have given Ray Finocchiaro an assist, and I don't mean out the door.

I've always been a sports-page fan. When I was growing up, my favorite authors were Tom Mercy and Maurie Cossman of the Flint Journal. I think the first time I got my name in print was as a tenth-grader on the junior varsity football team. Maurie wrote something to the effect that I had been a factor in a winning season. I felt as if he had put me in Yankee Stadium. That's when I began thinking that sports writers were not real people — that they had been created in heaven.

We check out the newspapers that cover our opponents during a season, plus our own area papers. Bob Depew of our staff is in charge of propaganda. If he sees a story that might help juice our club, he'll have it duplicated and post it.

I have been misquoted in my time, particularly when I fell into the trap of making comments I assumed would be off the record — or would you call that an unquote? Dave Nelson warned me about this bad habit a long time ago. One reporter may accept it as an off-the-cuff remark and not print it, but another would treat it as fair game and write it.

So I'm pretty careful what I say. I think that's one reason why they describe me in the press as very conservative, very pessimistic. I'm afraid that if I say exactly what I feel, it will be misinterpreted. An expression of confidence, a feeling that "this game is going to be easy," is the greatest detriment to playing well and playing intensively that a team can have. So no matter what team we're playing, I play it close to the vest in my pre-game comments. To be absolutely honest about it, though, there are very few ball games in which I do not expect trouble.

In the early years, there were times when I felt I would rather hide than face the press after a defeat. But I soon came to feel that if I wanted to be the kind of football coach I proposed to be, one with class, then I had better show up and stay as long as the writers had questions. I wanted to be like Dave Nelson. He could meet the press very nicely.

It takes some self-control. In 1967, we opened the season by losing to Rhode Island by 28-17. A Wilmington sports editor who has gone on to such things as writing books walked in after the game and his first question was, "How does it feel to lose to Elmira?", the implication being that we had been conquered by a Class C opponent. I had to get a grip on myself with that one because while Rhode Island may sound like the Elmira of football, they were a pretty good football team that year. They went on to win the Yankee Conference championship.

I object to a player's popping off in the press, using the media as an implement for himself. An incident of this nature once involved the late Chuck Hall, a tremendous player for us. He started every game in the backfield for three years and still holds a number of our rushing records. He gained more than 3,100 yards, scored 17 touchdowns as a senior, rushed for a career per-game average of 95.7 yards. Simply outstanding.

Chuck's girl friend, Patty, attended West Chester State and he wanted to play especially well against the Rams. For one incentive, he kept hearing Patty relay comments that the West Chester guys were making about what they would do to us.

Hall could hardly wait for the kickoff, and he had said a few words in an interview. After our pre-game meal, I picked up the morning paper and did a double-take. The advance on our game was built around a Chuck Hall claim that he was going to run all over West Chester. I exhaled slowly, folded the paper and walked over to Chuck as he was stashing his tray.

"Are you ready to play today?" I asked grimly.

He gave me a puzzled look. "I certainly am."

"Well, you better be," I said, biting off the words as I handed him the sports page.

Chuck's face turned red. He stiffened.

"I'm not a psychologist like you," he said. "All I do is play."

"That's all right with me," I said, "as long as you play well."

And just as he had predicted in the paper, Chuck ran all over West Chester as we won 39-22. He had his usual 150-yard day.

Steve Adamek of the Delaware State News in Dover met us for the first time at a pre-season orientation luncheon. He was introduced as one of the writers who would be covering us regularly. I had the feeling Steve didn't want to be impressed, if we had anything impressive going for us. His first article was one of questioning, dealing with alleged hypocrisy, cynical about our feeling that football is an educational opportunity. OK — he was entitled to his opinion, as the saying goes. But I think he wrote that when he really didn't know us very well. I hope we have convinced him that our program is all we say it is. In any case, he has been a pleasant addition to our press corps.

I might as well throw Joe Harris and Dick Dunkel and their weekly predictions into this chapter on the press. Sure, our ball players follow them. You can rest assured that everything written about our football team, numerical and otherwise, is read by the athletes.

Sometimes I read the Harris and Dunkel forecasts and wince, say when they have us favored to win by 30 points or so. You never want to be heavily favored when you're really not that strong. (See, I told you I was pessimistic).

The Dunkel ratings give us something to work on, even if it is a small thing. They are positive in the sense that we are not in a conference. We cannot look at a particular game and say that we will be in first place in the league if we win it. But we can look at the Dunkel list and if we're on it, try to stay on it. And if we aren't listed, we try to be. If Harris and/or Dunkel pick us to lose, that's a psychological ploy, too.

The Associated Press and United Press International polls were another recognition factor. They might encourage gambling on games involving the major teams, but I know that for us they were an incentive to do well and impress the writers, who voted in the AP poll, and the panel of coaches that did the ratings for UPI. Since 1976, the wire-service rankings on our level have been replaced by a poll of NCAA coaches. The incentive to excell in this "league" remains with us.

Our radio coverage is an important means of communication. Bob Kelley, the play-by-play man, is one of the best in the country — they tell me. Do you know that Kelley has been covering our games for a zillion seasons, and I've never heard him? For an obvious reason: I'm coaching the game he is broadcasting. I see him before and after the games, he travels with us, and that's it.

Bob has been covering for us so long and knows what we're doing so well that he doesn't meet with us during game week, as he once did. He has an unusual setup — he does not work for the radio station, but is under contract to the university. We think he's that good.

Now and then his act gets back to me. I was told that in one game he kept saying that Delaware was running to the sideline, and questioned this practice. So I explained to him, first chance I had, that the opponent was rotating its defense to the wide side with a 6-5 relationship, meaning five defensive men to the sidelines flank and six men to the wide side of the field. So by running into the sideline, which we did with success, we were really outnumbering them.

Careful, Kelley. My spies are everywhere.

17

Halftime Isn't Hollywood

What goes on in the Delaware locker room at halftime?

A friend asked that of Sue during an intermission at Delaware Stadium.

My first wife (that keeps her on her toes) looked around for possible eavesdroppers, then lowered her voice as if plotting a conspiracy while sitting among 20,000 people.

"Promise not to tell?" she asked. The friend swore she wouldn't.

"Well," Sue said, "there are ninety players in there, right? Plus five coaches, two trainers and a couple of student managers. And there's only one urinal. That's what goes on at halftime — they line up."

Most of the time, our halftimes aren't much more exciting than Sue's story. The coach's deportment between halves is one of the great popular misconceptions in football. I would like to say that I am Knute Rockne reincarnated, with perhaps a suggestion of Vince Lombardi, alternately breathing fire and recalling deceased predecessors and doing everything to provoke inspiration short of ushering in the Mormon Tabernacle Choir as a backup group.

I would like to say that, but I can't. I have breathed some fire in my time, but it all depends on the situation. I'm sure that while the customers are out there watching the pretty girls and the bands on the field, they also have a vision of me coming up with stunningly trick plays that will either turn the tide or turn the game into a rout — in our favor, of course. They have to picture me standing on a Coca Cola box, among the used orange slices and the old tape, making such a dramatic pitch to my tired but dogged troops that they will run right back to the field through the wall, without bothering to open the door.

In our regular-season game at Youngstown in 1979, we were miles behind when the half ended, 31-7. In what turned out to be the whackiest turnaround you ever saw, we outscored them 44-14 from there on in and won 51-45. The poets of the press box called it a shootout. So naturally, when the same teams got to the national finals in our division, it was billed as Shootout II.

You will understand when I say that I was not enraptured by our first-half performance. We were uninspired. We played far below our capability. Should I rip into 'em, let it fly, be ugly? That approach crossed my mind as I walked to the gloom of the locker room.

But there is a place where that kind of reaction from the coach can destroy a football team, not rally it. I decided this was not the situation for me to go into a Captain Bligh routine. Sure, we were trailing badly. But we still had a good offensive game plan. We had moved the ball well. We had some technical problems defensively, but we should have been behind no more than 17-14. For me to tear the roof off would shatter the good things we had going for us.

So it was the spot for almost a couch job — reality therapy, a sensitivity session, a complete regrouping, rather than a chew-out. I told them — but not calmly — I wanted them to get themselves together so we could leave town with respectability.

With that statement, Ed Wood, a junior halfback, jumped

up and shouted, "Yeah, and let's win the game while we're at it!"

The rest of the players looked at Wood as if he didn't have all his walls papered and didn't realize what the score was. But even that worked. We regrouped Youngstown to death.

I really don't have time to be Laurence Olivier, and run the gamut from plead to excoriate. Besides, I'm too little to be Olivier. The rulebook says a team is allowed fifteen minutes at intermission, but by mutual consent you can have twenty. It is usually twenty to accommodate the fans, who don't want to be cheated out of any halftime entertainment. So that means that by the time you reach the locker room, you have already spent three minutes. It is going to take another three to get back, so now you are talking a big 14 minutes.

My procedure is to give the players the first three or four minutes to themselves, a recovery time. And while they are doing this, meditating or cussing themselves or whatever, I meet with the defensive coaches and check the "split," which is a breakdown of the plays run against us that have been successful. Now I can make suggestions as to different calls, different stunts, different maneuvers, maybe taking two or more ideas from one defense and putting them together with another defense simply by calls.

There sometimes are boudoir comments we don't want the defensive players to hear: "Joe isn't doing the job . . . get rid of Sam . . . Let's crank up a replacement for Steve . . . I don't care if I ever see him again."

Now we join the athletes. The room is divided in half, the offense on one side, the defense on the other, with a blackboard for each. The defensive coaches move in with their respective groups. "Why did this happen?" is a common question, or accusation.

The offensive coach, who has been spotting from on

high, makes a report. Our basic formation was put on a blackboard before the game. We describe the basic defense the other team is throwing at it. Our quarterback entered the game with a "short list" of plays — maybe one or two outside plays from a couple of formations, one fullback play, perhaps two or three passes — and that's all we are armed with. So our immediate job from an offensive standpoint at halftime is to devise a new short list — if it looks as though we need one.

Everybody has plays they want to plug. The second-string quarterback, who has been on the sidelines, might have suggestions. The quarterback, the coaches, speak up.

It gets to the point where I have to knock all this off so I can think. With Ted Kempski's help, I will devise a new short list. It could be that we decide not to change anything. Finished with the offense, I go to talk to the defense.

And when I am through with the platoons, I give them all my message, or whatever you want to call it. The priority, though, goes to checking the machinery. After that, there isn't much time for any violins, or torture racks, or whatever the fans think is being employed in the locker room.

It would be wrong for me to give you the impression that I don't say something that might juice up the squad. Don't call it a pep talk — I despise that term. Pep talks went out with Jack Armstrong.

Two or three individuals or an area of the team might be in for some heat. There are times when you cannot be gentle with them: "Either play or get out . . . You told me you wanted to play and now it's obvious that you don't . . . If you don't want to play, let me know and I'll find somebody who does."

Those comments are related to the team's early orientation, back to when we set the theme of the season. That's when I would have told them "It doesn't make any difference what the score is; we're going to play sixty minutes of intensive football for eleven games." So many of the things that are said at halftime are connected to something we have been building all season.

I am not as cool at halftime as all this might hint. I am very emotional, and tend to be that way all the time when I'm with my football team. Dave Nelson was just the opposite. He was about as emotional as Steve Carlton. I never heard him say anything inspirational; it was all business with him. In the years since I succeeded him, I believe I have leaned a little to his approach.

There are times when you have to calm a team down, as if you are administering a sedative. Other times, you need to build a fire under them, needle them.

The important thing is to have a procedure for everything, including halftime. I think my halftime program has improved. In the early years, we were thrashing around a bit. If you have a procedure, that itself will transcend all the hysteria that might be present. If the team can anticipate what you are going to do, they will feel stronger for it.

This wasn't at halftime, but Fritz Crisler showed me something about indoor coaching when I was a hanger-on with the Michigan varsity. We were getting ready to go out and battle Michigan State. We could hear the jammed stadium screaming and yelling as if they were waiting for the lions. Everybody was sitting there in silence except our coach, who wasn't even in the place. There was a lot of snorting going on, but nothing else. I was hiding behind people, being as quiet as possible. Scrubs don't make noise.

At the very last second, Coach Crisler walked in rather melodramatically and said, "Gentlemen, there are 101,000 people out there. Just remember that you are Michigan and they are Michigan State." It was the greatest inspirational one-liner I've ever heard. We — or they, the guys who played — went out and murdered State.

I have another pre-game memory of Bennie Oosterbaan, Crisler's successor. Michigan was about to play Northwestern, with the Big Ten Conference championship riding on the score. You could taste the tension in the locker room. Bennie made a Crisler-like late appearance. "If you think you're tight," he said, "you should see them on the Northwestern side. They are scared to death. Loosen up and have a good time."

Sure enough, we did — or they did — and won. During my days at Ann Arbor, there weren't many losses. The coaches could afford to be smooth and business-like.

I learned a great halftime lesson as a spotter on top of the stands when I was coaching the backfield, in a game against the University of Buffalo. With about a minute and a half to go, we had them pinned back on their five-yard line. I figured nothing was going to happen. I cut out, hurrying to the locker room so I could get my defenses on the board for the offensive discussion. While I was hustling there, I heard an awful lot of noise from the stands, but I didn't know what was going on.

Suddenly, the Delaware football team came in dazed and all out of breath. "What happened?" I asked. I learned that a Buffalo receiver was completely naked (not covered by our defense, class) in our secondary and caught a 60-some-yard pass that almost turned into a touchdown. With a bit of luck, we held them as the gun went off.

I had no idea what the Buffalo pattern had been on their successful strike into our territory. So there I was scrabbling around the locker room, quizzing players, trying to patch information together. That was a mistake. I was bombarded with excuses, not answers. Like Buffalo had seventeen players on the field; four or five of them were in motion at the same time; the splits in the line were not the actual two feet but more like six feet. I heard all kinds of fairy tales. That taught me something: Don't leave your post.

Don't ever buy a ticket to see what goes on behind the locker curtain at halftime. Stick with the band. The scene inside is not entertainment, no matter what Hollywood thinks. There are another thirty long minutes to play, and even though you have what looks like a nice lead, a coach is wary of what could happen — and has happened. There are never any laughs. When you are trailing, or have but a slight edge, it is worry time. At halftime, we don't ever need Johnny Carson.

Blue Hens bury Choctaws 60-10

Sunday News Journal • • Dec. 2, 1979 —

Hal Bodley
sports editor

Blue Hen Comeback Nips Villanova, 14-13

Temple Muffles Delaware Offense

DELAWARE OWNS RICH POST SEASON HISTORY

Hens batter Temple

Supplement to The News Journal Papers, December 7, 1979

Hens' comeback at Youngstown unforgettable

Delaware explosions net national crown

By RICK OSTROW
Of The Bulletin Staff
Albuquerque, N.M. — The new NCAA Division II national champion Delaware Blue Hens can be called many things — explosive, self-confident, maybe even self-destructing — but one thing they most certainly are is resilient.

The Hens played with fire most of the first half yesterday, then d...

nated enough big pl... 38-21 victory ove... Youngstown State a... tory in three tries... old bowl game ... al champi...

Dela... averaging close to 280 yards per ... passes of 74 and 75 yards from lanky

"Our offense is so e...

Raymond Accustomed To Success

18

A Girl Named Sue

The real winner around the Raymond estate in Windy Hills, Newark, Del., is the lady of the house.

I win football games and plaques and, occasionally, a championship.

They are insignificant when you compare them to what Suzanne Raymond did. She won back her life.

It was a life that took a terrifying turn for the worse twenty years ago when she lost her hearing. Just like that. Sue has been legally deaf ever since.

She was putting in another routine morning alone at home. She was dusting. Straightening up to move to another piece of furniture, she became very dizzy. "I felt weird, like the whole world was going around," was the way she described it to me.

That is when we learned about Meniere's Syndrome. It confined Sue to bed for two weeks. Experts still do not know what caused her loss of hearing. One guess is that it was a virus.

Our happy little home was overturned. The kids wondered what was going on. Debbie was 7, Chris 5, David 3. Sue was upset and depressed. We went through all the emotions. Anger. Frustration. Bitterness.

We went for midnight walks, trying to settle her down —

and me too, I suppose. Name a top hearing specialist, and we have seen him.

She was 29 years old.

She said later we went through four stages. First was the depression. Then a mental rally, the feeling that what was happening to her couldn't be true; her hearing would return and everything would be OK. Next, the realization that she really was deaf, and the grief over a priceless loss. And finally — ten years later — the acceptance that she never would hear again.

What terrible times for her. And what a gallant, courageous person, to accept the challenge of a completely new way of life and then go out and conquer it. She literally fought herself out of a world of isolation.

Five years after Sue was stricken, she went to work as a teachers' aide at the Margaret S. Sterck School for the Hearing Impaired, in Newark. For the first time, she met people who had been deaf from birth. She forgot all about her own handicap. She thought she had known everything about being deaf, but this experience proved she knew absolutely nothing.

The school administration at the time did not believe in teaching its students the sign language, but the kids knew it nevertheless, and they taught it to Sue. She became fluent with it later when she worked with Lou Ann Simpson as a State Vocational Rehabilitation counselor.

Sue said it first: The language of the deaf is beautiful. I have learned to speak that way — at least basically — and I agree. To me, though, it is easier to send than to receive.

For a year and a half, she did rehabilitation work with people with various handicaps. The telephone made her decide to leave the job. She could handle two or three calls a day, but any more than that and she was out of it. She learned that the telephone is the handicap of most deaf people. Now she answers the phone and hears by placing its receiving end on what I irreverently call her electronic bosom.

She has total communication. She reads lips and gets some sound with a hearing aid. If we have trouble with a particular word, I clue her with its first letter. Men with mustaches, or smoking a pipe, do not get through to her.

In April of 1979, the Wilmington Quota Club, an international professional women's organization, announced the winner of its first Deaf Woman of the Year award: Suzanne H. Raymond. The citation honored outstanding achievement and contributions to the community, and it was presented at a luncheon in the Gold Ballroom of the Hotel du Pont. You can be sure the Raymond family had a ringside table.

Sue's education had been interrupted by our marriage. Ironically, she had been a speech and hearing major at the University of Michigan. Get this: She resumed her education as a deaf person, earning her bachelor's degree in psychology and then a master's degree in guidance counseling from the University of Delaware. She had gone back to Sterck School to intern as part of the requirement for the master's.

As an undergraduate at Delaware, she was the only one deaf and the only one over thirty years of age. I have to believe that was a bit tougher assignment than a football coach's trying to think of ways to win a game. Sue, you inferiorate me.

She now is a member of the Sterck School staff, and counsels 12-to-21-year-olds through the difficult transition years from high school to a career. She served on the State of Delaware's task force for the Conference on Handicapped Individuals.

When son Christian was married to Lee Ifflan in the spring of 1979, the vows were said in sign language. They did that for their mother. You talk about an emotional scene!

You know a problem is erased when you can joke about it. We do. I tell Sue she'd be nothing without her deafness, because she developed a great deal of character through it. When she was nominated for the Quota Club award, I told her to relax — she was a cinch to finish at least second because there were only two deaf women in town.

Sue countered by saying she never really appreciated how enjoyable a football game at Delaware Stadium could be until she lost her hearing — "now I can't hear the fans boo you every week."

Now some of my best friends are deaf. I like to think that it was because of my association with that community that I was invited to speak at the annual athletic banquet at Gallaudet College in Washington, D.C., the world's only liberal arts college for the deaf.

It was a strange experience, even though I was braced for it. I walked into a room crowded with five hundred people and all I heard was the occasional clinking of the dishes and the silverware.

I've had a lot of introductions as a veteran of the banquet league, some bad ones and some good, but this was my first silent one. A young man, so fast with his signs I couldn't field them, told the audience who I was and then motioned for me to stand. I was on. The students applauded, and because they could not hear, it was a most unrhythmic clapping.

Lou Ann Simpson went with me to interpret by speech. She was raised by parents who were born deaf, and she is an exceptional signer. It was quite a test for her, though. She had to convey my jokes, too — and they don't hold up too well even in spoken form.

If you managed to finish the chapter on my growin' up in Flint, Mich., you may recall that I met Sue Heinemann when I worked in her father's drug store. She was just a child

Dennis Johnson played defensive tackle on teams that lost only three games from 1970 through 1972. A Kodak Little All-American choice, he went into the pros with the Washington Redskins and then the Buffalo Bills.

Joe Carbone was AP Little All-American defensive end in 1972. He was one big reason we were 10-and-0.

Little Johnny Bush stuck it to Mike Siani of Villanova in 1971. He also ran back an interception a hundred yards against Temple in 1972, a record which still stands.

In my solitude . . . I suffer. I'm there in the debris of a steamy locker room after our 20-game victory streak was halted by Rutgers in 1973. I didn't appreciate the end of the pressure at the moment.

Three good men on the 1975 team. Left to right: Nate Beasley, who carried a record 248 times for more than 1,000 yards; Curt Morgan, the captain, and Kodak Little All-American defensive end Sam Miller.

Ivory Sully, who didn't get a nickel's worth of aid, played halfback for us for three years and led us in rushing his senior year. He went on to play for the Los Angeles Rams, just in time for the Super Bowl.

Wow! It looks as if we just did something spectacular, and we just did — we closed the 1977 season by trouncing undefeated Colgate.

Unheralded at the outset, Jeff Komlo, 1976-1978, finally got a start in the third game of his sophomore year. From then on, he rewrote almost all the quarterback records. In 1979, as a rookie, he started for the Detroit Lions after the two guys ahead of him came up sore.

Herb Beck, Scott Brunner and Captain Jim Brandimarte of the 1979 Division II National Champion Blue Hens.

Jay Hooks caught two long touchdown passes to help beat Villanova in 1979. His mother approved.

Scott Brunner (left) tied a Delaware record when he threw five touchdown passes against C.W. Post in 1979. The congratulations are from Mike Donnalley.

Ed Wood (38) and Lou Mariani celebrate after the first shootout with Youngstown State in 1979. We came back from the grave to beat the Ohioans, and did it again in the national championship game.

Bo Dennis (32) leads the blocking for Lou Mariani against Youngstown State in the 1979 NCAA Division II championship game.

Pete Bistrian and defensive backfield coach Joe Purzycki congratulate each other after the 1979 Zia Bowl victory that gave us the Division II title. Our defense turned the game around.

My championship ride in Albuquerque. It was Delaware's first national title won on the field. The others came in polls. I prefer the polls system.

Don't unhand me sir – I love it. This was part of the crowd that greeted us at Philadelphia Airport when we came back from Albuquerque with all the marbles. The face just above my head belongs to Chris Short, the former Phillies pitcher.

then, 10 years old. I was a manly 15. But I really didn't know she existed as a real, live person — dumb athlete that I was — until she was in high school. At graduation time, and af the suggestion of her father, she invited me to her senior prom. I was attending the University of Michigan and, well, I thought she'd never ask. I long ago had been attracted to her, and I guess you could say we were fond of each other.

Sue went on to Hillsdale College in Michigan — that's where Dave Nelson started his coaching career — for a semester, and then transferred to Michigan and became part of a social scene that included me and several better football players. We dated inconsistently for about a five-year period. The subject of marriage didn't rear its attractive head until I came back from one of my always-to-be-forgotten professional baseball seasons.

Sue's a great cook, but it took her ten years to get there. One night early in our stay in Maine, she served her brilliantly promising assistant-football-coach-husband peppers stuffed with rice and ground meat. She had neglected to use precooked rice, which means that the dish fought back at me a little. Sue also went on a streak of serving Italian dishes flavored heavily with garlic — for days at a time, it seemed. That was a stretch during which my fellow coaches at Maine weren't close to me.

One more bride-and-groom recollection: As newcomers to Maine, we lived in a log cabin. The bed was built into a wall. Sue slept on the wall side and kept complaining how cold her feet were. After a few nights of this, I mildly rebuked her for not having the pioneer spirit and, martyr that I am, swapped places with her. My feet didn't get cold — they almost froze.

The next night, I bundled up and checked out the exterior of the cabin in the vicinity of the bed. There was a hunk of log missing, an opening about two feet long and two inches wide. I filled that baby up completely. Thus, an early crisis in The Life of the Raymonds was solved.

The kids are grown-up now and have flown the nest. Debbie is Mrs. David Rahn, and they have presented us with two granddaughters. David is married to that Phillie Phanatic costume. We named him after Dave Nelson, and I don't know if Dave has ever forgiven us since David became what I call a Green Transvestite.

When Sue was acknowledging her Quota Club award, she looked at our table and made the comment that she was especially pleased to see that David had shown up in his dress clothes. He doesn't make many public appearances out of uniform.

19

And In Conclusion . . .

I'd go bananas (and you can see I'm a hip coach with that remark) trying to select an all-star team of players I have coached at Delaware since I took over the top spot in 1966. Don't ask. I've had so many great ones at all positions, it would be an impossible task.

Let's do it this way. I'll pick the best in categories, including intangibles. And you'll note that with the exception of two players, I still can't boil "the best" down to a single Blue Hen.

The Ideal All-Timers, in each case alphabetically:

Blocking – Bill Armstrong, Conway Hayman.

Conditioning – Paul Schweizer.

Fanaticism (or whatever you would call super dedication) – Bob Pietuszka, Joe Purzycki.

Hardness – Bill Armstrong, Bob Slowik.

Intelligence – Bob Depew, Yancy Phillips.

Know-how – Jim Colbert, Scotty Reihm.

Leadership – Gary Bello, Jim Brandimarte, Ed Clark.

Moves – Glenn Covin, Dick Kelley, Vern Roberts.

Nerve – Tom DiMuzio.

Passing – Scott Brunner, Jeff Komlo.

Poise – Scott Brunner, Jeff Komlo.

Power – Chuck Hall (incomparable).

Receivers – Bill Cubit, Ron Withelder, Larry Wagner.

Size (and something to go with it) – Dennis Johnson,
  Garry Kuhlman, Herb Slattery.
Speed – Gary Gumbs, Lou Mariani, Ivory Sully.
Stride – Gardy Kahoe.
Tackling – John Bush, John Favero.

*   *   *

Temper, temper. I've got one. But I like to think it's been
tempered over the years. It's one of the many things I learned
from Dave Nelson: You cannot lose control when you are the
boss. There has to be a personal demonstration of the discipline, which is the essence of your game, that you are teaching.

I lost a little control during the 1978 season. The team
was going through a lethargic period, not doing the job I
knew they were capable of. I walked into the locker room one
day and did a number on the big fiber-board sign that identified the "Home of the National Champions," listing the
years. Muttering "We don't need this any more," I un-
holstered a crowbar and totaled it.

A new "Champions" sign is back up for the 1980 season
— and with the addition of the year 1979.

I had a much shorter fuse when I was the baseball coach
— in my comparative youth. I was sort of the Billy Martin of
the varsity set.

I got thrown out of a game at Navy when the home team
wouldn't put the tarpaulin on the infield when a heavy rain
interrupted the game. Because Navy was leading, I protested
vigorously and was chased. I was almost annoyed all over
again when my club rallied and won without me.

We were making a southern trip in the late '50s and I
had warned the players to eat sensibly, not to go spending
their money on between-meals junk.

After a game with Duke — a loser — we were in a restaurant waiting for dinner when in walked Larry Catuzzi, our

shortstop — and also the football quarterback — eating a nice, dripping, grilled cheese sandwich.

"Your fat butt is going to sit next to me for the rest of the trip," I growled. He said he had bought it with his own money, but I reminded him that the problem was not economical but physical.

The next night, we were sleeping in a dormitory at East Carolina College. I always had a fungo bat with me, because I liked to talk to the players about hitting before we went to bed. I was awakened by something running across my face that just had to be a mouse. Jumping out of bed, I turned on the light and grabbed the fungo bat to attack the rodent.

Catuzzi awoke in the next bed and saw me standing with upraised bat, looking in his direction. He let out a yell. "I'm sorry, Coach! I'll never eat another grilled cheese sandwich as long as I live!"

*   *   *

Ever wonder what the winning coach says to the losing coach when they shake hands at midfield after a game?

Not much. Trite stuff. "Nice game . . . congratulations . . . good luck."

But an assistant coach at New Hampshire abruptly eliminated the banality after one game in which we had won rather convincingly. He must have felt we poured it on without mercy.

"Raymond," he said after the head coach and I had already exchanged the usual comments, "you are a jerk and you always will be." I asked him to repeat it — the new material had indeed startled me — and he did.

Jerk I may be, but you just don't say things like that on fields in our league. I reported it to the ethics committee of the National Football Coaches Association, and had an apology from the New Hampshire man the next week.

*   *   *

I'm going to need some tickets if the Phillies get into the World Series, so I'll remind Dallas Green of this story.

I was the freshman baseball coach my first year at Delaware, and Dallas was the pitching ace of the varsity. Because of my experience with the Michigan varsity and despite my experience as a catcher in the minor leagues, Bob Siemen, the baseball coach, had asked me to work with Dallas in the fieldhouse the previous winter.

Dallas went on to have a good spring, and Bob Carpenter invited him to audition with the Phillies in a workout at Connie Mack Stadium. I drove him to the ball park and introduced him to Robin Roberts, a friend of mine from the Michigan days. Robin suggested I catch Dallas to make him feel more comfortable, so I warmed him up and also caught batting practice for him.

Then we went out to dinner — on the Phillies — and when we returned to the park, they offered Dallas a contract. He was too young to sign it, so we brought it home and showed it to his mother and I explained the terms the best I could. With family approval, Dallas signed. I took the contract to the Phils the next day.

Make that six good ones behind first base, Manager Green.

Dallas also was a basketball star for us; he was an exceptional athlete. I think if he had not signed with the Phillies his junior year, he might have given football a try. He now says if I had been a decent coach, I would have recognized his ability and persuaded him to stay and used him as a spread receiver.

*   *   *

After all those years of spotting from press-box level, there I was head-coaching on the sidelines.

From the best seat in the house to the worst.

If you are talking about operations, then it would be

easier to coach from a booth on high. But then the game would take on the aspects of a basketball or baseball game, a geometric thing in which the intensity and the hardness of football would not be in your view. You would not get a feel for the game.

You've got to be with the troops, to have close contact — especially eye contact when they come out of the game or you are communicating with them. And that "touch" is more important than the technical information you are feeding them over a telephone.

*   *   *

My all-time fifteen-second man is Mike Lude. I don't mean sprinting. I mean recruiting.

Mike, who was the line coach when I was a fellow assistant, could dazzle a high school boy just by showing up. He was the greatest first-impression guy I've ever seen. He oozed effervescence and had an almost overpowering personality.

Recruiting was his responsibility, and he loved it so much he wanted to do it all by himself. Effective as he was, I think he had himself tied up in knots because he spread himself too thin geographically, and discouraged help.

*   *   *

Last year we handed Bill Narduzzi's Youngstown State team its only two defeats in a thirteen-game season, including one in the national championship playoff.

And yet Narduzzi was voted Coach of the Year in Division II by the American Football Coaches Association. I voted for him for an award I have won twice.

When the press asked me for a comment, I said I was not disappointed: that to win it once is a great feeling and you accept it as a tribute to your staff; to do it twice is a miracle, and if you do it three times, you're a pig.

Disappointed? No. Surprised? A little.

*   *   *

Allegations to the contrary, I have never coached a team in one game in such a way as to deliberately run up a score to impress somebody, such as a polls participant, or to humiliate an opponent.

I take you back to our losing season of 1967, which taught me a lesson and also gave me a sense of insecurity. When you lose five games in the last several minutes, seeing "comfortable" leads crumble, you realize that anything can happen and that your lead is not comfortable until the game's over.

So from that time on, I just let things fly. If we are rolling, I let us roll. I've been told I never appear to enjoy a ball game until I'm absolutely sure it has been won. What's so unique about that? I admit there were times when I might have played more people. Of recent years, I have been able to get more bodies into games because of the quality of the lower levels.

I don't worry about any "piling up" accusations. Those things come with the job. And I never have had the feeling somebody was out to get US, either.

*   *   *

Golf and sketching are my medicine. When I finished playing baseball, I was left with this enormous void in my life physically. After that first year at the University of Maine, I began playing golf with my father-in-law on trips back to Michigan and got down to the middle eighties on a pretty good course.

I liked the game, but there were priorities and I unwillingly kicked the habit until about twelve years ago. That's when Roy Donoho, our team physician and also our family doctor, suggested I return to the golf course and play rather seriously as an outlet from the heat of coaching. Good advice. It relaxes me, I shoot a little better, enjoy the game more and I can hold my own at the coaches' convention golf outings.

Even as a little kid I liked to draw things, and I was always sketching people in high school. But this was another hobby that was crowded out until I made a practice of painting acrylic portraits as a means of relaxing during the season. I think Roy Rylander, our trainer, was my first subject. Each Thursday morning, I do one of a starting senior and tack it on the locker-room bulletin board. They only take me forty-five minutes, so don't go looking for any Mona Lisas in the collection.

If you ever get mail from our football department, check out the letterhead. The chicken on it is an original H. Raymond.

*   *   *

Scheduling football games is the athletic director's problem. And a problem it has become at Delaware. There are a number of schools in the East that simply will not play us. Most of the teams that do schedule us now — outside of our regular opponents — do it to take advantage of what has become a fat guarantee at Delaware Stadium or for the opportunity to knock the University of Delaware from its traditional high perch.

So what were we doing playing the United States Merchant Marine Academy, a team that, frankly, was not of our caliber, last season? I'll put it this way: If Penn State can play Colgate, and some of the other schools on their schedule, then certainly we can play the Merchant Marine Academy. We were just part of an upgraded Merchant Marine schedule that also included Dayton and Boston University. They are pointing for Division I-AA recognition by 1981.

We're still playing a lot of Division I schools and many that have aid packages superior to ours.

I am not consulted on scheduling. Some years ago, Dave Nelson told me that we were no longer in a position to select our schedule, that it was becoming increasingly difficult to

find colleges that would play us. He did not go into the ups-
and-downs of scheduling; it would have been silly to spend a
lot of time with that on me because I am not involved in the
booking department. And I'm glad. I have enough headaches.
I just can't conceive of someone filling the dual role of head
coach and athletics director. But Dave did it, for fifteen years.
No wonder his growth was stunted.

*   *   *

I was born November 14, 1926. (Co-author's note: I know
you didn't want the book to be written chronologically,
Coach, but this is preposterous).

Delaware Blue Hen Football Statistics

from the
University of Delaware
Sports Information Office

Tubby's Awards and Appointments

1980
First Vice President, American Football Coaches Association
(President-Elect, 1981)

1979
District II College Division Coach of the Year
ABC Sports National Coach of the Year — Division II

1978
District II College Division Coach of the Year

1976
Assistant Coach in College All-Star Game

1974
District II College Division Coach of the Year
Elected to 12 member Board of Trustees
of the American Football Coaches Association
Assistant Coach for East in East-West Shrine Game

1972
District II College Division Coach of the Year
East's College Division Coach of the Year
as selected by the Football Writers Association of N.Y.
Kodak College Division Coach of the Year
as selected by the American Football Coaches Association
Assistant Coach for East in Coaches All-American Game

1971
District II College Division Coach of the Year
Kodak College Division Coach of the Year
as selected by the American Football Coaches Association
Assistant coach for East in Coaches All-American Game
Recipient of Governor's Medal for contributions
to the State of Delaware

1966
6-3

Middle Atlantic Conference Champions

Tubby's Top Teams

1979

13-1

NCAA National Division II Champions
ECAC Division II Team of the Year
Lambert Cup Recipient

1978

10-4

Finalist in NCAA College Division Playoffs
Washington Touchdown Club National College Division Title
ECAC Division II Team of the Year

1976

8-3-1

Quarter-Finalists in NCAA College Division Playoffs
ECAC Division II Team of the Year
Lambert Cup Recipient

1974

12-2

Finalists in NCAA College Division Playoffs
ECAC Division II Team of the Year
Lambert Cup Recipient

Tubby's Top Teams

1973

8-4
Played in first NCAA College Division Playoffs
Lambert Cup Co-Recipient

1972

10-0
AP National College Division Title
UPI National College Division Title
Washington Touchdown Club National College Division Title
National Football Foundation and Hall of Fame's
National College Division Co-Title with Louisiana Tech
University's first ever 10-0 regular season record
Lambert Cup Recipient

1971

10-1
AP National College Division Title
UPI National College Division Title
Washington Touchdown Club National College Division Title
Boardwalk Bowl Winners (72-22 over C. W. Post)
Lambert Cup Recipient

Tubby's Top Teams

1970

9-2

Boardwalk Bowl Winners (38-23 over Morgan State)
Lambert Cup Recipient

1969

9-2

Boardwalk Bowl Winners (31-13 over North Carolina Central)
Middle Atlantic Conference Champions
Lambert Cup Co-Recipient

1968

8-3

Boardwalk Bowl Winners (31-24 over Indiana State of Pa.)
Middle Atlantic Conference Champions
Lambert Cup Recipient

1966

6-3

Middle Atlantic Conference Champions

1968

8-3

Boardwalk Bowl Winners (31-24 over Indiana State of Pa)
Middle Atlantic Conference Champions
Lambert Cup Recipients

Tubby's Team Captains

1979 Jim Brandimarte	1972 Dennis Johnson
1978 John Morrison	1971 Ralph Borgess
1977 Dave Bachkosky	1970 Ray Holcomb
1976 Gary Bello	1969 Joe Purzycki
1975 Curt Morgan	1968 Bob Novotny
1974 Ed Clark	1967 Art Smith
1973 Jeff Cannon	1966 Ed Sand

1969

9-2

Boardwalk Bowl Winners (31-13 over North Carolina Central)
Middle Atlantic Conference Champions
Lambert Cup Co-Recipient

The Game by Game Results of Tubby's Teams

Delaware Score	Opponent	Opponent Score	Delaware Score	Opponent	Opponent Score
	1966 (6-3)			**1970 (9-2)**	
35	Hofstra	13	39	West Chester	22
3	Gettysburg	0	34	Gettysburg	7
23	Lafayette	15	53	New Hampshire	12
14	Villanova	16	31	Villanova	34
41	Lehigh	0	36	Lafayette	20
20	Temple	14	54	Rutgers	21
6	Buffalo	36	15	Temple	13
14	Boston University	42	13	Lehigh	36
45	Bucknell	20	51	Boston University	19
			42	Bucknell	0
			38	Morgan State	23
				(Boardwalk Bowl)	
	1967 (2-7)				
17	Rhode Island	28		**1971 (10-1)**	
13	Villanova	21	39	Gettysburg	7
31	Hofstra	33	40	New Hampshire	7
21	Rutgers	29	23	Villanova	15
21	Lafayette	2	49	Lafayette	0
17	Temple	26	48	Rutgers	7
19	Buffalo	38	47	West Chester	8
33	Lehigh	10	27	Temple	32
6	Bucknell	35	49	Lehigh	22
			54	Boston University	0
			46	Bucknell	0
			72	C.W. Post	22
	1968 (8-3)			(Boardwalk Bowl)	
35	Hofstra	0			
0	Villanova	16		**1972 (10-0)**	
28	Massachusetts	23	28	Lehigh	22
17	Buffalo	29	64	Gettysburg	7
28	West Chester	0	49	Boston University	12
50	Temple	27	27	Lafayette	0
14	Rutgers	23	32	Connecticut	7
37	Lehigh	13	31	West Chester	14
41	Boston University	13	28	Temple	9
38	Bucknell	12	14	Villanova	7
31	Indiana, Pa.	24	62	Maine	0
	(Boardwalk Bowl)		20	Bucknell	3
	1969 (9-2)			**1973 (8-4)**	
52	Gettysburg	0	45	Akron	24
33	Villanova	36	49	West Chester	14
33	Massachusetts	21	60	Gettysburg	18
28	Hofstra	13	21	Lehigh	9
24	West Chester	8	56	Baldwin-Wallace	18
33	Temple	0	35	Connecticut	7
44	Rutgers	0	7	Rutgers	24
42	Lehigh	14	8	Temple	31
14	Boston University	30	7	Villanova	24
49	Bucknell	21	23	Maine	14
31	N.C. Central	13	50	Bucknell	0
	(Boardwalk Bowl)		8	Grambling	17
				(NCAA Quarterfinals)	

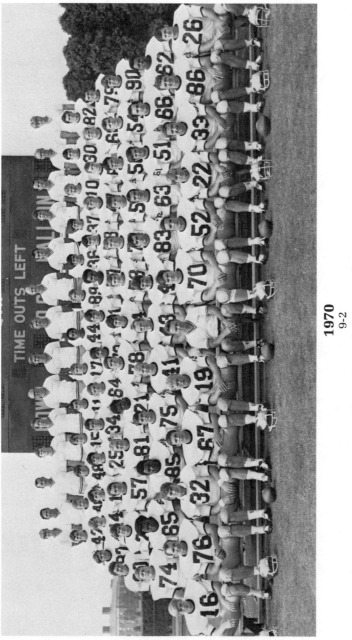

1970

9-2

Boardwalk Bowl Winners (38-23 over Morgan State)

Lambert Cup Recipients

The Game by Game Results of Tubby's Teams

Delaware Score	Opponent	Opponent Score	Delaware Score	Opponent	Opponent Score
	1974 (12-2)			**1977 (6-3-1)**	
14	Akron	0	7	Eastern Kentucky	24
48	The Citadel	12	17	West Chester	15
34	New Hampshire	10	29	Morgan State	29
29	McNeese State	24	3	Temple	6
15	Connecticut	6	23	The Citadel	7
14	Lehigh	7	16	Villanova	33
17	Temple	21	60	Middle Tennessee	7
49	Villanova	7	28	Connecticut	0
39	Maine	13	41	Davidson	7
31	West Chester	3	21	Colgate	3
51	Bucknell	16			
35	Youngstown State (NCAA Quarterfinals)	14		**1978 (10-4)**	
			37	Rhode Island	0
49	Nevada Las Vegas (NCAA Semifinals)	11	56	West Chester	0
			35	Western Illinois	7
14	Central Michigan (NCAA FINALS)	54	7	Temple	35
			17	Lehigh	27
			26	North Carolina A&T	0
			53	Middle Tennessee	3
	1975 (8-3)		14	The Citadel	21
10	V. M. I.	9	48	Maine	0
8	Wittenberg	14	23	Villanova	22
16	New Hampshire	7	38	Colgate	29
21	Akron	0	42	Jacksonville State (NCAA Quarterfinals)	27
29	Connecticut	0			
23	Lehigh	35	41	Winston-Salem (NCAA Semifinals)	0
0	Temple	45			
14	Villanova	13	9	Eastern Illinois (NCAA FINALS)	10
35	Maine	9			
35	West Chester	7			
46	Indiana State	7		**1979 (13-1)**	
			34	Rhode Island	14
			42	West Chester	6
			14	Temple	31
	1976 (8-3-1)		65	Merchant Marine	0
37	Eastern Kentucky	21	21	Lehigh	14
15	The Citadel	17	21	Villanova	20
59	North Dakota	17	47	C.W. Post	19
18	Temple	16	40	William & Mary	0
15	William and Mary	13	31	Maine	14
24	Villanova	24	51	Youngstown State	45
6	V. M. I.	10	24	Colgate	16
30	Connecticut	6	58	Virginia Union (NCAA Quarterfinals)	28
63	Davidson	0			
42	West Chester	7	60	Mississippi College (NCAA Semifinals)	10
36	Maine	0			
17	Northern Michigan (NCAA Quarterfinals)	28	38	Youngstown State (NCAA FINALS)	21

Tubby's All-Americans

First Team

1979
Herb Beck — AP — Offensive Guard
Scott Brunner — Coaches — Quarterback

1978
Jeff Komlo — AP and Coaches — Quarterback

1976
Bob Pietuszka — Coaches — Defensive Back

1975
Sam Miller — Coaches — Defensive End

1974
Ed Clark — Coaches — Linebacker
Ray Sweeney — AP — Guard

1973
Jeff Cannon — Coaches — Defensive Tackle

1972
Joe Carbone — AP — Defensive End
Bob Depew — Cosida Academic — Defensive End
Dennis Johnson — Coaches — Defensive Tackle

1971
Bill Armstrong — Universal Sports — Halfback, Fullback
Bob Depew — Cosida Academic — Defensive End
Gardy Kahoe — AP, UPI, Universal Sports, Coaches — Halfback

1970
Conway Hayman —AP and Coaches — Offensive Guard
Yancy Phillips — Cosida Academic— Offensive Tackle

Tubby's All-Americans

1969
John Favero — Coaches — Linebacker

1966
Herb Slattery — AP — Offensive Tackle

Second Team

1979
Scott Brunner — AP — Quarterback

1978
Herb Beck — AP — Offensive Tackle
John Morrison — AP — Offensive Guard

1977
Tony Glenn — AP — Center

1976
Gary Bello — AP — Linebacker
Tom James — Cosida Academic— Halfback
Paul Schweizer — Cosida Academic— Linebacker

1973
Sam Miller — Cosida Academic — Defensive End

1972
Dennis Johnson — AP — Defensive Tackle

1969
Tom DiMuzio — AP — Quarterback

Tubby's All-Americans

Third Team

1974
Nate Beasley — AP — Fullback

1970
Chuck Hall — AP — Fullback

Honorable Mention

1979
Bo Dennis — AP — Fullback
Mike Donnalley — AP — Center
Vince Hyland — AP — Cornerback
Guy Ramsey — AP — Cornerback
Mike Wisniewski — AP — Linebacker
Jaime Young — AP — Tight End

1977
Herb Beck — AP — Defensive Tackle

1976
Dave Fritz — AP — Offensive Tackle

1974
Bill Cubit — AP — Safety, End
Gene Fischi — AP — Defensive Tackle

1973
Jeff Cannon — AP — Defensive Tackle
Blair Caviness — AP — Halfback

Tubby's All-Americans

1972
Bob Depew — AP — Defensive End

1971
Dennis Johnson — AP — Defensive Tackle
Tom Morin — AP — Center, Guard

1970
Chuck Hall — Coaches — Fullback

1969
Joe Purzycki — AP — Defensive Back

The August V. Lambert
Memorial Cup

Lambert Cup Winners

The Cup is presented annually for outstanding achievement among middle-sized colleges in the East. Past winners, year by year, have been:

1979 DELAWARE	1968 DELAWARE
1978 Massachusetts	1967 West Chester
1977 Lehigh	1966 Gettysburg
1976 DELAWARE	1965 Maine
1975 Lehigh	1964 Bucknell
1974 DELAWARE	1963 DELAWARE
1973 DELAWARE/Lehigh*	1962 DELAWARE
1972 DELAWARE	1961 Lehigh
1971 DELAWARE	1960 Bucknell
1970 DELAWARE	1959 DELAWARE
1969 DELAWARE/Wesleyan*	1958 Buffalo

1957
Lehigh

*Co-Recipients

1971
10-1

AP National College Division Title
UPI National College Division Title
Washington Touchdown Club National College Division Title
Boardwalk Bowl Winners (72-22 over C.W. Post)
Lambert Cup Recipients

Delaware in the National Rankings

NCAA
Coaches Poll

1979 — FIRST
1978 — Third
1976 — Fourth

ASSOCIATED PRESS Writers and Broadcasters Poll	UNITED PRESS Coaches Poll
1976 — Fourth	1974 — Fourth
1974 — Fourth	1973 — Tenth
1973 — Thirteenth	1972 — FIRST
1972 — FIRST	1971 — FIRST
1971 — FIRST	1970 — Eighth
1970 — Eleventh	1969 — Tenth
1969 — Tenth	1963 — FIRST
1963 — Second	1962 — Ninth
	1959 — Fourth

Since 1976 the NCAA has had a coaches poll to replace wire service rankings.

1972
10-0

AP National College Division Title
UPI National College Division Title
Washington Touchdown Club National College Division Title
National Football Foundation and Hall of Fame
National College Division Co-Title with Louisiana Tech
University's First Ever 10-0 Regular Season Record
Lambert Cup Recipients

Delaware 1,000-Yard Rushing Club

		Yards
1.	Chuck Hall, Fullback (1968-70)	3,157
2.	Vern Roberts, Halfback (1972-74)	2,760
3.	Nate Beasley, Fullback (1973-75)	2,697
4.	Gardy Kahoe, Halfback (1969-71)	2,374
5.	Bill Armstrong, Halfback, Fullback (1969-71)	2,340
6.	Dick Kelley, Halfback (1968-70)	2,046
7.	Blair Caviness, Halfback (1971-73)	1,870
8.	Jack Turner, Halfback (1957-59)	1,785
9.	Craig Carroll, Halfback (1975-77)	1,762
10.	Mariano Stalloni, Fullback (1961-63)	1,719
11.	Mike Brown, Halfback (1961-63)	1,675
12.	Jimmy Zaiser, Halfback (1953-55)	1,628
13.	Brian Wright, Halfback (1965-67)	1,558
14.	Jimmy Flynn, Halfback (1951-54)	1,387
15.	Bo Dennis, Fullback (1978-79)	1,368
16.	Ivory Sully, Halfback (1976-78)	1,359
17.	Lou Mariani, Halfback (1977-79)	1,272
18.	Bill Hopkins, Halfback (1962-64)	1,265
19.	Tom James, Halfback (1974-76)	1,234
20.	Roger Mason, Fullback (1970-72)	1,227
21.	Tony Toto, Halfback (1955-57)	1,195
22.	John Spangler, Fullback (1966-67)	1,116
23.	Andy Wagner, Halfback (1953-55)	1,053
24.	Theo Gregory, Fullback (1972-73)	1,041
25.	Bob Moneymaker, Halfback (1954-56)	1,031

1973
8-4

Played in First NCAA College Division Playoffs
Lambert Cup Co-Recipients

Individual Blue Hen Records

Rushing

MOST ATTEMPTS (one game) — 45
 Roger Mason vs. Temple, 1972 (gained 182 yards)
MOST ATTEMPTS (one season) — 248
 Nate Beasley, 1975 (1,077 yards)
MOST ATTEMPTS (career) — 604
 Chuck Hall, 1968-70 (gained 3,157 yards)
MOST YARDS GAINED (one game) — 220
 Gerald "Doc" Doherty vs. Gettysburg, 1946
MOST YARDS GAINED (one season) — 1,397
 Nate Beasley, 1974 (236 attempts)
MOST YARDS GAINED (career) — 3,157
 Chuck Hall, 1968-70 (604 attempts)
HIGHEST AVERAGE YARDS GAINED PER GAME
  (one season) — 143.0
 Tony Toto, 1957 (715 yards in five games)
HIGHEST AVERAGE YARDS GAINED PER GAME (career) — 95.7
 Chuck Hall, 1968-70 (3,157 yards in 33 games)
LONGEST RUN FROM SCRIMMAGE — 98
 Jim Zaiser vs. Muhlenberg, 1953
 Harold (Buck) Thompson vs. Western Maryland, 1946
BEST AVERAGE PER CARRY (one season) — 8.5
 Tony Toto, 1957 (715 yards)

Passing

MOST PASSES COMPLETED (one game) — 22
 Tom DiMuzio vs. Lehigh, 1969
 Frank Linzenbold vs. Rutgers, 1967
MOST PASSES COMPLETED (one season) — 188
 Jeff Komlo, 1978 (332 attempts)
MOST PASSES COMPLETED (career) — 359
 Jeff Komlo, 1976-78 (686 attempts)
MOST PASSES ATTEMPTED (one game) — 42
 Frank Linzenbold vs. Buffalo, 1967, and vs. Rutgers, 1967

MOST PASSES ATTEMPTED (one season) — 332
  Jeff Komlo, 1978 (14 games)
MOST PASSES ATTEMPTED (career) — 686
  Jeff Komlo, 1976-78 (36 games)
MOST PASSES INTERCEPTED (one season) — 16
  Scott Brunner, 1979 (268 attempted)
  Jeff Komlo, 1976 (143 attempted)
MOST PASSES INTERCEPTED (career) — 43
  Jeff Komlo, 1976-78 (686 attempted)
MOST YARDS GAINED PASSING (one game) — 369
  Tom DiMuzio vs. Lehigh, 1969 (22 completions)
MOST YARDS GAINED PASSING (one season) — 2,677
  Jeff Komlo, 1978 (14 games)
MOST YARDS GAINED PASSING (career) — 5,256
  Jeff Komlo, 1976-78 (36 games)
TOUCHDOWN PASSES (one game) — 5
  Scott Brunner vs. C. W. Post, 1979
  Tom DiMuzio vs. Lehigh, 1969
TOUCHDOWN PASSES (one season) — 24
  Scott Brunner, 1979 (14 games)
  Tom DiMuzio, 1969 (11 games)
TOUCHDOWN PASSES (career) — 38
  Tom DiMuzio, 1967-69 (29 games)
BEST PASSING EFFICIENCY (one season) — .619
  Jim Breyer, 1958 (39 completions in 63 attempts)
LONGEST COMPLETED PASS — 87
  Tom DiMuzio to Pat Walker vs. Villanova, 1969

Total Offense

MOST PLAYS (one season) — 443
  Jeff Komlo, 1978 (332 passes, 111 rushes)
MOST PLAYS (career) — 840
  Jeff Komlo, 1976-78 (686 passes, 224 rushes)
MOST YARDS GAINED (one game) — 376
  Tom DiMuzio vs. Lehigh, 1969 (41 plays)
MOST YARDS GAINED (one season) — 2,620
  Jeff Komlo, 1978 (14 games)
MOST YARDS GAINED (career) — 5,417
  Jeff Komlo, 1976-78 (36 games)

Scoring

MOST POINTS (one game) — 27
  Ed Thompson, 1936
MOST POINTS (one season) — 144
  Gardy Kahoe, 1971 (11 games)
MOST POINTS (career) — 268
  Vern Roberts, 1972-74
MOST TOUCHDOWNS (one season) — 24
  Gardy Kahoe, 1971 (11 games)
MOST TOUCHDOWNS (career) — 42
  Vern Roberts, 1972-74
MOST FIELD GOALS (one season) — 12
  Brandt Kennedy, 1978 (19 attempts)
MOST FIELD GOALS (career) — 21
  Brandt Kennedy, 1977-1979 (42 attempts)
LONGEST FIELD GOAL — 48
  Hank Kline vs. Villanova, 1976
MOST PAT BY KICKING ATTEMPTED (one game) — 10
  Larry Washington vs. C. W. Post, 1971
MOST PAT BY KICKING ATTEMPTED (one season) — 64
  Brandt Kennedy 1979 (14 games)
MOST PAT BY KICKING MADE (one game) — 10
  Larry Washington vs. C. W. Post, 1971
MOST PAT BY KICKING MADE (one season) — 62
  Brandt Kennedy, 1979 (64 attempts, 14 games)
MOST CONSECUTIVE PAT BY KICKING — 33
  Hank Kline, 1975-76 (last 26 of 1975 season,
    first 7 of 1976 season)

Pass Receiving

MOST RECEPTIONS (one game) — 12
  Brian Adam vs. Villanova, 1977
MOST RECEPTIONS (one season) — 57
  Pete Ravettine, 1978 (14 games)
MOST RECEPTIONS (career) — 118
  Ron Withelder, 1967-69
MOST YARDS GAINED RECEIVING (one game) — 208
  Pete Ravettine vs. Middle Tennessee, 1978 (9 receptions)

MOST YARDS GAINED RECEIVING (one season) — 1,036
  Jay Hooks, 1979 (14 games, 49 receptions)
MOST YARDS GAINED RECEIVING (career) — 1,880
  Ron Withelder, 1967-69
MOST TOUCHDOWN RECEPTIONS (one game) — 3
  Pete Johnson vs. New Hampshire, 1971
  Paul Mueller vs. Lehigh, 1965
  Mike Purzycki vs. Rutgers, 1964
MOST TOUCHDOWN RECEPTIONS (one season) — 12
  Pat Walker, 1969 (11 games)
MOST TOUCHDOWN RECEPTIONS (career) — 15
  Pat Walker, 1968-70

Punting

MOST PUNTS (one season) — 63
  Al Brown, 1973 (12 games)
BEST PUNTING AVERAGE (one season) — 39.1
  Tom Van Grofski, 1965 (37 kicks)

Interceptions

MOST INTERCEPTIONS (one game) — 3
  K. C. Keeler vs. Jacksonville State, 1978
  Mike Randolph vs. Colgate, 1977
  Ken Bills vs. Buffalo, 1964
MOST INTERCEPTIONS (one season) — 9
  Joe Purzycki, 1969 (11 games)
MOST INTERCEPTIONS (career) — 15
  Ron Klein, 1968-70
MOST YARDS INTERCEPTIONS RETURNED (one game) — 106
  Clint Ware vs. Lehigh, 1962
MOST YARDS INTERCEPTIONS RETURNED (one season) — 195
  Jim O'Brien, 1971 (5 interceptions in 11 games)
MOST YARDS INTERCEPTIONS RETURNED (career) — 245
  Bruce Fad, 1968-70
LONGEST INTERCEPTION RETURN — 100
  John Bush vs. Temple, 1972
MOST TOUCHDOWNS BY INTERCEPTIONS (one season) — 2
  Jim O'Brien, 1971
  Jack Istnick, 1963

Punt and Kick Returns

MOST PUNT RETURNS (one season) — 31
   John Bush, 1971 (11 games)
   Herky Billings, 1973 (12 games)
MOST PUNT RETURNS (career) — 50
   Steve Schwartz, 1973-75
MOST YARDS PUNTS RETURNED (one season) — 310
   John Bush, 1971
MOST YARDS PUNTS RETURNED (career) — 488
   John Bush, 1970-72
LONGEST PUNT RETURN — 83
   Bruce Carlyle vs. Boston U., 1965
MOST KICKOFF RETURNS (one season) — 21
   Steve Schwartz, 1974 (459 yards)
MOST KICKOFF RETURNS (career) — 39
   Sam Brickley, 1968-69
MOST YARDS KICKOFFS RETURNED (one season) — 460
   Sam Brickley, 1968 (11 games)
MOST YARDS KICKOFFS RETURNED (career) — 793
   Sam Brickley, 1967-69
LONGEST KICKOFF RETURN — 99
   Buck Thompson vs. Western Maryland, 1946

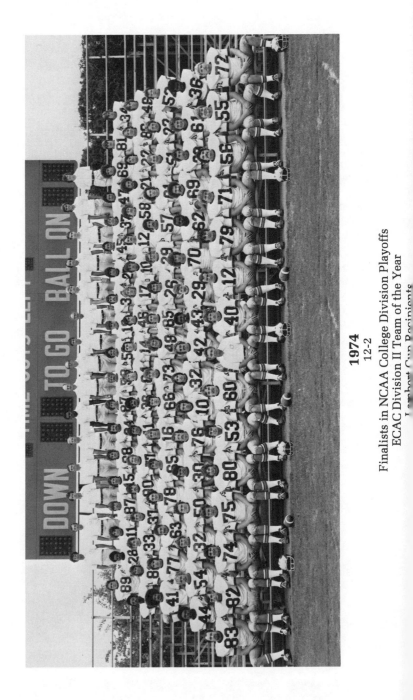

1974
12-2

Finalists in NCAA College Division Playoffs
ECAC Division II Team of the Year
Lambert Cup Recipients

Blue Hen Team Records

	Delaware	Opponents

FIRST DOWNS

Most, Game	42 vs. Baldwin-Wallace, 1973	24 by Buffalo, 1964
Fewest, Game	4 vs. Bucknell, 1964	2 by Connecticut, 1957

RUSHING

Carries, Game	82 vs. Temple, 1968	69 by Lafayette, 1956
Fewest Carries, Game	27 vs. Lafayette, 1956	18 by Lehigh, 1962
Yards, Game	520 vs. Lehigh, 1971	367 by Villanova, 1977
Fewest Yards, Game	−23 vs. Grambling, 1973	−55 by C. W. Post, 1971
Yards, Season	4,256 (11 games) 1970	

PASSING

Attempts, Game	44 vs. Rutgers, 1967	51 by Colgate, 1978
Fewest Attempts, Game	2 vs. Temple, 1962	2 by Connecticut, 1957
Completions, Game	23 vs. Rutgers, 1967	31 by Colgate, 1978
Fewest Completions, Game	0 vs. Marshall, 1959	1 by Lafayette, 1958
	0 vs. West Chester, 1970	Connecticut, 1957, 1958
	0 vs. Temple, 1973	Bucknell, 1955, 1972
Yards, Game	380 vs. Lehigh, 1969	482 by Colgate, 1978
Fewest Yards, Game	0 vs. Marshall, 1959	4 by Connecticut, 1957
	0 vs. West Chester, 1970	
	0 vs. Temple, 1973	
Yards, Season	2,926 (14 games) 1978	2,202 (14 games) 1978
Interceptions, Game	6 vs. West Chester, 1978	4 by Eastern Ky., 1976
		Villanova, 1979
Interceptions, Season	35 (9 games) 1946	

TOTAL OFFENSE

Yards, Game	676 vs. Baldwin-Wallace, 1973	520 by Villanova, 1969
Lowest, Game	76 vs. Bucknell, 1964	16 by Temple, 1969
Yards, Season	6,553 (14 games) 1978	3,843 (14 games) 1979

SCORING

Quarter	59 vs. William and Mary, 1915 (W 93-0)	
	39 vs. Middle Tennessee, 1977 (Second Quarter) (W 60-7)	
Game	93 vs. William and Mary, 1915 (93-0)	89 by Pennsylvania 1919 (89-0)
	72 vs. C. W. Post 1971 (72-22)	89 by Pennsylvania 1921 (89-0)
Season	546 (14 games), 1979	222 (9 games), 1967
	494 (11 games), 1971	
	358 (10) games, 1946	

ATTENDANCE

Opening Day	Wittenberg, 1975 (H) 20,132
Regular Season	Temple, 1973 (H) 23,619
All-Time Single Game	Temple, 1974 (A) 37,265

VICTORIES

Most Wins, Season	13 (1979, 13-1)
Consecutive Wins	26 (1941-1947)

1976

8-3-1

Quarterfinalists in NCAA College Division Playoffs

ECAC Division II Team of the Year

Lambert Cup Recipient

Delaware Stadium Records

INDIVIDUAL

Rushing

Most Attempts — 35, Beasley (Del.) vs. Akron, 1975
Most Yards Gained — 217, Kelley (Del.) vs. Mass., 1968
217, Roberts (Del.) vs. Akron, 1973

Passing

Most Completed Passes — 31, Marzo (Colgate), 1978
Most Passes Attempted — 51, Marzo (Colgate), 1978
Most Yards Gained Passing — 482, Marzo (Colgate), 1978

Receiving

Most Receptions — 10, Purzycki (Del.) vs. Bucknell, 1966
10, Cubit (Del.) vs. Bucknell, 1973
Most Yards Gained Receiving — 209, Lenhard (Bucknell), 1966

Field Goals

Longest — 52, Leggett (Maine), 1975

TEAM

Most First Downs — 42, Del. vs. Baldwin-Wallace, 1973
Most Yards Rushing — 520, Del. vs. Lehigh, 1971
Most Passing Attempts — 51, Colgate, 1978
Most Completions — 39, Temple, 1967
Most Yards Passing — 482, Colgate, 1978
Total Offense — 676, Del. vs. Baldwin-Wallace, 1973
Punts — 12, West Chester, 1969
Fumbles Lost — 8, West Chester, 1975
Highest Attendance — 23,619 vs. Temple, 1973
Highest Score — 71-7, vs. Temple, (Del. Wins), 1957

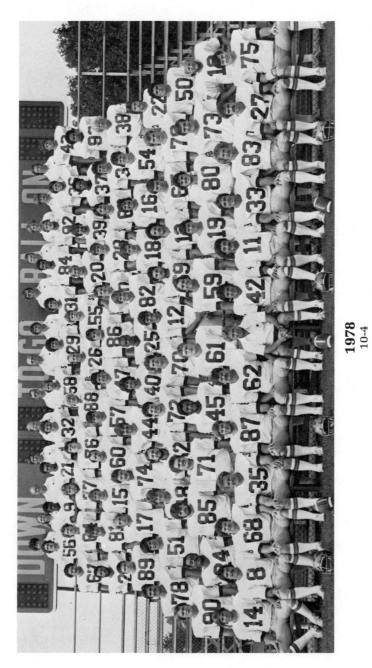

1978
10-4

Finalist in NCAA College Division Playoffs
ECAC Division II Team of the Year

Delaware Stadium Attendance
Ranking and Per Game Average

IN THE EAST		IN THE NATION
10th	$\dfrac{1979}{19,644}$	89th
9th	$\dfrac{1978}{19,009}$	90th
9th	$\dfrac{1977}{19,032}$	87th
10th	$\dfrac{1976}{17,392}$	88th
7th	$\dfrac{1975}{18,939}$	81st
11th	$\dfrac{1974}{19,112}$	82nd
10th	$\dfrac{1973}{19,037}$	83rd
10th	$\dfrac{1972}{18,881}$	80th
13th	$\dfrac{1971}{18,971}$	80th
11th	$\dfrac{1970}{16,438}$	88th
13th	$\dfrac{1969}{13,831}$	99th

1979

13-1

Washington Touchdown Club National College Division Title
NCAA National Division II Football Champions
ECAC Division II Team of the Year
Lambert Cup Recipient

Blue Hen Game by Game Total Offense
1968 - 1979

Opponent	Score	Won Lost	Total Yards	Year
Baldwin-Wallace	56-18	W	676	1973
Boston U.	54-0	W	675	1971
Gettysburg	52-0	W	646	1969
Middle Tennessee	53-0	W	646	1978
West Chester	47-8	W	624	1971
C. W. Post	72-22	W	623	1971
Maine	48-0	W	611	1978
William & Mary	40-0	W	602	1979
North Carolina A&T	26-0	W	599	1978
Lehigh	49-22	W	598	1971
Lafayette	49-0	W	593	1971
Mississippi College	60-10	W	590	1979
Rutgers	54-21	W	588	1970
Maine	39-13	W	582	1974
Lehigh	37-13	W	578	1968
Boston U.	41-13	W	573	1968
Rutgers	44-0	W	572	1969
Bucknell	46-0	W	570	1971
Merchant Marine Academy	65-0	W	567	1979
Rhode Island	37-0	W	564	1978
Bucknell	38-12	W	556	1968
Nevada LasVegas	49-11	W	553	1974
Youngstown State	51-45	W	552	1979
Bucknell	51-16	W	551	1974
North Dakota	59-17	W	549	1976
Villanova	49-7	W	544	1974
West Chester	56-0	W	537	1978
Hofstra	35-0	W	534	1968
Temple	33-0	W	533	1969
Maine	36-0	W	530	1976

Opponent	Score	Won Lost	Total Yards	Year
Lehigh	42-14	W	529	1969
N. Carolina Central	31-13	W	527	1969
Morgan State	38-23	W	526	1970
Bucknell	49-21	W	523	1969
New Hampshire	40-7	W	520	1971
C. W. Post	47-19	W	519	1979
West Chester	35-7	W	519	1975
Gettysburg	60-18	W	517	1973
Jacksonville State	42-27	W	516	1978
Middle Tennessee	60-7	W	514	1977
Temple	50-27	W	513	1968
Western Illinois	35-7	W	513	1978
Villanova	21-20	W	509	1979
Davidson	63-0	W	508	1976
Winston-Salem State	41-0	W	508	1978
Villanova	33-36	L	502	1969
Temple	27-32	L	501	1971
The Citadel	48-12	W	501	1974
Lafayette	36-20	W	500	1970
Maine	35-9	W	499	1975
West Chester	39-22	W	496	1970
West Chester	24-8	W	493	1969
New Hampshire	53-12	W	492	1970
Rutgers	48-7	W	487	1971
Gettysburg	64-7	W	486	1972
Indiana, Pa.	31-24	W	482	1968
Hofstra	28-13	W	482	1969
Youngstown State (Championship Game)	38-21	W	477	1979
Indiana St. (Ind.)	46-7	W	475	1975
Boston U.	49-12	W	465	1972
Gettysburg	34-7	W	461	1970
Akron	45-24	W	458	1973
The Citadel	14-21	L	457	1978

Opponent	Score	Won Lost	Total Yards	Year
New Hampshire	34-10	W	456	1974
Massachusetts	33-21	W	455	1969
Bucknell	50-0	W	452	1973
Virginia Union	58-28	W	449	1979
Lehigh	21-9	W	449	1973
Lehigh	23-35	L	446	1975
Maine	31-14	W	445	1979
Colgate	24-16	W	442	1979
Rhode Island	34-14	W	442	1979
Villanova	24-31	L	439	1970
West Chester	49-14	W	435	1973
Bucknell	42-0	W	435	1970
Lehigh	14-7	W	433	1974
West Chester	28-0	W	432	1968
West Chester	31-3	W	428	1974
Maine	62-0	W	426	1972
Boston U.	51-19	W	425	1970
The Citadel	23-7	W	423	1977
Morgan State	29-29	T	422	1977
Akron	14-0	W	422	1974
Colgate	21-3	W	419	1977
Lafayette	27-0	W	415	1972
Connecticut	32-7	W	414	1972
Colgate	38-29	W	413	1978
West Chester	42-7	W	409	1976
Bucknell	20-3	W	403	1972
West Chester	31-14	W	399	1972
Gettysburg	39-7	W	389	1971
West Chester	42-6	W	388	1979
Eastern Illinois	9-10	L	387	1978
VMI	6-10	L	386	1976
Massachusetts	28-23	W	383	1968
Villanova	24-24	T	378	1976
Akron	21-0	W	376	1975

Opponent	Score	Won Lost	Total Yards	Year
Connecticut	29-0	W	373	1975
Connecticut	28-0	W	364	1977
West Chester	17-15	W	364	1977
Boston U.	14-30	L	359	1969
Villanova	16-33	L	354	1977
Central Michigan	14-54	L	354	1974
Temple	15-13	W	350	1970
McNeese State	29-24	W	348	1974
William & Mary	15-13	W	346	1976
Lehigh	28-22	W	344	1972
Temple	3-6	L	340	1977
Connecticut	35-7	W	326	1973
Buffalo	17-29	L	323	1968
Eastern Kentucky	37-21	W	316	1976
Connecticut	15-6	W	314	1974
Northern Michigan	17-28	L	314	1976
Maine	28-12	W	310	1973
Davidson	41-7	W	304	1977
Lehigh	13-36	L	302	1970
Villanova	23-22	W	302	1978
Lehigh	17-27	L	300	1978
Temple	18-16	W	295	1976
Wittenberg	8-14	L	292	1975
Rutgers	7-24	L	288	1973
Lehigh	21-14	W	283	1979
New Hampshire	16-7	W	283	1975
Connecticut	30-6	W	263	1976
Villanova	0-16	L	255	1968
VMI	10-9	W	254	1975
Youngstown State	35-14	W	253	1974
Eastern Kentucky	7-24	L	252	1977
Villanova	14-13	W	252	1975
The Citadel	15-17	L	249	1976
Temple	7-35	L	248	1978

Opponent	Score	Won Lost	Total Yards	Year
Villanova	7-24	L	244	1973
Temple	28-9	W	238	1972
Temple	14-31	L	232	1979
Villanova	14-7	W	220	1972
Temple	8-31	L	217	1973
Villanova	23-15	W	200	1971
Temple	17-21	L	187	1974
Temple	0-45	L	164	1975
Grambling	8-17	L	85	1973

Overall Blue Hen Football Record
1889-1979

Year	Won	Lost	Tied	Year	Won	Lost	Tied
1889	1	1	1				
1890	2	2	0	**Stan Baumgartner**			
1891	5	3	1	(2—5—0)			
1892	1	2	2	1917	2	5	0
1893	2	1	0				
1894	1	1	0	**Lt. Milton Arronwitz**			
1895	1	3	0	(1—2—2)			
1896	0	5	0	1918	1	2	2
1897	2	4	1				
				H. B. Shipley			
Herbert L. Rice				(5—10—2)			
(14—15—2)				1919	2	5	1
1898	1	6	1	1920	3	5	1
1899	6	2	0				
1900	2	3	1	**Sylvester R. Derby**			
1901	5	4	0	(5—4—0)			
				1921	5	4	0
C.A. Short							
(3—5—1)				**William J. McAvoy**			
				(15—9—2)			
1902	3	5	1	1922	6	3	0
				1923	5	3	1
Nathan A. Mannakee				1924	4	3	1
(8—13—2)							
1903	4	4	0	**R. M. Forstburg**			
1904	1	5	1	(9—14—1)			
1905	3	4	1	1925	4	4	0
				1926	3	5	0
C. A. Short				1927	2	5	1
(5—1—0)							
1906	5	1	0	**Joseph J. Rothrock**			
				(2—6—0)			
E. Pratt King				1928	2	6	0
(0—5—1)							
1907	0	5	1	**A. B. Ziegler**			
				(6—10—2)			
William J. McAvoy				1929	0	7	1
(27—34—11)				1930	6	3	1
1908	3	4	1				
1909	1	6	1	**Charles Rogers**			
1910	1	2	2	(12—9—4)			
1911	2	5	2	1931	5	1	2
1912	1	6	1	1932	5	4	0
1913	2	4	2	1933	2	4	2
1914	7	1	1				
1915	6	3	0	**J. Neil Stahley**			
1916	4	3	1	(4—3—1)			
				1934	4	3	1

Overall Blue Hen Football Record
1889 - 1979

Year	Won	Lost	Tied	Year	Won	Lost	Tied
Lyal W. Clark				**Harold R. Raymond**			
(5—18—1)				(119—38—2)			
1935	2	5	1	1966	6	3	0
1936	2	6	0	1967	2	7	0
1937	1	7	0	1968	8	3	0
				1969	9	2	0
Stephen J. Grenda				1970	9	2	0
(4—12—0)				1971	10	1	0
1938	3	5	0	1972	10	0	0
1939	1	7	0	1973	8	4	0
				1974	12	2	0
William D. Murray				1975	8	3	0
(49—16—2)				1976	8	3	1
1940	5	3	0	1977	6	3	1
1941	7	0	1	1978	10	4	0
1942	8	0	0	1979	13	1	0

1943-45—no formal teams during World War II

Year	Won	Lost	Tied
1946	10	0	0
1947	4	4	0
1948	5	3	0
1949	8	1	0
1950	2	5	1
David M. Nelson			
(84—42—2)			
1951	5	3	0
1952	4	4	0
1953	7	1	0
1954	8	2	0
1955	8	1	0
1956	5	3	1
1957	4	3	0
1958	5	3	0
1959	8	1	0
1960	2	6	1
1961	4	4	0
1962	7	2	0
1963	8	0	0
1964	4	5	0
1965	5	4	0

88 Seasons — 394 Wins — 293 Losses — 43 Ties

Blue Hen Football Lettermen
1889-1979

A

Adam,B.: 1975, '76, '77
Adams,M.: 1950, '51
Adkins,J.B.: 1906, '07, '08
Ainsworth,C.: 1975
Akin,M.A.: 1920, '21, '22, '23
Albertson,J.B.: 1969
Alexander,H.B.: 1920
Allan,C.C. Jr.: 1937, '38
Alleman,T.: 1964
Allen,G.: 1974, '76
Allen,J.: 1951, '52, '53
Allen,R.: 1974
Allen,W.: 1954, '55
Ameche,A.: 1975
Anderson,E.: 1965
Angeli,R.: 1971
Apostolico,M.: 1953, '54
Apsley,W.V.: 1937, '39, '40
Armor,J.P.: 1918, '19
Armstrong,E.S.: 1892
Armstrong,J.P.: 1889, '90, '91
Armstrong,W.: 1969, '70, '71
Aschenback,A.A.: 1916
Attix,J.G.: 1909, '10, '11
Avery,C.: 1968, '69, '70
Ayerst,D.B.: 1910

B

Bachkosky,D.: 1975, '76, '77
Bachman,K.M.: 1978, '79
Baer,G.L.: 1939, '40, '41, '42
Baker,J.: 1979
Baker,O.: 1960, '61
Baldwin,J.F.Jr.: 1904, '05, '06, '07
Baldwin,W.R.: 1895, '96, '97
Ball,J.Jr.: 1889
Barbieri,M.: 1968, '70, '71
Barkley,F.W.: 1925
Barlow,G.E.Jr.: 1942
Barrabee,B.: 1963, '64
Bartlett,F.R.: 1894
Barton,A.S.: 1927, '28
Baston,S.: 1976, '77
Bauman,J.: 1966
Baxter,W.P.: 1924
Beasley,N.: 1973, '74, '75
Beatty,E.H.: 1924, '26

Beck,H.: 1976, '77, '78, '79
Bedford,T.A.: 1889
Beinner,D.: 1958, '59, '60
Belcher,V.M.: 1978, '79
Belicic,B.: 1974, '75, '76
Bell,H.A.: 1903, '04
Bell,R.: 1971, '72
Bello,G.: 1974, '75, '76
Bennett,J.: 1970, '71, '72
Benson,D.A.: 1926, '27, '28, '29
Bergh,B.: 1970
Betzmer,H.J.: 1920
Bevan,W.T.: 1901, '02, '03, '04
Bianco,R.: 1962, '63, '64
Bice,J.B.: 1909
Bills,K.: 1964, '65, '66
Bistrian,P.: 1977, '78, '79
Billings,H.: 1972, '73, '74
Bilski,S.W.: 1947, '48, '49
Bitter,J.: 1979
Blair,M.: 1968, '69, '70
Boc,J.: 1979
Boggs,J.C.: 1929
Bogovich,H.M.: 1939, '40, '41, '42
Bonodonna,R.: 1966
Boneli,T.: 1949, '50
Bookhammer,S.A.: 1889, '90, '91
Boorse,D.: 1948, '49, '50
Booth,J.M.: 1978, '79
Booth,J.W.: 1977, '78, '79
Booth,W.: 1973, '74
Borgess,R.: 1969, '70, '71
Borreson,A.J.: 1976
Borreson,J.: 1951, '52, '53
Bosher,T.: 1973, '74, '75
Bowen,M.: 1979
Bowler,R.W.E.: 1904
Bowman,J.: 1956, '58, '59
Bowman,U.: 1957, '58, '60
Boyce,W.D.: 1922
Boyd,M.: 1959, '60
Boyer,W.B.Jr.: 1926, '27
Braceland,E.: 1978, '79
Brandimarte,J.R.: 1978, '79
Branner,J.D.Jr.: 1930, '31, '32, '33
Bratton,H.J.Jr.: 1915
Bratton,T.: 1971
Bratton,W.J.: 1907
Brayer,R.: 1961

Crocker,E.G.: 1935
Crothers,J.A.: 1914, '15
Crothers,J.L.: 1918, '19
Crowe,J.J.Jr.: 1932, '33, '34
Csatari,W.: 1964, '65
Cubit,W.: 1973, '74

D

Dalton,L.: 1950, '51, '56
Daly,J.P.Jr.: 1936, '37
Davis,E.C.: 1902
Davis,G.: 1972, '73
Davis,G.N.: 1895, '96, '97
Davis,J.: 1933
Davis,J.C.: 1925
Dean,A.H.: 1911, '12
Dean,F.: 1911
DeCarlo,M.: 1971, '72
DeGasperis,J.: 1949, '50, '51
DeLuca,J.J.: 1918, '19, '20
DeLucas,T.: 1955, '56, '57
Dennis,K.B.: 1977, '78, '79
Depew,R.: 1971, '72
Detar,D.T.: 1977
DeVries,C.: 1979
DiBartolomeo,M.: 1971, '72
DiJoseph,L.C.: 1926, '27, '28
Dillon,H.V.: 1930, '31, '32
Dillon,J.F.: 1934, '35, '36
DiMaio,B.: 1973, '74
DiMuzio,T.: 1967, '68, '69
Doan,W.R.: 1908
Doherty,G.P.III: 1941, '46, '47
Dolente,D.S.: 1977, '78
Dombroski,L.: 1957, '58, '59
Doppstadt,W.: 1951, '52
Donalson,J.H.: 1920, '21, '22, '23
Donnalley,M.F.: 1977, '78, '79
Donofrio,N.: 1968, '69, '70
Donohue,J.T.: 1908
Donolli,J.: 1964
Dougherty,H.F.: 1978, '79
Dowling,R.: 1961, '62, '63
Draper,W.R.: 1925, '27, '28
Drozdov.P.A.: 1934, '35, '36, '37
Drueding,W.: 1963, '64, '65
Duerr,R.: 1958
Duncan,R.B.: 1946

E

Eberle, J.: 1951
Ebersole,B.: 1972, '73, '74
Edmonston,G.H.Jr.: 1890, '91, '92
Edwards,L.P.: 1906, '07, '08

Elder,T.: 1960, '61
Elliott,I.S.: 1920, '22, '23
Emmons,L.: 1967, '68, '69
Emslie,C.: 1976
Ennis,D.: 1960
Ennis,H.T.: 1911
Evan,J.: 1955
Evans,H.C.: 1900, '01
Evers,R.: 1961

F

Fad,B.: 1968, '69, '70
Fad,O.: 1957, '58, '59
Falcione,R.: 1974, '75
Falivene,T.: 1975
Fannon,T.: 1951, '52, '53
Farrand,D.: 1973
Favero,A.: 1974
Favero,J.: 1967, '68, '69
Fay,M,: 1964
Federici,M.: 1974
Feller,J.: 1959
Ferguson,B.: 1901, '02, '03
Ferrell,C.: 1937
Fetterman,B.: 1959, '60, '61
Fidance,M.J.: 1914, '15, '16
Figg,C.: 1979
Fischi,G.: 1972, '73, '74
Fitzpatrick,W.S.: 1915
Flynn,J.: 1951, '52, '53, '54
Flynn,J.J.: 1927
Ford,D.: 1951, '52, '53, '54
Ford,J.: 1951
Foster,H.M.: 1913
Foster,R.: 1971, '72, '73
Foulk,R.N.: 1918, '19, '20
Fox,G.: 1972, '73
Frame,T.C.Jr.: 1889
Francis,W.M.: 1905, '06
Frankofsky,F.W.: 1936
Frantz,K.: 1957, '58, '59
Frantz,P.: 1972
Frazer,J.H.: 1900, '01
Freebery,J.: 1964, '65
Frey,J.: 1963, '64
Frith,W.: 1962, '63, '64
Fritz,D.: 1975, '76
Fugazzi,R.: 1973, '74, '75
Fulling,R.W.: 1929
Funk,V.: 1971, '72
Furman,R.G.: 1941, '42

G

Galeone,G.: 1974, '75
Gallagher,J.L.Jr.: 1946, '47, '48, '49
Gallira,C.: 1971, '72, '73
Garrick,J.F.: 1903, '04
Garvin,J.: 1958, '59
Garvine,P.: 1923
Gaszynski,R.: 1979
Gearhart,W.: 1971, '72
Geisler,J.D.: 1968, '69, '70
Gemp,R.: 1960
Genther,P.D.: 1947, '48, '49
George,E.: 1936, '37, '38
Gibbons,J.: 1963, '64, '65
Gibson,C.W.: 1924
Gill,M.: 1977
Girman,T.: 1974, '75
Glaspey,A.S.: 1937, '38
Glasser,M.: 1925, '26, '27, '28
Glenn,S.: 1975, '76, '77
Glisson,R.: 1946, '47, '48
Glover,J.S.: 1934, '35
Godek,J.: 1966
Goffigon,O.W.: 1921, '22
Good,P.: 1977
Gouert,C.E.: 1933, '34, '35
Graham,E.F.: 1936
Graham,H.: 1952, '53
Grande,V.: 1954, '55
Graves,R.: 1918, '19
Gray,V.T.: 1914
Green,H.: 1898
Green,J.F.: 1930, '31, '32, '33
Green,L.: 1902, '03
Green,R.B.: 1974, '75
Green,S.: 1964, '65, '66
Green,W.J.: 1926, '27
Greenwood,L.W.: 1908
Gregory,T.: 1968, '69, '70
Gregory,Theo.: 1972, '73
Grieves,H.D.: 1914
Griffin,D.: 1956
Griffith,B.: 1970, '71
Groetzinger,W.: 1949, '50
Grossman,W.: 1960, '61, '62
Groff,F.: 1913, '14
Groves,J.S.: 1900
Grundy,J.W.: 1938, '39, '40
Gudzak,P.: 1979
Guerriero,M.: 1967
Gumbs,G.E.: 1978
Guthridge,F.: 1949, '50
Gyetvan,F.: 1952, '53, '54

H

Hackney,L.: 1966, '67
Hagerty,B.: 1951, '52
Haggerty,F.V.J.: 1929, '30, '31, '32
Haley,G.G.: 1908, '09
Hall,C.W.: 1968, '69, '70
Hamel,A.R.: 1910, '11
Hammer,R.: 1958, '59, '60
Hancock,W.A.: 1939, '41, '42
Handel,W.: 1955, '57
Handy,J.B.: 1889, '90, '91, '93
Handy, V.H.: 1910, '13, '14, '15
Haney, J.A.: 1930, '31
Hanley,B.: 1968, '69
Hanson,A.M.: 1925
Harrington,C.: 1894
Harrington,W.W.: 1893
Harrington,W.F.: 1899, 1900, '01
Harrison,T.: 1961, '62, '63
Hart,P.L.: 1943, '46
Hartman,A.H.: 1897, '98, '99
Harvanik,J.: 1955, '56, '57
Hauber,A.: 1902, '03, '04, '05
Hauptle,C.D.: 1946, '47, '48
Hayes, H.M.: 1889
Hayman,C.: 1968, '69, '70
Hayman,L.T.: 1936
Hayman,W.: 1969, '70
Hays,G.W.: 1976, '77, '78
Hearn,J.: 1946
Hebert,G.: 1959, '60, '61
Heckler,W.: 1975, '76
Hellig,F.: 1950, '51, '52
Heinecken,M.: 1958, '59, '60
Helley,R.: 1958
Henry,R.: 1972, '74, '75
Herkness,F.G.: 1934
Hess,D.M.: 1976, '77, '78
Hessler,G.W.: 1902, '04
Heyer,R.: 1979
Hidell,T.: 1972, '73, '74
Higgins,W.: 1962, '63
Hill,A.W.: 1928
Hill,F.: 1946, '48
Hines,K.: 1971, '72, '73
Hirst,T.: 1965
Hocker,T.: 1952
Hodgson,J.A.: 1934, '35, '36
Hodgson,L.G.: 1931
Hoey,J.: 1967
Hoffman,W.R.: 1974, '75
Hogan,W.R.: 1940, '41
Holcomb,R.: 1968, '69, '70
Holton,W.D.: 1917, '21

Photography Credits